The *Travel Detective*

The *Travel Detective*

How to Get the Best Service and the Best Deals from
Airlines, Hotels, Cruise Ships, and Car Rental Agencies

PETER GREENBERG

VILLARD NEW YORK

Library of Congress Cataloging-in-Publication Data

Greenberg, Peter.
    The travel detective: how to get the best service and the best
deals from airlines, hotels, cruise ships, and car rental agencies /
Peter Greenberg.
        p.   cm.
    ISBN 0-375-75666-3
    1. Travel.   I. Title.
G153.4 .G74 2001
910'.2'02—dc21   00-069329

98

This book is dedicated to my mother, who always encouraged me to travel; to my sister, who understands why I still travel; and to my late father, who continues to show me the way home.

PREFACE

Some years ago, when I was trying to find my way as a writer, I had lunch with a good friend who is also a gifted journalist, Chris Barnett. I had worked for nearly seven years as a correspondent for *Newsweek* and had traveled extensively while on the job. So frequently was I on airplanes, in fact, that I kept two packed suitcases in the trunk of my car.

But at *Newsweek* I was a generalist, assigned to one of the magazine's bureaus on the West Coast. I could—and did—write for different sections of the magazine each week. After six years, I was drifting, looking for a way, as a writer, to pursue my creative passions and to focus.

It didn't take long for Barnett to put the pieces together. "You should be a travel writer," he said. My response? I laughed. In those days, most of the travel writers I knew were failed journalists, escaped librarians, or schoolteachers looking to find someone who would give them a free cruise. In fact, not that long ago, most travel journalism was more or less an oxymoron. And travel sections of newspapers were perceived as nothing more than advertising vehicles.

But Barnett proceeded to convince me. After all, he argued, I loved to travel. More important, I loved the process of travel. Even on stories that had nothing to do with travel, I could be found up in the cockpit talking to the pilots, or in the galley with flight attendants, or on cruise ships I'd be on the bridge talking with the officers.

No one was writing about travel as news, or explaining the process of how things really worked.

It began with a weekly column in the *Tribune,* "The Savvy Traveler" (a name I later gave to my close friend Rudy

Maxa, who was at *The Washington Post* when I was at *Newsweek,* and who started the very successful public radio show and newsletter now bearing the same name).

And it soon expanded to nearly 60 newspapers. It was the first investigative travel column—it didn't address subjects like Lovely London or Beautiful Bermuda. Instead, I wrote about which cruise ship was a mechanical disaster, as well as which had a great safety record; which hotel had a pattern of bad fire safety as well as which trained its staff well; which airline consistently lied to consumers on its pricing, as well as which performed ethically and professionally.

PETER GREENBERG

ACKNOWLEDGMENTS

Harriet Choice at the *Chicago Tribune* took a big chance on me, and for that I will always be grateful. Grateful as well to Jerry Hulse, a tough editor and a great boss, the former travel editor of the *Los Angeles Times*. When Jerry decided to run my column, my work was nationally recognized. Jerry will always be a giant in my eyes because he did it all—he not only edited a complete Sunday newspaper section each week, he also wrote for it, and, sometimes it seemed as if he wrote all of it! Thankfully, he knew what he was writing about. And I like to think he felt the same about me. He was and still is a traveler in the truest sense of the word.

Thanks, too, goes to Michael Jackson, who will always be the dean of radio talk show hosts in my eyes, who was enormously generous in allowing me time on his show. He is one of the few radio interviewers who understands the questions he asks as well as why he asks them, because he always does his homework beforehand.

Over the years, I have been blessed with assistants who also became friends—they helped me so much, and they shared many things in common, among them that they are strong and incredibly capable women: Jodie Sternberg and Meredith Patterson, Jessica Nathan, and the rock solid Jessica Milligan.

I have so many people to thank in the travel industry itself that my biggest fear in writing these acknowledgments is the highly likely possibility of forgetting some. And so, I apologize now for any omissions.

Having said that, there are the legendary, and unforget-
table hoteliers who helped me and pointed me in the right
direction, even if it wasn't always flattering to them or their
hotels: Stan Bromley and Wolf Hengst at Four Seasons, two
men who really know how to run hotels; Wolfgang Hultner
of the Mandarin Oriental in San Francisco, and John Toner
at the Ritz Carlton in Maui, who have mastered the art of
making the impossible look effortless; Bill Marriott, who
continues to amaze me by being so accessible and helpful;
then there's the legendary Kurt Wachveitl at the Oriental in
Bangkok, who IS the Oriental in Bangkok, Tom Guertner at
the Regent in Hong Kong and Bill Black, most recently at the
Regent Hotel in Bangkok, who can explain Thai culture and
nuance—and service better than anyone else I know; Speaking of legends, Sally Bulloch at the Athenaeum in London,
who has limitless energy, and is the consummate hostess.
But she also knows everything and everybody—and shares
her information with an impossible combination of great
flair as well as discretion. Thanks to Jon Tisch, who has been
a friend and supporter, even when he didn't have to be.

Most guests who stay at the Mark Hotel in New York
don't know the name Birgit Zorniger. But she knows their
name, and thankfully, she knows mine. She quietly, effi-
ciently and with limitless strength has turned this hotel into
a gracious home and my favorite hotel. It is almost an under-
statement to say that this book would not have been possible,
even conceivable, without the incomparable Raymond Bick-
son, general manager of the Mark, whom I unabashedly wor-
ship as a hotelier but above all as a friend.

Thanks also to Jane Mackie and Deb Bernstein and Katie
Meyer at Starwood hotels, for always having an answer for
every one of my questions.

And some true professional public relations women: Vi-
vian Deuschl, Stephanie Platt and Colleen Evans at Ritz Carl-

ton, who have been so generous with their time, their support their information, and their honesty. I can't just thank them. Instead, I have to say "my pleasure and certainly" for reasons they know all too well. Also thanks to Lou Hammond, Yvonne Middleton, Jeannie Datz, Anita Cotter, Nancy Friedman and Florence Quinn, who know the difference between promotion and presentation, puffery and the truth.

Anchors of thanks away to Julie Benson of Princess, Juli Chase of Holland America, Mimi Weisband of Crystal, Liz Jakeway of Celebrity, and Jennifer Schott of Silversea Cruises.

A special, special thanks to Sheila Donnelly, my dear friend, and one of the most wired, informed, smart people I know. Outside of being a great PR executive, she knows the difference between promotion and presentation, between spin and truth, and was never afraid to tell the truth, even when it hurt. She was always there for me as a constant and selfless source of support, inspiration and direction.

My love-hate relationship with the airlines includes some people who still helped me immeasurably—Tim Doke at American, who will hopefully still have his job after his superiors learn I thanked him; Jon Austin at Northwest, Joe Hopkins and the late Chuck Novak at United; Ned Walker at Continental, Stephanie Ackerman at Aloha, Scott Mowrer at Cathay Pacific. Mark Abels at TWA, Gareth Edmonson-Jones at Jet Blue (formerly at Virgin), John Lampl at British Airlines, Peter McLaughlin and Ken Groves at Qantas and John Selvaggio at Delta.

My column is no longer syndicated in newspapers. It now appears on the Internet, on MSNBC.com, thanks to the stewardship and guidance of Robin Dalmas, my editor.

At NBC, I have been lucky to work with some great producers, ranging from Beatrice Myers and Kim Bondy to the total professional, Linda Finnell, who never asked me for anything other than hard, good work—when she wasn't gently asking me to get out of her office!

At the Travel Channel, Jay Feldman, with whom I once worked at KNXT in Los Angeles, hired me on as chief correspondent, and developed a great and ambitious show, Travel Daily along with another KNXT alum, Nancy Jacoby, who served as executive producer, and with whom I still work with today at MSNBC.

And, most recently Steve Cheskin, who didn't have to keep me at the channel when he came onboard, but thankfully, did.

My career as a television journalist specializing in travel was actually started by Merv Griffin, who first allowed me a national audience; then came the steady hand of Jack Reilly, who took a chance on me at *Good Morning America*. Seven years later, when Jack left ABC, I moved over to NBC and the *Today Show*, and it was—and is—the experience that changed everything. Bryant, Matt, Katie Al and Ann welcomed me to their special family. Few people outside of television know how hard their job really is, and even fewer know how easy they make mine.

Most importantly, it is Jeff Zucker, until recently executive producer of the *Today Show* (and now president of NBC Entertainment) to whom I will always owe my success. He truly recognized travel as news, and treated it as such. First, he invited me on the show as a guest. Then he asked me to stay. A tougher, more fair boss I will never find.

I can think of few things more fulfilling than travel. In the course of writing this book, in fact, in the course of my entire career as a journalist, I have had the wonderful opportunity of meeting and spending time with literally hundreds of the most important people in travel: bellhops, skycaps, ticket agents, train conductors, flight attendants, cabin stewards, taxi drivers, doormen, waiters and busboys, maids, ramp drivers, maintenance jockeys, security officers, airplane cleaners. They were also some of the most interesting people I will ever meet. I learned so much from them, and I will forever be in their debt, as an author as well as a traveler.

My heartfelt thanks to Nancy Marcus Land at Publications Development Company for the design and copyediting of this book; to my television agent, Adam Leibner, who continues to toil in the trenches with and for me; and to my book agent, Amy Rennert for her persistence in first believing in this book and its author,and then staying on my case and helping me to stay the course to finish it. Not last, and certainly not least, thanks to my editor Bruce Tracy, first for his vision in embracing the need for this kind of book, and also for his incredible patience in waiting for this often delayed flight.

Finally, I am indebted to Kari Haskell of the *New York Times,* for tirelessly organizing the mountains of constantly changing information, following endless but essentially important paper trails, for tracking down previously unreachable or unwilling sources, and for researching this book.

P.G.

CONTENTS

The *Travel Detective*

1

Before Leaving

GETTING WHAT YOU WANT
BEFORE THE FACT

Most of us love to travel. That's the good news.

The bad news: We hate the process of travel.

We've been abused. And after each trip, we tell ourselves we'll never do it again.

And yet, we can't wait to do it all over again. And we do.

To many people, travel remains a voyage—or a flight or an Interstate trip—of discovery. But to most of us, travel remains a ritual of reassurance. Where there's a whim . . . there's a way. And even though we hate the process, we continue to travel.

In 1999, more than 1.3 billion people traveled by air. The average American traveler is 44 years old. Of all American adult travelers, 49 percent are men, 64 percent are married, and 48 percent have children.

We travel to escape, or to explore, or to rest. Travel is, for many of us, an exercise in renewal, or a test of our limits. And some of us travel, simply, because we *CAN*.

And we *DO*. In a recent American Express study of 200 developing and developed countries, travel and tourism were found to be the biggest industry. In fact, if travel and tourism were a country instead of an industry, its gross national product (GNP) would rank among the top five in the world.

As an industry, it is one of the world's largest employers—one of every eleven jobs worldwide is held by someone in the travel business.

I've been traveling since I was six months old, when my parents took me on a very long DC-6 flight from New York to Los Angeles.

Since then, I've flown on virtually every commercial aircraft ever made, from DC-3s to Comets, Fokkers, Ilyushins, Fairchilds, and Boeings.

Over the years, my passports have bulged with the entry and departure stamps of more than 120 of the world's 187 countries.

And many readers of this book have passports that are fatter than mine.

There has been an exponential jump in the number of travelers and in the frequency of their trips.

In 1978, at the beginning of airline deregulation in the United States, only about 17 percent of all adults had ever taken an airplane flight.

With deregulation came dozens of new airlines. Airfares started matching bus fares, and the numbers of passengers soared.

Today, more than 84 percent of adults have flown.

An impressive number, but also a scary one because a majority of that 84 percent feel abused by the process.

But the key question remains: Are we tourists or travelers?

To me, the definition of *tourist* is *victim waiting to happen.*

I know very few people who define themselves as tourists. Instead, they call themselves *travelers.*

But that doesn't mean they're *good* travelers.

I always get a laugh on Mondays. That's when my incoming-call volume soars.

Nearly everyone who calls is angry. They've just returned from a trip and there were problems.

And the calls seem to share the same structure, language, and intonation.

"It was a HORRIBLE flight," one will say. "The service was TERRIBLE." And, they add, they will NEVER do it again.

"Really?" I respond. "A horrible flight?"

"Absolutely," they answer. "Horrible."

"Let me ask you something," I continue. "At any time during your flight, did the airplane hit a mountain and disintegrate?"

"No."

"And when you landed, did the wing hit the runway and did you cartwheel and explode?"

Again, "No."

"And," I conclude the questioning, "are you calling me from your . . . destination?"

"Yes."

"Well, hang up the phone. It was a GREAT flight. You arrived!"

A funny thing then happens between the time my phone rings on Monday and the time it rings again—the same person is calling—on Thursday.

The person who had insisted that his or her experience was horrible on Monday, that he or she would NEVER do it again, is now in a mild panic. Why? Because it's THURSDAY and he or she is desperate for the information necessary to get to the airport, get out of town, and try it all over again!

We have become a nation of travel junkies. And our addiction seems to be incurable.

And yet, for many of us, the decisions involving the PROCESS of travel are flawed. We have a serious entitlement problem. Half of us don't think we're entitled to anything when we travel. And the rest of us think we deserve EVERYTHING.

Result: A nation of unhappy, but addicted travelers.

So, what do we REALLY want when we travel?

Chances are, if you've traveled lately, you now have a list. You may not have written it down or committed it to memory, but you've got it—your list of all the ways a trip can be ruined.

What tops that list as the one item or experience that guarantees your vacation will be a disaster?

A few years ago, travel researcher Stanley Plog decided to find out, and the results might surprise you. They seem to indicate that, on the whole, we don't do our homework as travelers before we take our trips. We do little research or planning.

To find out our pet travel peeves, Plog tracked travel trends and preferences for virtually every major hotel and airline in the United States. He then picked a random sample of the U.S. population with incomes above $20,000.

Plog's staff asked the travelers to rate—on a scale of 1 to 10—the thing that they felt ruined their trip the most.

Was it rude people? High prices? Feeling ripped off by locals? How about weather, crime, bad food, or a feeling that the destination visited was too much like other places they've visited?

No. First on the list of factors that ruin a trip was dirt. That's right, *dirt.* Hoteliers and housekeepers, take note: Of 13,526 travelers surveyed, 77 percent said that if a hotel is dirty or run-down, the trip is ruined.

Second on the list? Dirt again. Of those surveyed, 72 percent indicated that if things were "dirty everywhere," their trip would be similarly destroyed.

What about the actual expense of a trip? After all, aren't we all looking for a great deal when we travel? Expense ranked fifth on the list of trip spoilers, behind "poverty."

Poverty? Forty-three percent of the travelers indicated that if there was "poverty evident" at their destination, their trip would be a bummer. Forty percent cited the high cost of a trip as the number-one trip destroyer.

There were lots of surprises among these responses, and no one was more surprised than Plog, who has been doing specific travel research for nearly 30 years. To Plog, the survey was a stunner.

A majority of those surveyed wanted things to be tidy, clean, almost antiseptic, and planned. They wanted no surprises when they traveled.

These travelers don't take risks. In fact, when Plog listed things like "Too many tourist traps" or "Too many fast-food outlets or souvenir shops" as candidates for ruining a trip, or suggested that the destination was "Too much like other places visited," no one seemed to care.

Why is that significant? Think about what the findings really say. *We* pick cleanliness and organization, but we neglect to note the rampant development that tends to destroy foreign cultures.

In a way, that's like going to a McDonald's in a foreign country because you are familiar with its clean operation, and prefer not to discover something new about a place, its people, and its customs. In fact, only 9 percent of those surveyed thought their trip would be ruined if the place they picked was "Too much like other places visited."

Another interesting finding: The number of sophisticated American travelers is growing, but the bulk of American travelers don't do adequate trip planning, and they are willing to concentrate more on cleanliness than on culture, and more on known creature comforts than on price.

We are also geographically challenged as a people. Only 11 percent of all Americans actually hold a passport, and fewer use one.

Heard this story of a couple just returned from their vacation. "Where did you go?" a friend asks. "Aruba," they respond, happily. "We had a great time."

"That's terrific," their friend says. "And by the way, where IS Aruba?

Without hesitation, the husband shrugs, then answers, "I don't know . . . we flew!"

The point is—hopefully—that while we know some of these people, we desperately do not want to *be* these people.

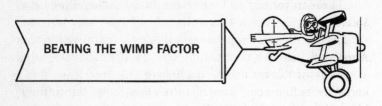

BEATING THE WIMP FACTOR

What's amazing is that our vacation couple actually went to Aruba and weren't scared of the island country.

But how much do we really know about travel? About where we are going, what we are experiencing, and, yes, even where we are?

Two nationwide surveys have attempted to find out.

The results are surprising, amusing, even disturbing. And they reveal some widely held misconceptions that Americans harbor about travel.

When the National Geographic Society conducted an international study to determine how the United States compares with other countries in geographic literacy, Americans ranked near the bottom in the test of geographic knowledge. Only Italians and Mexicans scored lower.

Adults in nine countries (including France, Japan, Sweden, and the United Kingdom) were asked to locate thirteen selected countries. The Swedes came in first, averaging 11.6 places out of a possible sixteen.

Not only did the Americans score poorly, but our 18- to 24-year-olds who took the test performed abysmally. They averaged only 6.9 places right—worse than their counterparts in all other countries.

Only 15 percent could name the world's largest city—Mexico City.

In another survey, none could point to Iraq on the map, and about the same number had trouble finding Illinois!

So much for our lack of geographical knowledge. What about basic travel common sense?

Omni Hotels conducted a survey to try to determine Americans' travel IQ.

Some of the results: Seven out of ten Americans don't know the difference between a direct and a nonstop flight. More than six out of ten Americans are not sure whether they must pay travel agents a commission for their services. And nearly half think it is cheaper to drive an automobile than it is to take a plane to a destination.

How many time zones does the United States span? Seven out of ten Americans surveyed by Omni said four. (The correct answer is eight: Atlantic (including Puerto Rico and the U.S. Virgin Islands), Eastern, Central, Mountain, Pacific, Alaskan, Hawaiian/Aleutian, and Samoan.)

Test yourself on some other questions asked in the Omni survey.

True or false? The economy-class section of a plane is at the rear of the plane, behind full-fare, coach-class seats. False again. But more than six out of ten Americans think it's true. Economy class is not a physical section of any plane. It's a fare category.

The Omni survey also revealed what Americans DO know about travel. For example, 83 percent knew that a federal law prohibits smoking on domestic flights.

About 67 percent knew that airlines have the legal right to give your seat away if you check in at the gate after the designated time. And 64 percent were correct in identifying a major area of airline confusion. You are not entitled to any compensation if an airline bumps you from a flight but is able to get you to your destination within an hour of your original arrival time.

(If the delay is more than one hour, you are entitled to "denied boarding compensation" equivalent to the one-way fare to the destination but not more than $200. If the delay is more than two hours, compensation must be doubled. Each airline may also offer bumped passengers a voucher for a free flight in lieu of the denied boarding compensation.)

Last, the Omni survey asked Americans whether they needed a passport to travel to Mexico, Bermuda, the Bahamas, Puerto Rico, Toronto, or Honolulu. The majority of Americans—60 percent—knew a passport was not required to travel to any of those destinations.

However, one out of ten Americans surveyed thought a passport was required to visit Honolulu.

Ouch!

The sad fact remains: Americans can be some of the least adventurous people in the world when it comes to travel. In the summer, we go to Europe. In the winter, we go skiing. We're easily scared by world events: One terrorist incident, and we retreat.

And yet, a statistical look at the real numbers concerning travel, safety, and terrorism might surprise you.

Between 1992 and 1999, according to the U.S. State Department, ninety-two American CIVILIANS were killed by acts of political terrorism overseas.

Want a scarier statistic? Can you guess how many of us slip, fall, injure ourselves, or even die, each DAY, stepping out of our bathtubs?

According to the Consumer Product Safety Commission, it's a staggering 187,283. (That works out to more than 500 of us each day!)

So, every time friends of mine balk at traveling overseas because of safety concerns, I tell them not to worry. They're free to stay home and take a bath instead, but I caution them: They're on their own!

With exceedingly few exceptions, it is safe for Americans to travel virtually anywhere in the world.

In fact, in recent years, the U.S. Government prohibited Americans from traveling to only one country: Lebanon. And that travel ban was removed in 1997.

But what about North Korea, Vietnam, Nicaragua, Iran, South Africa, Ethiopia, or Haiti?

Before you wince and run for cover, consider this: You can get there from here. And with a little advance planning, you can have a great time while learning something about the rest of the world. A growing number of specialty tour and travel agencies offer such trips on a regular basis. And you don't have to be a mercenary in military fatigues to sign up.

The U.S. State Department is no longer cautioning Americans about travel in the Soviet Union within a 100-mile radius of Chernobyl, and travel to Kiev (about 60 miles from the site of the April 28, 1986, nuclear disaster) is slowly rebounding.

Grenada, the beautiful 13-by-21-mile Caribbean island distinguished by a 1983 invasion by the United States, is still eagerly awaiting American tourists.

How can you find out the score before traveling somewhere?

The U.S. State Department issues "advisories" and stronger "warnings" on trouble spots around the world. Currently, the State Department has these alerts on a few dozen locations within eight geographic regions. The advisories and warnings deal with civil unrest, natural disasters, and disease.

To receive a travel advisory is relatively simple. Dial (202) 647-5225 and specify the country—assuming there is an advisory in effect for that country.

Some advisories are strongly worded and should be heeded. A few years ago, one advisory on Afghanistan warned that "a high level of risk" existed there. Prospective travelers were informed that the U.S. embassy had been evacuated of all American personnel. It stated that anyone who had to go to the region should avoid travel on the national airline, which had an extremely poor maintenance record.

Fair enough.

Another advisory warns against trekking along the Thai-Burmese (Myanmar) border, since there have been reports of bandits and drug traffickers.

Other travel advisories should be interpreted with simply a large dose of common sense. As the situation in the Middle East continues to be tense, the State Department warns us to refrain from traveling there, and adds that we should stay away from large crowds and avoid taking buses.

What kind of advice is that? I've lived in Los Angeles for nearly thirty years and I stay away from large crowds and buses HERE!

Translation: The words "State Department Advisory" carry an unfortunate negative connotation.

If I told you there was a State Department Advisory on Turkey, would you refrain from going there?

Many of you would, merely after hearing the word "advisory."

Now, let's look at what a recent advisory said: that U.S. travelers should be aware that Turkish drivers pass on the right as well as the left.

Here's a small news bulletin: Cab drivers do that all the time on the East River Drive in Manhattan!

The important distinction here is: Just because the State Department issues an advisory does not necessarily mean that a country is unsafe. It just means the U.S. Government is covering its rear, and with good reason.

In early December 1988, the U.S. Embassy in Helsinki received what was regarded as a "credible" threat—a U.S.

airliner would be blown out of the sky during the Christmas holiday, on a flight from London or Frankfurt to the United States.

The State Department took the threat so seriously that it immediately informed all U.S. embassy personnel worldwide to avoid taking U.S. airlines over the period. One small problem: the State Department neglected to inform U.S. citizens.

And on December 21, 1988, Pan Am Flight 103 was blown out of the sky over Lockerbie, Scotland.

From that moment on, if someone tears a fingernail in Peru, has a purse snatched on the streets of Montego Bay, or slips and falls in Oman, the State Department rushes to issue an advisory or bulletin.

The net result: Those advisories fuel our fears—more often than not, unnecessarily.

For example, Fiji experienced two coups in 1987, and the State Department issued advisories. Few Americans traveled there. But there was hardly any violence, and no foreigners were killed. Another coup in 2000—the same dropoff in tourism, and the same U.S. casualty count: zero.

Place the State Department advisories in their proper perspective as they relate to your specific travel needs.

Certain myths do persist. Just ask the Turkish government how many Americans didn't go to Turkey—and still don't go there—after viewing the movie *Midnight Express*. Or ask the Greek government what happened after the *Achille Lauro* incident, which didn't even occur in Greece.

Until recently, the United States took a hard line against any of its citizens' traveling to Cuba or North Korea. Does that mean you can't go to those countries? Absolutely not. What it does mean is that no U.S. travel agent can sell you a ticket or book you a hotel room there.

If you want to go to Cuba, Canadian travel agencies can easily arrange such a trip and will obtain the proper Cuban visas. (The U.S. Treasury Department says American citizens may not spend U.S. currency in Cuba without a "license.") And any U.S. travel agent can book you a flight to Beijing (for separate flights to Pyongyang), or Bangkok.

At the height of our government's problems with the Sandinistas in Nicaragua, 40 percent of the 100,000 tourists who went there in 1984 were Americans.

Did the American tourists shoot it out with the Contras or the Sandinistas? No; many of them went to the beach.

I have always argued that an advisory is just that—an advisory. You are well advised to read it. But I strongly encourage you to put any advisory in perspective.

Recently, a friend told me she would not be getting off her cruise ship when it docked in Lisbon, because she had heard there was a State Department advisory. Had she read the advisory? No. She made her decision simply because one had been issued. Well, I DID read the advisory. It warned only of an increase in pickpocketing and purse snatching in the Portuguese capital. Based on that warning, she should NEVER get off the ship at ANY port!

Not surprisingly, the Middle East and Asia are targets of a continuous flow of State Department advisories. Some are specific and quite helpful.

For example, in Indonesia, a number of groups identifying themselves as Islamic organizations showed up in some areas of the country. They demanded names of American guests and delivered an ultimatum that U.S. citizens must leave Indonesia within 48 hours. The State Department advised Americans to "defer" travel to Jakarta. And for those Americans already in Indonesia, the State Department advised "extreme caution" in their travels.

In this instance, there was a credible, implied threat, and the State Department's advisory was to be taken seriously.

However, Indonesia is a country of more than 17,000 islands, and the major tourist areas of Bali, Sumatra, and North

Sulawesi have traditionally remained calm during times of major unrest in Jakarta.

And yet, would that State Department advisory keep most people from going to Indonesia? Yes.

And therein lies the sad story of State Department advisories. I support the efforts of any government to inform its people of inherent dangers abroad. But I also support an effort to arrive at a definition of terms when a danger is real.

Based on the current State Department criteria for issuing most advisories, if our government issued advisories for most U.S. cities, using the same State Department criteria for determining danger and other warnings, none of us would ever leave our own towns.

One piece of additional advice: You don't have to depend on only the U.S. State Department for advisories. An excellent alternate source is the British Foreign Office (www.fco.gov.uk).

- *Bottom Line:* Read the advisories, but use them ONLY as advisories and not as outright prohibitions. The State Department currently has no fewer than three dozen such advisories warning of certain dangers abroad.

If an advisory tells you to defer all travel to a particular country, or indicates that all Americans there have been urged to leave—as recently occurred with Liberia—you should definitely avoid going to that country. And, as long as you want to read State Department advisories, consider reading some of the advisories foreign governments give THEIR citizens about traveling to certain locations.

One of the most informative (and often more candid) sources about medical situations abroad is also the British Foreign Office (BFO, Great Britain's equivalent of our State

Department). It's particularly good about medical information concerning foreign locations—specifically, disease and epidemics.

As with U.S. State Department advisories, the BFO messages are meant only as advisories and should be read in that context.

You can access the reports easily at www.fco.gov.uk /travel/.

If an advisory simply states that you should avoid going to a particular region of a country, because of political instability or an outbreak of disease there, just avoid that individual region. You don't have to avoid the entire country.

Keep a generous dose of common sense on hand.

What should you do overseas, if you believe there's a potential problem?

First, consider some obvious precautions:

- Don't advertise yourself as an American. Don't wear excessive amounts of jewelry. Don't look like a bad golfer or a professional tourist. (Keep those plaid pants in your suitcase; leave the stupid logo T-shirts at home.)

- On an airplane or at an airport, no need to show your U.S. passport unless an airline official or customs agent demands to see it.

- Pick a window seat. As my friend Neil Livingstone, chairman of Global Options (an international risk management firm), likes to say, few terrorists or hijackers will climb over two other people to get to you. More than likely, they'll pick the person in the aisle seat as a hostage or violence target.

Think about this: If the commonsense advice is "Stay away from large crowds," then why travel in one? If there ever was an argument against group tours, this is the best one. And, if you must take a group tour, when checking into a hotel or major tourist site, don't stand with the entire group at the counter or the entry gate.

And what happens if a real problem erupts?

This is where I will be accused of being unpatriotic.

In the past, when I have been in dangerous areas, the absolutely last place I head for is the U.S. Embassy. Think about it. The U.S. Embassy is the first place that either is attacked or, in anticipation of a threat or attack, is immediately closed, even to its own citizens.

Instead, head for the Canadian Embassy. Recent history proves that our neighbors to the North are the real heroes when the proverbial you-know-what hits the fan.

If you're ever in a difficult area, you're concerned, worried or need information, and it just so happens to be a Friday, definitely head for the Canadian, British, or Australian embassies. Why? In the diplomatic world, these embassies traditionally hold TGIF parties. If you're particularly nice, you might just get invited. And sometimes, when you're in the middle of dusty Khartoum—a broken-down city that looks like it was evacuated in 1955 but someone forgot to tell a few million people—- it is most comforting to be invited to one of these parties!

It has been argued that travel does more to promote world peace than just about anything else. Slowly but surely, Americans are beginning to realize that they can visit most countries without undue fear. They can vacation in Central and South America, and they can visit Eastern European countries and the Middle East safely.

By the way, if you're THAT concerned about safety—or even potential hijacking—you might think about making your travel plans on charter flights. The hijacking risk is severely reduced in this manner. Most terrorists won't even consider a charter flight. Charters rarely leave or arrive on time, and some often cancel at the last minute. And, after all, how many terrorists book at least 30 days in advance?

Well-informed travelers who break down misperceptions are doing all of us a great service. And the first thing these travelers pack is common sense.

That's what this book is about—common sense, and beating the airlines, hotels, cruise lines, and rental car agencies at their own game, playing by their rules. If you look around you, you'll see plenty of disclaimers masquerading as advice on or in virtually every product you buy: In case you needed further proof that the human race is doomed on account of stupidity, here are some actual label instructions that have been found on consumer goods:

- On a bar of Dial soap: Directions: Use like regular soap.
- On some Swanson frozen dinners: Serving suggestion: Defrost.
- On a Sears hair dryer: Do not use while sleeping.
- On a bag of Fritos: You could be a winner! No purchase necessary. Details inside.
- Printed on the bottom of one grocery chain's box of Tiramisu dessert: Do not turn upside down.
- In England, printed on Marks & Spencer Bread Pudding: Product will be hot after heating.
- On a bottle of children's cough medicine: Do not drive car or operate machinery.
- On a bottle of Nytol: Warning: May cause drowsiness.
- On a Korean kitchen knife: Warning: Keep out of children.
- On a string of Chinese-made Christmas lights: For indoor or outdoor use only.
- On an American Airlines packet of nuts: Instructions: open packet, eat nuts.

- And my favorite, on a hotel shower cap: Instructions: fits one head.

OK, so much for overly cautious lawyers trying to protect their deep-pocketed clients from outrageous litigation.

And so much for what most of us would easily classify as the obvious.

Here's something else that's obvious: Travel isn't much fun these days. And we don't need a set of self-evident instructions to figure that out.

I'll try to stay away from the painfully obvious as we explore the ridiculous and often draconian world of the travel experience. The advice I'm offering in this book comes from my own travel experience, as well as the experiences of countless other road warriors who have been kind enough to share some of their secrets with me.

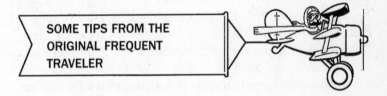

SOME TIPS FROM THE ORIGINAL FREQUENT TRAVELER

Someone once told me that you know you've been traveling too long when you wake up, panicked, in the middle of the night in a strange hotel room, and you have absolutely no idea where you are.

But, as I learned firsthand—and, I'm ashamed to say, only recently—you've REALLY been traveling too long when you get a case of "minthead."

I first heard about minthead when I sat down with another frequent traveler, Jay Leno. At the time, he was doing more than 150 one-night comedy stands a year—and guest hosting on *The Tonight Show*. And, he was the most frequent flier I knew.

As we sat in his dressing room at NBC in Burbank, he decided to tell me the frequent flier meaning of life.

"It's all about minthead," he told me.

Minthead?

"That's right. Minthead," he confided, "is what happens when you get back to your hotel room and go to sleep. But the maid has put a chocolate mint on your pillow, and you end up sleeping on it. You wake up with all this white cream in your hair. If you travel as much as I do, it happens all the time."

In those days, Leno would leave his stint on *The Tonight Show,* pack a carry-on bag with three shirts, two jackets, and an extra pair of pants, and head for the airport and one-night comedy stands across the country.

"Travel isn't fun," he sighed, "and I'm not one of those who believes that you're entitled to have fun on the road. For me, it's work, but if you do it as much as I do, you learn that there are certain things you must always do, and certain things that, if you are stupid enough to try them, you may never come back sane."

In those days, he had already accumulated so many frequent flyer miles that he was one of the top members of the American Airlines and Delta programs. What did Leno do with all his frequent flyer miles?

"Upgrade to first class," he said. "Or I give my friends tickets. But I never buy a first-class ticket. Instead, I buy a full coach ticket and upgrade. Even though the difference between coach and first class isn't that great," he says. "There's not much reason to fly first class. The legroom isn't that much better. The seats are not particularly comfortable. But I like being up front."

The reason, he explained, is simple—he can keep his options open. "I'm like everyone else. I despise delays. I've developed my own approach to coping with it. The trick is to be the first one on the plane under any circumstance. Because once you put your bags in the overhead bin, that's it. There's room for maybe three other people. So I have to be first on. How do I do it? I limp."

Limp?

"When they ask at the gate if anyone needs a little extra time in boarding, I limp up. 'Oh jeez, my leg; oh please, sir.' It always seems to work. But then, as I boarded one flight, I limped to the front, and there was a woman in a wheelchair, and she said, 'Oh, go ahead, dearie, I see you've hurt your leg.' I felt like that guy on the *Titanic* who put on that dress so he could get into a lifeboat."

Of course, Leno was joking. He never limped. He doesn't limp. Oh yes, he doesn't schlepp either.

Luggage for Leno? Carry-on. Always and only. "Never, never check anything . . . ever . . . under any circumstances. It would be better to throw them away than check them in."

Delays? "I protect myself by checking the schedules beforehand. I always book the first flight out in the morning, and I'm also holding reservations on the next one, and the next one. Sometimes I go so far as to buy two or three tickets which I cash in later if I don't use them. And since you can always be sure your flight is not going to leave on time, I never book a reservation on the last plane out."

What about delays once the plane leaves the gate and you're trapped, a virtual hostage?

"That's when I use the insulin routine. I begin screaming, 'My insulin! My insulin! I have to have it, and I have to get back to the gate!' That always works." (Leno is not a diabetic.) "Actually," he advised me, "you should employ just about any excuse to get off that plane and back to the gate. Because once you're stuck on that plane, you have no options. You have to assume that airlines push their planes back from the gates on time so that they can say they had an on-time departure. But you have to be prepared to smell a rat."

Weather? In the winter, Leno avoids flying through both Denver and Chicago. "Especially Denver. In Denver, you don't get stuck for hours, you get stuck for days. In the summer, I try to fly through Dallas/Fort Worth on American. Or through Atlanta on Delta."

Seat selection? Leno always sits in an aisle seat. "I don't understand the attraction for a window seat," he said. "You sit there and you're trapped. I also want to be near the door, so I'm first out. So I always get an aisle at the bulkhead because it has extra legroom."

Once seated, Leno prides himself on his mechanical skills and performs some structural work on the airline seat. Whether he's in coach or in first class, Leno pulls out the middle armrest between the seats.

"On some planes, they make it tough to do," he warned, "and it may require the use of a small adjustable wrench, which I do bring with me. Then I take the bolt out. And the flight attendant will say, 'Those don't come out, sir,' and throughout the course of the flight, I become a little bit like a prisoner tunneling out with a spoon. About halfway through, I'll look at her and say, 'Oh no . . . look! It came out!' Then I'll stretch across the two seats."

Like many frequent fliers, Leno insisted he wouldn't go near airline food. "It's abysmal. You can't even tell jokes about it, because it's no longer funny," he said. "It's beyond bad. I think you have to sample the food on foreign airlines to realize how bad the U.S. food is. To me, first class on a U.S. carrier is now what coach used to be. Everything has been moved back one notch."

Airports? Leno cannot figure out why so many airports are so poorly designed. "For years, you needed a pedometer just to see how far you had to walk at O'Hare," he said. "But the new United Airlines terminal in Chicago is a little better, because at least it gives you the appearance that you're much closer to your plane. Of course, you're not."

All right, what about once he's back on the ground? What about the hotels? Jay Leno has seen the inside of thousands of hotel rooms, and offered some choice stories from his experience.

"They've ranged from places where the towels are chained to the wall and you had to dry yourself by rubbing up against it, to suites with every possible amenity. But great goodies in the room don't necessarily make a great hotel," he argued. "It's the attitude of the staff.

"But," he added, "a good hotel tends to be one where I don't really notice it's a hotel. Where the bed is comfortable, the remote control works, and you have a real key, not one of those plastic cards. I think those little key cards are terrible. First, I'm always losing them, and even when I don't lose them, they don't work. And when they do work, I forget my room number."

Another peeve, he charged, is "why some hotels feel they need to glue the remote control unit to the furniture. And they always do it so that it doesn't face the TV. And the unit has this huge lock on it, like I'm going to steal it. You have to be a contortionist to be able to turn on the TV or change the channel."

Leno most despises hotels that try to be something they're not. "If you want to be a classy hotel and have a concierge," he suggested, "why not have a concierge who can speak English? I find this all over. Now, I have nothing against people who speak a foreign language. I come from a family of immigrants. But there's no excuse at a hotel. I was at a hotel recently, and I had just checked into the room. I wanted to watch a comedy program on cable but didn't know if the hotel got HBO. So I called downstairs to the concierge and asked.

"'Crebblega,' the guy says. I say, 'Excuse me?' And he says, 'Crebblega.'

"'Crebblega'? What the hell is that? It took me five minutes before I realized what he was saying was 'cable guide.' OK, now we've established the hotel had a cable guide. When I asked the concierge where it was, he said, 'Biroda.' Again, I didn't know what he was saying. This went on for another five minutes until the concierge, who was getting as crazed as I was, said:

"'It's in the bi-ro-da.' Finally! It was in the bureau drawer."

Leno admitted that he is different from most travelers. After all, he's a celebrity with a forum (*The Tonight Show*), and that gives him a rare natural advantage: he can always invoke the Fear Factor.

"The great thing about being in show business is: People are in dread fear that somehow they will wind up in a *Tonight Show* monologue. Not long ago, I had trouble with my washer. Let's just say it's a brand famous for having a repairman that doesn't work very often. So I called the repair service. They told me they'd send someone out in four days. 'Oh, four days, really,' I say. 'Let me write this down. When I mention this on *The Tonight Show* . . . it's going to be four days. . . .' An hour later, the guy is at the door. So that's the great advantage to being on TV.

"Being in show business is like being retarded," he says. "There are always people along the way to lead you. 'Mr. Leno, come with us.' 'Mr. Leno, walk this way.' You ever hear people talk about celebrities? Sometimes you can hear them whisper, 'He even drives himself to the airport!'"

Is there anything to be said in favor of a life on the road?

"The shampoo bottles. The little shampoo bottles. I haven't bought shampoo in fifteen years. I have hundreds of them. That's how I know when it's time to go on the road again. When I'm down to maybe 1,500 bottles, I call the airline and make a reservation."

Two weeks after I spoke with Leno, I was in a hotel in Denver. I returned from a late dinner and sat down on the bed to watch—as luck would have it—*The Tonight Show.* Five hours later, I awoke in a panic. The television was still on. All the lights in the room were aglow. Suddenly I forgot where I was. Couldn't remember the city, or the name of the hotel. And my face and forehead felt funny, and sticky. Slowly, I put my hand to my face. It was all gooey. Was I bleeding? What happened?

And then I smelled it. Chocolate, with more than a slight hint of mint. It had happened. I had fallen asleep on the mint on the pillow. At that moment, I felt I had been inducted into the official frequent-traveler hall of shame.

Minthead notwithstanding, it is really the LEAST of our concerns when traveling.

When it comes to the travel experience, it seems we've evolved into a society where most of us want to find a line just so we can stand in it. And yet, we claim to be desperate for the very information that will help us stay off any lines.

With luck, this book will help us to avoid the lines and still get what we want in travel.

Indeed, there has been a quantum shift in our travel priorities, not to mention our life philosophy. In a recent travel survey, when people were asked, "Would you prefer more free time or more money?" a majority opted for the extra free time.

Among other trends, business travelers like control over their travel arrangements. A majority like to choose the airline they fly and the hotels they stay in.

The pivotal factor in choosing an airline? A convenient schedule.

And how do we like to spend our time on planes? British, Hong Kong, and Singaporean business travelers like to watch the in-flight movies. American, French, and German travelers seem addicted to in-flight phones, and Asian flyers want to play computer video games.

Here's a no-brainer. Most business travelers say they don't want to sit next to anyone during a flight. (Believe it or not, 40 percent of those surveyed admitted moving their seats so they wouldn't have to sit next to anyone.)

How often do business travelers fly? An average of 18.6 trips per year.

Interesting behavioral differences were revealed when the sexes were separated. In 1970, only one percent of business travelers were women. Today, nearly 51 percent are women. Women business travelers are younger (60 percent are under 45), and more of them are interested in using their frequent flyer rewards for leisure, rather than business, travel.

Women are as likely as men to prefer sitting next to an empty seat. Also, one in ten reports being sexually harassed during a flight.

There's also a booming interest in family travel. Three of ten adults took at least one vacation with children last year. This finding seems to match other indications that the number of families consisting of two married parents, and their children, increased by 700,000 in a recent five-year period.

It also confirms another trend: More business travelers are crossing the line into leisure travel—extending their business trips into the weekends and including their spouses and children. Another interesting finding: Half of those surveyed said they were willing to take their kids out of school to gain that extra vacation time together.

There's also a financial incentive from a surprising source: the very airlines that love to stick it to the business traveler.

The airlines' once-dreaded Saturday night stayover restriction has suddenly turned into an ally.

If you agree to stay over a Saturday night, your air fare can drop almost 70 percent. Because of this, a number of corporations are encouraging their hardest workers to take the weekend off. Some companies even pick up the air fare for a spouse or significant other. An extra Saturday night is more economical, even with two discount tickets, than paying for one full-fare seat.

The results: Happy employee, happy spouse, happy company ledger sheet. And happy hotels.

Word of mouth continues to play a significant role in travel decisions. Seventy-nine percent of those surveyed said they had confidence in the recommendations of a friend. Only 28 percent reported confidence in the information found in travel advertisements.

Once viewed as a luxury, leisure travel is now considered, by seven out of ten Americans, to be a psychological necessity.

There also seems to be a change in the class of service for airline flights. In 1994, 14 percent of domestic trips were in first or business class.

That figure—at least in first class—is dropping.

Then there's the extended business-class trip. In 1994, 10 percent of business travelers were accompanied by a spouse, and 3.6 percent brought a child. In 1995, 25 percent took their spouses and 5 percent took a child. Today, nearly 35 percent bring a spouse, and 10 percent bring a child.

I found one statistic most amusing. When American Express did a survey of its Platinum cardholders, the company discovered that male Platinum cardholders said the one thing they wanted to take with them on business trips was their spouse. Women platinum cardholders preferred to take personal items.

One particularly interesting response came when cardholders were asked what they considered the most important factor for a comfortable overnight stay in a hotel. Their answer: Great water pressure in the bathroom. Are you hoteliers listening? Forget the fruit-basket welcome. Work on the plumbing.

Some travel-research dollars are spent trying to understand the psychology of travel. For example, psychologists were consulted before the interiors for the Concorde were designed. Because some believed high-speed travel would produce higher levels of tension and stress for passengers, the Concorde interiors were subdued instead of flashy. And psychiatrists continue to be consulted on what makes us happy when we hit the road and become angry when the road seems to hit us.

A Harvard University study of 700 business travelers concluded what we already know: We have a love-hate relationship with travel.

The study found that business travelers fall into four distinct groups:

1. *Tightrope walkers:* Inexperienced travelers "who report high levels of stress and feel they lose a part of their private lives while on the road."

2. *Eagles:* Folks who enjoy business travel, "but at the same time admit high levels of stress."

3. *Family-ties:* Married travelers who say that business "puts a lot of stress on their spouses, causing a conflict between career and family."

4. *Road warriors:* People who travel a lot "but report lower levels of stress than other business travelers and are more likely to feel like a hero or warrior on the road."

What do these different groups want? Less stress and an ability to develop a sense of humor and plan for things to go wrong, considering they're dealing with variables over which they have little or no control.

Changing demographic trends can often impact travel psychology. The American population is aging, and because older Americans have been traveling more and rewriting the vacation calendar, off-peak travel is booming.

Average Americans take a day and a half to unwind at the start of their vacation. But one in ten Americans says he or she never unwinds.

And what about vacation "afterglow," that period of "feeling good" right after a trip? According to an American Express survey, the average vacation "afterglow" lasts six days. But again, nearly one in every ten of us says it lasts only a day.

This book is about improving the PROCESS of traveling. It's about realizing that the destination has become incidental to the experience. It's about finesse, and understanding the process so we can better handle the product. And in the end, it's about taking some risks, asking some important questions, and thinking outside the box when it comes to both our leisure and our business travel.

And most of all, it's about finding common ground—in the air, at a hotel, inside a rental car, or on the high seas. Travel converts our dreams into the power of discovery.

The bottom line here is: We're all frustrated. We seek information that will help us finesse the process of travel so that we can have a great experience.

Remember, a tourist sees a destination. A traveler EXPERIENCES it.

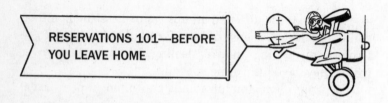

RESERVATIONS 101—BEFORE YOU LEAVE HOME

OK. So much for international acts of terrorism and fear of travel.

Now it's time to discuss some *real* fears of travel, like making reservations for hotels and airlines, getting a good deal, and asking the right questions.

When it comes to travel, everyone seems to have an opinion. And every time someone asks me for advice, I'm reminded of the story of Bill and Joe.

Bill is sitting in the chair at Joe's barber shop, getting his regular haircut. And as Joe is snipping away, he asks Bill, "What's up?"

Bill tells Joe the good news. He's finally taking a vacation.

"Where are you going?" Joe asks.

"Rome," says Bill, excitedly.

"Rome?" Joe says. "Why would you want to go there? It's a crowded, dirty city full of crazy Italians. You're nuts if you go there. So . . . how are you getting there?"

"We got a deal on TWA," Bill replies.

"TWA?" Joe yells. "TWA is a terrible airline. They have old planes, their flight attendants are mean, and the airline is always late. So . . . where are you staying in Rome?"

"Well," Bill answers, somewhat hesitatingly, "we got a pretty good package at the Hilton."

"That's a dump!" Joe screams. "Without a doubt, it's the worst hotel in the city. The rooms are small and dingy, the service is terrible and slow, and they're way overpriced. And what are you gonna do when you get there?"

"We were sort of hoping to go to the Vatican and see the Pope."

Joe laughs. "Yeah. . . . You and a million other people are going to crowd in there. You'll never see the guy, and even if you do, he'll look like an ant."

A month later, Bill returns to the barber shop for his regular haircut. Joe cuts to the chase. "So how was your trip to Rome? Let me guess, TWA was the flight from hell."

Bill shakes his head. "Actually, it was great. Brand new plane. Terrific food, and we landed in Rome ten minutes early. But the best part is that because they were booked full, they bumped us up to first class, and the flight attendants couldn't be nicer."

Joe can't believe it. "Well, I'm sure that hotel was the worst."

Again, Bill shakes his head. "Quite the opposite. They had just finished a major multimillion-dollar remodeling and it's now the hottest hotel in Rome. Even better, because they were fully booked, they upgraded us to the Presidential suite at no extra charge!"

"Wait a minute," Joe says, in disbelief. "Don't tell me you actually got to see the Pope?"

Bill sighs. "Talk about luck. As we toured the Vatican, a Swiss guard tapped me on the shoulder and explained that the Pope likes to personally meet some of the visitors, and asked if I wouldn't mind stepping into this private room. So I did, and five minutes later, the Pope walked through the door, and he walked right up to me. And then he actually spoke to me."

"He spoke to you?" Joe asks. "He actually spoke to you? What did he say?"

"Well, not much, but he did want to know where I got that awful haircut!"

So be prepared. If people perceive themselves as travelers, you will inevitably be second-guessed on every travel decision you make.

The key is to make the right decision from the start. Toward that end, it's actually more important to realize what resources you should avoid than to seek out the ones to use. As part of defining your resources, keep each one in proper perspective.

Let's start with brochures and the brochure mentality. I have a built-in aversion to any word that ends with "st." Can any one hotel, resort, airline, destination, or travel experience be the "best?" The "most?" The "greatest?" The "cleanest?"

How many things are actually "unique?" Is there really only one of them in the universe? And what about the words "beautiful," "gem," and "jewel?" Are we sick of them already? To navigate the travel maze and negotiate some very good travel deals, you must start by burying the brochures.

Why? How many brochures promise an "ocean-view" hotel room? But when you arrive, you need high-powered binoculars to make out the sea a mile away.

A brochure for a package tour to the Soviet Union promises "tickets to the theater where the Bolshoi Ballet performs." Tourists who sign up for the tour are excited at the prospect of watching top-flight ballet.

But it is not to be.

The tourists do indeed arrive at the theater where the Bolshoi performs, but the brochure gave no promise that the Bolshoi itself would perform. The brochure promised tickets to that theater, and, instead of ballet, these unwitting visitors get a disappointing performance of Russian folk songs.

A resort is described as being "five minutes from restaurants, shopping, and entertainment." But the ad doesn't reveal whether that five minutes is by walking or by being beamed up by the cast of *Star Trek*.

One Honolulu hotel claimed in its brochure that it was "steps from the beach."

I actually counted, and it wasn't pretty. If I could have walked there in a straight line, it was half a mile away, but there was no direct route to the beach. I had to walk across heavily traveled city streets, through a construction site, a park, another construction site, and then to the beach. Distance: nearly a mile. That's a lot of steps.

Then there are the visual deceits. A hotel in Santa Barbara airbrushed its brochure photo to show the hotel not just on the beach, but on the ocean itself. Reality: the hotel was across a four-lane state highway. (Translation: If you believed the brochure, went to the hotel with your kids, and told them to go play at the beach, you would have heard the screeching sound of automobile brakes!)

Welcome to the wonderful world of travel promotion and hyperbole, a semantic battlefield where seductive but often misleading words persuade you to journey to a particular country, stay at a certain hotel, fly one airline instead of another, or rent a specific car.

In this highly competitive business, unfair advantage with the language is often taken at travelers' expense.

Most of the time, these descriptive words aren't blatant lies. But, in many cases, they are intentionally misleading—

or, at the very least, not exactly structured to help would-be visitors find the truth.

All too often, if you don't read a travel ad or brochure carefully, you could find yourself a victim of greater expectations of your vacation than logical thinking might otherwise allow.

Here are some of my favorites:

- A cruise-line brochure boasts that "you will sail on a classic vessel." Real meaning: The ship is 38 years old and only months away from the salvage yard, if it ever makes it that far.

- "A travelers' oasis." You'd better like solitude. You could be miles from nowhere.

- "Fully equipped spa." Does a solitary exercise bike qualify? You'd be surprised how many hotels think it does.

- "Beautiful swimming pool." Yes, but how large? And where is it located? It may be beautiful but only ten feet long.

- "You'll love our secluded beaches." Does this mean so isolated that no other services are provided? Or does it mean the beaches are secluded because of the interesting marine life—sharks, perhaps?

- From a package-tour brochure to Egypt: "You will see the Great Pyramids." You will see them, but you won't be getting off the bus as it speeds by.

Then there are the outright lies: "The weather is beautiful all year 'round." That's a statistical impossibility and an insult to our intelligence.

Traditionally, the biggest abuses of descriptive language have taken place on package-tour brochures.

Who can forget the ubiquitous airline statement: "Some restrictions apply"? This all-purpose disclaimer has created unending confusion and anger.

Then there's the cruise-line brochure that says: "We are proud of our crew, representing 47 nationalities." The idea of a floating United Nations sounds great—until you need to talk with crew members, only to discover they don't speak English and, in the event of an emergency at sea, they won't even be able to communicate with each other!

When tackling any brochure, try to decipher the true meaning of the words used to describe the destination and services.

Before sending in a deposit or paying for your ticket, question your travel agent about what is being promised. If he or she doesn't know the answers, demand that the agent find out.

When booking an airline ticket, remember that a "direct" flight doesn't mean nonstop. It may mean you will make one or two stops en route. If it's a "connecting" flight, you must change planes.

So now you know what it means when Alitalia boasts that it offers the only "direct" service from Los Angeles to Italy. If you want to take a plane from Los Angeles to Rome, be prepared to make a stop in Milan.

Inevitable language problems are associated with tour packages. "Includes superior room." If anyone can give me the absolute definition of "superior," I'll send, in return, a matching set of luggage.

The same vagueness often applies to "ocean front" and "ocean view." Does "ocean front" mean that the hotel room actually is fronting the ocean or is facing a distant sea? The words "ocean view" get the worst abuse. At some hotels, the rooms do indeed have an ocean view—provided you bring your own binoculars.

How many times have you seen a very attractive hotel room rate quoted, followed by the disclaimer "double occupancy"? Double occupancy is the price *per person,* based on two people sharing one room.

Ever hear of something called "run of house" rooms? You will often see this term in Hawaii tour packages. It means, quite simply, that you will be given whatever room the hotel feels like giving you. If you agree to a "run of house" room, you are throwing yourself at the mercy of the hotel gods, and your odds of getting a large room, a room with a view, or one with a king-size bed are greatly reduced.

Hungry? Check out various meal packages carefully. In Caribbean destinations, some hotels offer something called "exchange dining." This means that you can eat at specially selected hotels and restaurants as part of a preset meal plan. Caution: Many of these restaurants and hotels look upon that meal plan as nonexclusive—a number of menu items feature surcharges.

Many hotel meal plans are confusing. European Plan (EP) means that no meals are included in the room rate. The American Plan (AP) includes all meals, and the Modified American Plan (MAP) includes two meals (usually breakfast and dinner) as part of your hotel room rate.

Some hotels and resorts allow you to choose either lunch or dinner as your second meal, and, to further confuse things, some hotels market the Continental Plan, which usually means bed and breakfast.

But does this mean a continental breakfast? Not necessarily.

In most of Europe, chances are it does mean a continental breakfast: coffee, tea, and rolls. However, in Scandinavia, it usually means a full buffet breakfast.

Hotels that offer something called the "Bermuda Plan" include a full breakfast.

Meal rates can be confusing. At many hotels and resorts, American Plan and Modified American Plan rates are quoted "per person." If your budget is tight, determine before you go what these terms mean at your destinations.

Here are a few more of my favorite seductive (but misleading) terms used to lure travelers to the wrong countries, cruise lines, and hotels:

"Secluded hideaway": Impossible to find.

"Carefree natives": Terrible service.

"Warmed by the Gulf Stream": Cold.

"Cooled by the Humboldt Current": Hot.

"Old World charm": No bath.

"Family Style": You'll be sharing a bath!

"Tropical": Rainy.

"Undiscovered": Not worth discovering.

"Off the beaten path": People have stopped coming here.

"Ocean view": Bring binoculars.

"Beachfront": Hold on to those binoculars.

"Some restrictions apply": Don't even bother trying to qualify for this fare.

And, as mentioned earlier, any word ending in the letters "st" is usually suspect.

What about guide books? Definitionally, they are guides, *NOT* bibles. And, there's another inherent problem. By the time most guide books are published, they're already out of date.

So, I'm not telling you not to buy them and read them (after all, THIS is a guide book of sorts), but I am strongly encouraging you to use them only as something to depart from.

NOTHING BUT NET

Which brings me to the subject of the Internet. Like the guide books, "the Net" can be extremely useful, but, once again, you cannot always depend on Web sites to get you what you need.

Currently, everyone and his mother—with the possible exception of MY mother—has a Web site. In 1998, there were already 320 million Web sites, and a large percentage of them contained travel information. By the end of 2000, the number of Web sites had soared to more than 800 million. Many Web sites are nothing more than graphically interesting extensions of dreadful brochures.

The rapid growth of travel Web sites is certainly entertaining, and people driven by low-fare obsessions will find no shortage of supposedly great deals. More than 25 million Americans booked travel on the Internet in 2000—up a whopping 60 percent from the previous year.

For some activities—for example, booking on Southwest Airlines— the Web is perfect. People who fly on Southwest are price-driven. They want the cheapest deal. They're not on the plane for a movie or a meal (neither is offered) or for luxurious comfortable seats. Chances are good they'll get stuck in a center seat facing a photo of the bag of peanuts they would have been given two years ago! But that's part of the charm of the Southwest flight experience. Passengers are there only because of price.

Southwest's Web site has been hugely successful. People can log on, buy their cheap tickets, and log off. Period.

In 2000, Southwest became the first airline Web site to book more than $1 billion in travel!

As a label for other travel Web sites, I suggest "Supposedly good deals" because their offerings all come down to a definition of terms. Want a cheap ticket to Los Angeles? You can find one on the Net, but what you often don't learn is that your itinerary may require track shoes for sprinting to connecting flights in both directions.

Many informational Web sites are thinly veiled transactional Web sites that often don't allow any browsing. Instead, you may quickly find yourself locked into a fare or itinerary, and before you know it, your credit card has been charged.

Please don't get me wrong. I love surfing the Net. But I like *riding* the wave, not getting creamed by it. It is but one informational tool I use. And if you approach the Net this way, you'll be a happier traveler.

Now, having said that, let's get down to the questions you need to ask when you are booking an airline ticket, a hotel room, or a cruise.*

If you don't ask these questions right away, you put yourself at an immediate disadvantage.

AIRLINE RESERVATIONS

Let me give you a typical airline reservation dialogue:

AIRLINE AGENT: Good morning. Draconian Airways. May I help you?

ME: Yes, I'd like to fly from Los Angeles to New York.

AGENT: And when would you like to fly?

ME: I'd like to leave next Thursday and come back a week later.

Anyone find anything worrisome in that conversation?

---

* You will find more information on the Web in Chapter 6.

The minute I told the agent *when* I wanted to fly, I was a dead man. I had given the agent too much information and placed myself at an immediate disadvantage.

Now, consider this approach. This time, the agent isn't doing the questioning. *I* am.

AGENT: Good morning. Draconian Airways. May I help you?

ME: Yes. I'd like to fly from Los Angeles to New York, but before you ask me when I want to fly, can you please punch up on your computer every published fare you have on that route? Thanks. I'll wait.

The wait isn't long. When the agent has punched up the information on the airline's screen, I ask a second question.

ME: OK, could you scroll to the bottom of the list? . . . Great. Now, could you tell me what that fare is?

AGENT: Oh, that's the fare that's only good on Wednesdays at midnight if your middle name is Murray, you own a snowmobile, and you can hop.

ME: And how much is that fare?

AGENT: $249.

ME: [Well, I can fly on Wednesday, change my middle name, and borrow a snowmobile.] I'll take that fare.

The moral of the story: If you volunteer when you want to fly, you will invariably be "stepped up" to a higher fare by the airline. Do it my way and you get to back into the fare, starting at the lowest rate that you can handle, if you're flexible.

One important caution is also a reassurance. Let's say you get an airline agent on the phone who WON'T scroll down on the computer screen. No problem. You dialed a toll-free 800 number. Politely end the conversation, hang up, and *call back!* You WILL get someone to help if you keep trying.

For example, a New York to San Francisco trip has eleven fares currently listed in United Airlines' computers. They range from full-premium first class, all the way down to a VE21NTV fare, which just about requires that snowmobile. It's a 21-day advance purchase, requires a Saturday night stay, is nonrefundable, and is time-specific. From JFK to SFO, it's only valid on United flights departing between 6:30 A.M. and 12 noon. On return flights to JFK, you can fly only between 6:30 and 8:30 in the morning, or 3:00 to 11:00 P.M.

These are just the basic fares. About 20 others pop up from time to time, depending on the season, the demand, and other factors.

Whenever you buy a ticket, it's imperative to understand the fare basis that is printed (in code) on that ticket.

The fare basis code provides information about the specific fare in addition to the class of service required for booking. Every published fare has a fare basis code. On your ticket, the code appears in the fare basis box. The codes can get confusing. Some tickets represent a combination of fares; thus, more than one fare basis code may exist for each class of service for booking. For example, two fares for H class may exist—one for midweek travel and one for weekend travel.

Consider this example: A return fare across the country has the fare basis code HL7LNR (an American airlines fare). The first letter (H) refers to the class of service for booking (in this case, H class). The L refers to low season, the 7 refers to the requirement for seven-day advance booking, the next L refers to long haul, and the NR means nonrefundable. The fare would presumably be different if the ticket were purchased fourteen days in advance or during a high season. In that case, both the fare and the fare basis code would be different. Often, you will see the letters X or W, referring to midweek or weekend travel, respectively.

As another example, your fare basis code may be ME7NR. M is the booking class code. E stands for excursion.

Fare Codes and Definitions

New York to San Francisco

Fare Basis Code	Definition
PS	Premium first-class product (only on NYC transcontinental flights), one way, no restrictions, refundable
FUA	First-class product, one way, no restrictions, refundable
CUA	Business class in a 3 cabin aircraft, first class in a 2 cabin aircraft, one way, no restrictions, refundable
YUA	Full fare walkup, one way, no restrictions, refundable
BUA	Full fare walkup, one way no restrictions, refundable
BA3	3-day advance purchase, one way, no restrictions, refundable
ME14NQ	14-day advance purchase, round trip, valid all days of the week, Saturday night stay, nonrefundable
MOE14NQ	14-day advance purchase, round trip, valid only Tuesday and Wednesday, Saturday night stay, nonrefundable
HE21NQ	21-day advance purchase, round trip, valid all days of the week, Saturday night stay, nonrefundable
HOE21NQ	21-day advance purchase, round trip, valid only Tuesday and Wednesday, Saturday night stay, nonrefundable
VE21NTV	21-day advance purchase, round trip, Saturday night stay, nonrefundable, valid on certain flights Valid only to JFK: 6:30 A.M.–8:30 A.M. or 3:00 P.M.–11:00 P.M. daily Valid only from JFK: 6:30 A.M.–12:00 P.M. daily

Chicago to Denver Pricing

Fare Basis Code	Definition
FUA	First-class product, one way, no restrictions, refundable
FUA3FS	First-class product in 3 cabin aircraft, one way, no restrictions, refundable
FUA2FS	First-class product in 2 cabin aircraft, one way, no restrictions, refundable
YUA	Full fare walkup, one way, no restrictions, refundable
BUA	Full fare walkup, one way, no restrictions, refundable
MFSNR	Walkup fare, one way, valid all days, nonrefundable, valid on certain flights
	Valid only to Denver: 5:50 A.M.–7:15 A.M. or 6:55 P.M.–7:25 p.m.
	Valid only from Denver: 6:00 A.M.–6:30 A.M. or 7:45 P.M.–8:45 p.m.
MA3NX	3-day advance purchase, one way, valid all days, nonrefundable, fuel surcharge exempt
ME31NX	3-day advance purchase, round trip, valid all days, 1 night minimum stay, nonrefundable, fuel surcharge exempt
MA7NX	7-day advance purchase, one way, valid all days, nonrefundable, fuel surcharge exempt
HA7NX	7-day advance purchase, one way, valid all days, nonrefundable, fuel surcharge exempt
QE7NX	7-day advance purchase, round trip, valid all days, Saturday night stay, nonrefundable, fuel surcharge exempt
HE14NQ	14-day advance purchase, round trip, valid all days, Saturday night stay, nonrefundable
HOE14NQ	14-day advance purchase, round trip, valid only Tuesday and Wednesday, Saturday night stay, nonrefundable

Chicago to Denver Pricing (Continued)

Fare Basis Code	Definition
HA14NX	14-day advance purchase, one way, valid all days, nonrefundable, fuel surcharge exempt
QE14NRX	14-day advance purchase, round trip, valid all days, Saturday night stay, nonrefundable, fuel surcharge exempt
VE1423NX	14-day advance purchase, round trip, valid only Tuesday and Wednesday, Saturday night stay, nonrefundable, fuel surcharge exempt
QE21NQ	21-day advance purchase, round trip, valid all days, Saturday night stay, nonrefundable
QA21NX	21-day advance purchase, one way, valid all days, nonrefundable, fuel surcharge exempt
QOE21NQ	21-day advance purchase, round trip, valid only Tuesday and Wednesday, Saturday night stay, nonrefundable
VA21NX	21-day advance purchase, one way, valid all days, nonrefundable, fuel surcharge exempt
VA2123NX	21-day advance purchase, one way, valid only Tuesday and Wednesday, nonrefundable, fuel surcharge exempt
WE21NRX	21-day advance purchase, round trip, valid all days, Saturday night stay, nonrefundable, fuel surcharge exempt
WE2123NX	21-day advance purchase, round trip, valid only Tuesday and Wednesday, Saturday night stay, nonrefundable, fuel surcharge exempt

The 7 and NR indicate that the ticket was purchased seven days in advance and is nonrefundable.

And now, an important note about the dreaded word "nonrefundable." Surprisingly, a number of people actually believe that if they buy a nonrefundable ticket and they don't use it, they've lost the entire value of their ticket. They either throw the ticket into a desk drawer or, worse, throw it away, when in fact the ticket has substantial value and can often be applied to the purchase of another ticket. Remember, nonrefundable does NOT mean worthless.

Why are there so many fares for the same type of coach seat? It all gets down to something called *yield management,* the dark science of the travel industry. For each flight, an airline allocates only a certain number of seats at each fare level or "bucket." That number is a closely guarded secret. In fact, that information is considered highly proprietary. Access to the specific count (how many seats are being sold in which "bucket") is limited to only one or two people at any one airline. And if they tell you, they have to kill you.

Then there are the different TYPES of tickets: student fares, group fares, convention fares, VUSA (Visit USA) fares, senior coupon fares, consolidator tickets, military fares, Internet fares, and rtw (round the world) fares.

How do all of these get priced?

This is where things get sticky.

Let's say you don't understand the fare bases, you buy a cheap ticket, and, later, you want to change your flight. For example, you bought a $250 ticket and now you want to change the outbound flight (the first leg of your trip). You're in for a painful surprise. When you buy a cheap ticket, you can't disregard the restrictions that apply. If you try to change the ticket, you will end up paying more money than you wanted to. For example, your $250 ticket entitles you to a restricted fare. If you want to change your outgoing flight, you may be told that it will cost $1,000 to make that change. To change any outbound flight after you've bought a restricted ticket can be excessively expensive. Most people don't understand that the price of the ticket is based on the *outbound* flight. It sets the fare for the entire ticket.

Any way to get out of paying the extra fees?

Here's something that should make you angry. The airlines make more pure profit for their $75 rewriting/change fees on tickets than they make from actually flying you with your original tickets.

On principle alone, you should try to do anything within your power—or someone else's—to avoid paying those charges.

And, more often than not, your payment of those charges depends on the discretion of the counter agent at the airport. If he or she is in a good mood, the agent can easily waive the charges.

On the other hand, if the agent is trying to get high marks for living in the uncompromising world of literal interpretation, then you're stuck with the charge.

Sometimes you just get lucky. At other times, you need to MAKE your luck. Too many people look at their flying experience in one-dimensional terms. Every flight is a new flight. It's as if they've never flown before, and, to them, the people who work at the airport are faceless and nameless. Yet these same travelers wonder why they don't get treated better.

To me, it's obvious. They've spent absolutely no time developing a relationship with that counter or gate agent. Got a problem? Quite simply, the airlines can—if they want to—make it all better.

And it all gets down to the relationship, or relationships, you've built along the way.

Also, it becomes a matter of understanding, and then embracing, a much bigger view of the travel experience. At the same time, it also becomes a matter of reducing the travel experience to the very basics.

Why are you really flying? To go from A to B. You're really *not* there to be pampered, fed well, comforted, coddled, and cared for. If you believe you're entitled to that kind of attention, you've been brainwashed by too many misleading airline ads.

You're on the plane because it will transport you to where you want to go.

But here's the problem. Most people—and, I'm sad to say, a number of my friends—don't get this simple message.

Imagine that Los Angeles was being invaded by outer-space aliens, and there was only one flight at the gate to rescue everyone. Most of my friends would be eaten by the aliens. Why? Because they'd still be at the counter saying, "But I wanted a WINDOW seat."

No, the concept here is: Get on the plane. Period.

The unwritten, unspoken, but acted-upon rule is that people who understand the basics—people who at least try to comprehend the actual *process* of travel—are invariably better treated by the airlines.

Short of alien invasion, understanding ticket lingo and codes doesn't have to be an extraterrestrial experience. What follows is a basic primer.

When it comes to tickets and fares, everything is contingent on inventory. On every flight, you have varied inventory. For example, full coach (y) and full first-class (f) fares are almost always available, and with good reason. They are full fare, totally unrestricted tickets and give the airline the highest yield per ticket. But you may have only one or two K14NR fares, meaning a discounted, 14-days-in-advance, nonrefundable ticket. Or, NONE of those fares may be available. It all depends on how many full-fare coach, business, and first-class passengers are already booked on your flight. And, perhaps more important, it depends on how many full-fare passengers flew on the same flight last month and last year.

Each airline has a computer-driven model of the projected "load factor" for every flight. It provides a historical pattern that may date back five years. This model determines, more than anything else, how an airline will price the inventory for the same flight this year.

It also affects how quickly the airline will break into the inventory and change fares if the projections don't materialize. For example, Flight 204 from San Antonio to Dallas flew at 82 percent capacity last year and a majority of the passengers paid full fare. This pattern was consistent with previous years, so an abundance of low-fare seats is extremely unlikely for the same flight on the same day of the same month this year.

But if, two weeks before the departure date, the airline realizes that only 61 percent of the plane is filled, the carrier will begin to dump tickets through consolidators, mailings to the airline's frequent flyer program, or the Internet.

How can you find out the exact inventory on a flight—in other words, how many buckets and how many seats are left? The information you get really depends on the questions you ask the agent. Remember, the reservations agent on the other end of the phone is trained to ask you questions that will more or less limit your options.

When you get the lowest fare offered over the phone, make a reservation. You'll have twenty-four hours to pay for the ticket. This gives you enough time to be a comparison shopper. Call competing airlines, and then check the Internet.

Here's another unwritten rule. Let's say an airline will sell you a discount ticket—$400 to fly to Boston from San Francisco—for an 11:00 A.M. departure, but tells you the 8:00 A.M. departure—the flight you REALLY wanted—is not available.

When an agent tells you a flight is "not available," the REAL interpretation, in most cases, is that the flight is not available at the fare you want to pay. There could be dozens of available seats. Your retort should be: But are there SEATS available?" If there are, here's where you can get creative.

Go to the airport at 7:00 A.M. holding your 11:00 A.M. ticket. Go to the counter or the gate and say you came out early and would like to depart early if there's space available.

And, if there's space, you get to go out on the flight you originally wanted, at the fare you wanted to pay.

Airport airline counter agents are not only encouraged to do this, they are EMPOWERED to do it by their companies.

The logic, from the airlines' point of view, is that the earlier they get people out and fill the departing planes, the better they'll be if they have a cancellation later and have to spend money for accommodations, meals, and even denied-boarding compensation if the later flights operate but are overbooked.

The airline reservations agents will never tell you this. Unless you're traveling during a peak holiday period, this almost always works, and it is totally within the scope of the airline agents' discretion.

THE BEST DAY OF THE WEEK
TO BUY CHEAP TICKETS

Believe it or not, there really IS a best day of the week to make your best deal on an airline ticket, and it's neither Monday nor Friday. It's Wednesday! And there's even a best time on Wednesday to buy that ticket.

Why Wednesday? Thank the small upstart airlines. In the airline business, fare wars are started by the weakest competitors, and the big guys tend to be the ones to raise fares. And all of that tends to happen on Fridays.

So how did Wednesday become the ideal day to strike a deal?

Let's say Airline A decides to raise fares. It usually does so at a late hour on a Friday night.

By Saturday, Airline A's major competitors will probably match that fare increase. Warning: Book your tickets over a weekend, and you might spend a whole lot more than you should.

But what if the major competitors DON'T match the higher fares? Then the instigator of the fare increase drops back down late on Sunday night or on Monday morning. If you already paid a higher fare, you still may be out of luck. Why? Because although you might still qualify for a lower fare and a ticket exchange, that terrible $75 change fee might wipe out your savings!

Here's another example. Let's say upstart Airline B decides to begin a fare war. Again, it happens late on a Friday night. Usually, some (but not all) of the majors will match that fare on routes where they compete with Airline B. Does that mean you should still book tickets over the weekend? Absolutely not. Remember, I said some, but NOT ALL of the majors will match that fare. By late Monday, depending on how that new fare is doing in the marketplace, Airline C might jump into the battle and offer an even LOWER fare, so look for all the other airlines to rush to match THAT one— usually, by Tuesday—and the war is on. Prices might go even lower on Wednesday. And that's when you strike. Wait any longer than Wednesday, and you may be in trouble. The wars usually end by Thursday morning.

Why? Friday is just around the corner! And the cycle starts all over again.

What's the best time to buy your ticket on Wednesday? One hour after Tuesday midnight (1:00 A.M. Wednesday morning). Why? At about midnight, the airlines usually reload their computers with the latest low-cost fares that were announced the previous day but will be canceled if they are not purchased within twenty-four hours.

THE CLASS SYSTEM

The overall numbers are indeed staggering. By conservative estimates, the airlines update the fares in their computer systems OVER 250,000 TIMES A DAY!

That's how much the allocations of inventory change. Different classes; same economy seats!

In airline reservation computer systems, the allocation of seats into different fare categories is designated by "class of service" codes. Do not confuse these codes with the actual class of service (e.g., first class, business class, coach— or, for that matter, where you sit on the plane). First class and business class do have their own class-of-service codes, but many different class-of-service codes are used for the coach cabin, even though all of the passengers sit in the same place.

It happens all the time. A full-fare business traveler and the gen Xer on a budget may sit next to each other in the coach cabin—and often do—but their reservations were made with different class-of-service codes.

So how do you read your airline ticket? Start with the class of service printed on the ticket, and then go to the "fare basis."

First class is generally coded as F or P; business class is either C or J; and full-fare coach is Y.

Any other letter on your ticket refers to a different—and discounted—fare class. Most of these fare classes have restrictions. They are the dreaded "subclasses," and their letters are: M, B, H, K, Q, L, and V. Things get confusing because each airline has a different hierarchical structure for these letters and a different interpretation as to the restrictions they represent.

Those letters, combined with a "fare basis," will tell you what your ticket really means.

When you are checking whether a particular flight is available, what you really want to know is what classes are available. If you are looking for a low fare requiring booking in Q class, you must find a flight for which Q class is available.

If you see a fare marked U, you are looking at an Internet fare that can only be purchased online.

See a ticket with an L class? That could be the lowest-class ticket, which has the most restrictions. Generally, L class tickets are not upgradable.

THE AIRLINES' REAL
MILEAGE PROGRAM

What most passengers don't know is that international fares are based on mileage, and North American fares are based on the routing of the trip. International fare tariffs relate to an established amount of mileage—called the maximum permitted mileage (MPM)—between every point A and point B. The carriers interested in the traffic between these two points can use their own hubs, provided the maximum permitted mileage is not exceeded.

In the event that the mileage is exceeded by 5 percent (or 10, 15, 20, or 25 percent), a surcharge of 5 percent (or 10, 15, 20, or 25 percent) can be assessed. Beyond 25 percent additional mileage, the through fare must be split and recalculated.

This means that you CAN backtrack on your route overseas, but you can't use your destination as an intermediate point in the same fare breakdown. So, when planning an international trip with a number of stops, determine the farthest destination point, go there first, and then return to your original starting point, stopping over en route.

Under MPM rules, you can travel via the same intermediate point more than once, but you can only stop there once.

But these rules also allow you to play the "open jaw" game.

An "open jaw" allows you to travel, for example, from Seattle to Miami and then fly to Los Angeles from Miami (with no ticket between Los Angeles and Seattle). Hence the open jaw. And the fare? Usually, the same low fare as a Seattle-Miami round trip, instead of two full-fare one-way tickets: (1) Seattle to Miami (point A to point B) and (2) Miami to Los Angeles (point B to point C).

The caveat here is that the distance between points B and C must be less than the distance to and from points A and B. In this example, an open jaw on the Seattle-Miami-Los Angeles ticket is allowed because the distance between Miami and Los Angeles is less than a round trip between Seattle and Miami.

Another way to look at it: The distance between Los Angeles and Seattle must be shorter than the shortest distance actually flown on the ticket.

OPEN RETURN

If money is no problem, an open return gives you the most options. An open return is a totally unrestricted ticket that

allows you to fly between the destination city and your originating city with no set date or flight. You still have to make
a reservation when you want to fly, but, with an open return
ticket, you fly home when you want to fly.

THE CONFUSION OF STANDBY

Standby remains one of the more confusing terms in the airline business. Standby meant a special discounted fare during
my college days at the University of Wisconsin—the days of
the much-abused "student standby" fare. At that time, it WAS
a fare. The deal was: Get a student standby card and show up
at the airport. If there was a seat, you got to go for half price.

In those days (yes, I did actually do this), if a group of us
wanted to go to New York for the weekend, I'd phone the airline and make a phony reservation for a family of eight.
Then my friends would call and make phony reservations,
on the same plane, for other large families. The airline must
have thought it was family reunion time. Within two hours,
when I called the airline back, I was told the plane was sold
out. Bingo! Run to the airport. Get a cheap ticket. Get on the
plane and surprise! Forty empty seats!

Thanks to the thousands of college students who, like
me, tried this tactic—and given today's more sophisticated
and computerized airline reservations systems—those fares
no longer exist. But they were fun while they lasted.

There were even standby fares on the New York-to-
London route—not just for students, but for everyone—if
seats were available.

Today, with exceedingly few exceptions (Air Tran has a
limited, restricted standby program for students), standby is
simply a status, not a fare.

And, if you're flying standby, that means you're also on the waitlist.

But a waitlist isn't democratic. It's not first-come, first-served, no matter what the airlines tell you.

Getting on the waitlist is easy. But making the jump from the waitlist to an actual seat on the flight you want is something else altogether.

Your status on the waitlist has nothing to do with what time you got placed on that waitlist. It has to do with the class of service, the amount of money you paid for your ticket, and your status as a frequent flyer. If all else fails, there's always the hope that the counter or gate agent likes you and will look kindly on your plight.

If an airline agent tells you that he or she can put you on the "waitlist," ask him or her to interpret that status for you. Don't ask: "How many people are ahead of me?"

Instead, ask how many people are ahead of you "with priority status." If they number more than twelve and you're flying on a narrow-body plane, you're not only waiting for Godot, but Godot has a better chance of getting on that flight than you do. Look for alternate connecting flights immediately—or alternate airports.

On a wide-body plane with three classes of service, a waitlist with twelve people is actually promising! Ask immediately: Is the flight sold out in all classes? If not, you have an excellent chance of getting off that list and onto the plane.

OK, now you've got the fare you want. Or do you?

These are just the fares in the airlines' reservation computers. They aren't the fares offered on the Internet (by consolidators) or the fares being marketed to specific income and ethnic groups.

OTHER TICKET AND FARE SOURCES

Chances are, you've seen consolidator ads in newspapers. Consolidators offer low-cost round-trip tickets to major destinations around the world: $600 tickets to Hong Kong from San Diego; $478 to Paris from New York; and $500 tickets from Chicago to Madrid. The lowest regular airline fares on these routes often can be twice to three times as much.

Are the consolidators too good to be true?

Sometimes.

Consolidators are airline wholesalers who get tickets at fares far below the officially published tariffs, in exchange for committing to sell large numbers of seats for airlines. They sell to travel agents, ticket brokers, and, more often than not, directly to the public.

Each airline has a reasonably good estimate of its future bookings. If those bookings are low on certain flights, many airlines will dump tickets on the consolidator market.

The excess inventory is sold to consolidators for a low fixed price. Consolidators then sell these tickets to the public for a small profit. In the past, airlines argued that they didn't dump excess tickets on what was essentially a gray market. But that was tantamount to the Claude Raines character in *Casablanca,* who expresses shock and indignation that illegal gambling is going on inside Rick's café, and then collects his winnings from the previous evening.

Through consolidators, the airlines sell seats they otherwise might not sell, and they can say that they have not discounted their tickets. In fact, many consolidator tickets showed that full coach fare was paid (along with endorsements on the ticket that it was totally nonrefundable, nonexchangeable and was good on that airline on one specific flight).

Is it legal? The Federal Aviation Act of 1958 prohibits the sale of international airline tickets below published fares. But the Act—designed to protect airlines—is not being enforced, because the airlines are the ones violating it.

Consolidators thrived for years in this nether world of dumped tickets. But it's a tougher market these days.

Major international airlines are offering discounts themselves, so the consolidators have little room to maneuver and still offer meaningful discounts.

That's where misleading ads have become prevalent. Many consolidators are promoting fares that they cannot deliver.

A few years ago, and after receiving many consumer complaints, New York's metropolitan Better Business Bureau (BBB) decided to investigate.

The BBB read the ads and shopped them.

BBB staffers pored through newspaper ads, made calls, and, in some cases, even bought tickets to see which consolidators were telling the truth. They tested one consolidator's ad by trying to buy an advertised high-season cheap ticket between New York and Paris, but they couldn't buy a single ticket.

During the low season, the BBB investigators could buy the advertised low-fare tickets at only one out of five consolidators promoting them. After the BBB complained, it received documentation from a few consolidators that some tickets had been sold at advertised prices.

It bordered on bait-and-switch. It was like an electronics store ad selling a new $50 television set and only having one for sale.

The investigation also revealed that, in two-thirds of the cases, BBB investigators would have paid the same amount if they had purchased the ticket directly from an airline, or they couldn't get a confirmed seat or were put on a never-ending waiting list.

In each case, the advertised price was not available, and the investigators were offered a higher priced ticket.

In fairness, that's not always the case.

I surveyed six consolidators' advertising in *The Los Angeles Times*. From three of the six, the advertised price WAS available. And, the best deals I found were $179 less than the airline's lowest rate for the same dates.

Here are four rules to live by if you want to play the consolidator game (by the way, I buy tickets from consolidators all the time):

1. Always pay with a credit card. Paying by check offers no protection.

2. Watch out for surcharges. A number of consolidators try to impose an additional charge if you pay by credit card. In New York, where many of these consolidators are based, this is against state law (it doesn't matter where you live; where the transaction takes place is key).

3. Be aware that many consolidator tickets carry severe cancellation penalties, and most tickets are totally nonrefundable.

4. Make sure you have a confirmed seat. One BBB shopper bought a ticket to Paris, but there was no confirmed seat, and even the waiting list was closed. Then the consolidator tried to charge a $100 cancellation fee!

Most consolidators are not scam artists. They are, in fact, bona fide operations that don't always advertise honestly. That's not to say you can't find savings through consolidators. You just need to be an obsessed comparison shopper.

SURFING THE NEWSSTAND

Sound silly? It's not. Some of the best airline deals overseas can be found right at your local newsstand.

In your neighborhood, look for a newsstand that carries foreign—particularly British—newspapers. Buy any two of them. Take them home, and turn to the travel section. You will see numerous advertisements for great discount fares to virtually anywhere in the world. It's a safe bet that many of the fares will NEVER be offered in the United States; Some of the destinations aren't even marketed here—especially for discount fares.

As an example, let's say you want to fly from New York to the Canary Islands, or from Chicago to Nairobi. Looking for a discount fare? Good luck. You won't find one.

But you'd have to be dead not to be able to find a great discount fare to London. American, United, TWA, Northwest, Continental, and USAir fly there. So do British Airways, Virgin Atlantic, El Al, Kuwait Airways, and Air India—and I've probably forgotten a few others. With that much capacity over the North Atlantic, London remains an intense discount route.

So, getting to London is easy. You can often fly for as little as $298 round trip—sometimes, for even less.

And that's where the newspapers come in.

Go ahead. Price out the New York-Tenerife (Canary Islands) flight, and you'll be hit—even in coach—for fares that exceed $1,800.

London is a major international hub. Not only do all the big *and* small airlines fly there, but virtually every foreign country flies FROM there!

Begin with a cheap fare from New York to London. Now check the newspapers. I recently found a *round-trip* airfare from London to Tenerife for 89 *pounds* (that's about $150)!

This theory works on just about any itinerary you could imagine. In fact, it is sometimes cheaper to fly from Los Angeles to London, and then take a cheap flight to Hong Kong or Bangkok, than to take a nonstop flight from Los Angeles to Hong Kong.

RTW

But what if you want to stop in more than one destination? Point-to-point travel will kill your wallet. Instead, investigate an RTW (round the world) ticket. (These tickets are heavily promoted in the UK papers.)

Airlines don't promote these fares, and travel agents tend to hate them because they are labor-intensive to process.

But if you're stopping in more than one destination overseas, the RTW ticket is more than your friend. It's your lover!

For example, the regular coach fare between Los Angeles and Singapore is $1,300 each way. Other examples: New York City to Rome, coach, $1,100 each way; Chicago to Frankfurt, coach, $1,400 each way.

If you buy APEX (advance purchase excursion) tickets, the fares drop, but, in most cases, you can fly to only one destination, and you are allowed no stopovers or flexibility in departure dates on your outbound or return flights.

Enter RTW fares. They allow you not only tremendous flexibility but also an opportunity—quite literally—to see the world, sometimes for less money than a regular coach fare between the United States and Europe.

Round-the-world tickets have been quietly sold since 1978, when Pan American offered its "Round the World in 80

Days" fare. Initially, the highly promoted fare angered world airlines because the price of the RTW ticket was less than half the cost of a regular economy fare to circle the globe.

When Pan Am flew around the world, the fare made sense to the airline, to customers who wished to combine business with pleasure trips, and to passengers who wished to extend their vacations beyond one or two foreign destinations.

Pan Am ceased operations in 1991, and no one airline currently flies around the world. But the fare lives on.

Almost every international airline offers a special RTW ticket—usually, in conjunction with one or two other airlines. The fares are nothing less than terrific when compared to regular coach and even to other discount routings to foreign destinations.

Remember the Singapore Airlines fare of $1,300 each way between Los Angeles and Singapore?

That's $2,600 round trip. But a round-the-world ticket bought on Singapore Airlines (in conjunction with another airline) can cost as little as $2,570.

Here's what you can do with the RTW ticket. Fly to Tokyo on American Airlines, then on to Singapore, Athens, and Paris, all on Singapore Airlines. In Paris, switch to American, fly to New York, and stop numerous times as you cross the United States on your way back to Los Angeles.

That's just a westbound option. You can also start your flight by heading east on TWA and visiting cities such as Frankfurt, Brussels, and Bangkok via Singapore Airlines.

Here's the best news: To buy an RTW ticket, you need only make your reservation and buy your ticket fourteen days in advance. There's no minimum stay requirement.

The ticket is good for a year; you can fly when you want. There are two important restrictions:

1. You must continue in the same direction—no back-tracking.

2. After you start your trip, if you want to add more cities, the airline will charge you $25 for each change in the original itinerary.

You can buy the same ticket in business class for about $3,700, or in first class for about $6,000. (Some cost comparisons: A round-trip point-to-point business-class ticket between Los Angeles and Paris is more than $6,800, and a first-class ticket weighs in at more than $8,100!)

This example is just one of dozens of possible combinations of routes and airlines.

Singapore Airlines has teamed with Delta, Air New Zealand, and American Airlines to offer various itineraries. Air Canada has joined with Japan Air Lines, and British Airways has paired with American and United to offer similar RTW bargains.

The combinations on RTW tickets are almost endless. Their sheer economy may explain why, with very little promotion or advertising, a growing number of passengers are buying RTW tickets. And they're not just coach passengers.

You will realize even greater savings if you buy your RTW ticket on another continent. One travel agency in England recently offered a RTW ticket for 1,100 pounds (about U.S. $1,800).

On some RTW tickets, provisions are made for side trips, and some airlines offer discounts on itineraries not flown by them or their RTW partners. (For example, few international airlines have extensive routings in South America, but some offer attractive side packages with local airlines for trips within that continent.)

A typical Japan Airways/TWA round the world itinerary might start with a trip from New York to Los Angeles. From Los Angeles you could fly to Honolulu and from there to Tokyo, Seoul, Osaka, Hong Kong, Bangkok, Delhi, Cairo, Athens, and Paris. A TWA European connection could then bring you home to New York.

One of the more exotic RTW itineraries was offered not long ago by American Airlines, Korean Air, and Royal Jordanian Airlines. Passengers flew from New York to Los Angeles, then on to Honolulu on American. From Honolulu to Tokyo, they were on Korean Airlines, which offered a continuing itinerary that included Osaka, Seoul, Taipei, Hong Kong, and Bangkok.

Royal Jordanian flew them from Bangkok to Amman, Jordan, then on to Cairo and Paris. The leg from France to the United States was an American flight.

Itinerary offerings change frequently, but once you're ticketed, you're in.

One of the great things about RTW tickets (other than the fares) is that you don't have to fly to all these destinations. You can fly to as many or as few as you wish, just as long as you circle the globe.

(Some travelers book flights to a dozen or so destinations on the route structure of one of the airlines. If they later decide to skip a city or two, they can usually bypass them without incurring additional costs.)

Perhaps the best news about RTW tickets is that if you're a member of a frequent-flier program on any of the participating airlines, you can earn mileage. In the airline mileage game, this is tantamount to nuclear fusion. Considering the distances involved, your RTW adventures could conceivably earn enough mileage points to qualify you for a free ticket upon your return.

AIR PASSES

Air passes aren't RTW tickets, but the concept is the same. In conjunction with round-trip tickets between two points, many airlines offer great deals for travel within certain countries or continents. When you buy a round-trip ticket, always check with foreign carriers to see what particular promotions they offer. In South America, a Latin Pass, for a nominal amount, gives you great flexibility in flying around that continent. British Airways (BA) has seasonal deals featuring booklets of flight coupons. For as little as $50, you can fly from London to many European cities if you've bought a round-trip ticket to London on BA. In the South Pacific, there are similar deals. But remember, you MUST buy these deals when you buy your round-trip tickets in the United States. If you wait until you get overseas, the deals do not apply.

COUPONS

Every once in a while, an airline will issue (or some travel agents will be incentivized to issue) promotional coupons. These coupons offer either a specific dollar discount or a sliding scale, depending on the initial fare you're paying.

An even better coupon is the one that offers a flat percentage off the cost of any published fare. But the next time you see one of these coupons, read the fine print. It may actually benefit you even more. For example, I recently received one of these coupons, and the ticketing instructions, printed on the back of the coupon, specifically delineated the deal: 50 percent off any published fare/itinerary. The key word was itinerary.

I combined the coupon with another coupon. (I save all those that come my way.) That gave me an upgrade to the next class of service on any "itinerary."

I then booked the following itinerary, which included two open jaw tickets, at the cheapest coach fare I could find: Los Angeles to Paris, then Paris to Orlando (open jaw number one), then Orlando to New York, and New York back to Los Angeles (open jaw number two). Total fare on this one "itinerary": about $1,526 in coach. I used my 50-percent-off coupon to bring the total fare down to $763, and then assigned my upgrade coupon to the same itinerary. I flew business class or first class on this itinerary for a total fare of $763! And, I accumulated lots and lots of future mileage.

ALTERNATE AIRPORTS

Have you considered alternate airports?

On a flight from Los Angeles to New York, you can get even cheaper fares by flying from secondary or tertiary airports—Burbank, Ontario, Long Beach, or San Diego—to Newark, LaGuardia, or Islip instead of Kennedy (JFK).

Every once in a while, even JFK becomes the desired alternate airport. Most people don't realize that, of the three major New York-area airports, JFK is the LEAST congested. With the exception of the 3:00 P.M. to 7:00 P.M, time slots, when most international flights either arrive or depart, JFK is operating at nowhere near its capacity.

This fact wasn't lost on the folks who started a new low-fare airline, Jet Blue, early in 2000. Jet Blue flies between JFK and Orlando, Fort Lauderdale, and Tampa (Florida), Buffalo (New York), and other East Coast cities. (It recently expanded to offer flights to the West Coast as well.)

Consider this: a one-way walk-up fare between New York and Orlando, flying out of congested LaGuardia on American Airlines. Cost: an average of $560—one way! Cost of the same trip from JFK on Jet Blue: $169 (and that's Jet Blue's HIGHEST fare). The irony is that, on some flights, the taxi time and delay time out of LaGuardia exceeds Jet Blue's flight time from JFK to Orlando!

One of the best airports for discount pricing is Newark (New Jersey). So many low-fare carriers fly there that the majors often match their fares.

The same deal can often be found at Kennedy, ask. Then ask again. Airlines may not always volunteer their time-specific discounts.

For example, American Flight 34 is an 8:00 A.M. departure from Los Angeles to JFK. It is not an inexpensive flight. But if you ask about a time-specific discount on the same route, American throws in its 7:00 A.M. departure, and there are significant savings.

Most of the time, that flight actually begins in Honolulu as the red-eye to California from Hawaii. American then needs to get the aircraft to New York so it can assign the plane, later that day, to the profitable 5:00 P.M. or 6:00 P.M. premium flights back to Los Angeles. And those are the flights you want.

Other positioning flights are deeply discounted by the airlines. Check the flight schedules for unusual departures. For example, Northwest Airlines has a late-night (10:30 P.M.) departure from Detroit to Washington, DC.

Does anyone ever take that flight? No.

Then why is it scheduled? Because Northwest flies the aircraft to Washington, where it undergoes basic overnight maintenance and becomes the popular first flight out of the District to Detroit the next morning. During that night positioning flight back to the nation's capital, you can literally go bowling on the plane. It is THAT empty ... and is often priced accordingly.

I DON'T HATE TRAVEL
AGENTS, BUT MANY TRAVEL
AGENTS THINK I DO

Once, for a segment I was preparing for ABC's *Good Morning America,* I decided to see how competitive travel agents were, and whether I could get better fares on my own.

I polled thirty travel agents around the United States. I asked them all the same question: "I'm traveling tomorrow between city A and city B. What's the lowest fare you can get me?" I then called individual airlines and asked the same question.

In every case, I got a lower fare from the airline.

We did the segment on *Good Morning America* a week after the survey, and we talked about the results. In one case, the fare differential between the travel agent's price and the price when I called the airlines directly was something like $831.

That was a major blow to travel agents. Before I was off the air, ABC and its affiliated stations around the country were being inundated with angry telephone calls. Within two hours of airing the segment, an organized letter-writing and faxing campaign began, led by the American Society of Travel Agents (ASTA).

Each letter or fax had essentially the same message. Each claimed that I was irresponsible, unfair, and biased against travel agents, and each demanded to have ASTA come on *Good Morning America* to dispute my report.

By the end of the first day, the angry letters and faxes numbered 7,000. By the next day, incoming messages were up to 14,000, a one-time record of negative responses.

I had not yet returned to Los Angeles. I was called into the New York office of Phil Beuth, the executive who ran *Good Morning America.* "What is this all about?" he queried. "This is the most negative response to a segment I've ever seen. Have we been fair here?"

I reminded him that, without exception, every letter was from a travel agent, and each letter's wording was virtually identical. I asked him: "Have there been any angry letters from consumers complaining that I saved them $831?"

We agreed that, in the interest of fairness, we should invite ASTA to appear on the show.

ABC then invited ASTA to send a representative to the show the following week, to discuss the segment.

ASTA refused, insisting that they would not send someone to any show on which I would also appear. I countered that I would simply sit and say nothing during the first four minutes of a six-minute segment, to give ASTA the opportunity to state its case.

Again, ASTA refused.

I then got on an airplane and returned to Los Angeles.

A funny thing happened during my transcontinental flight home.

ABC producers, confronted with thousands of protesting letters from individual travel agents, each demanding to come on *Good Morning America,* decided to simply pick one at random and extend the same invitation that was delivered to the ASTA executives.

When the ASTA executives heard about this proposal, they did an about-face and sent Richard Knodt, then their

Chief Operating Officer, to New York. ABC called and told me to fly back.

The resulting ABC segment made history, of sorts. Tape from that segment is now being used during media training sessions for executives, to teach them what NEVER to do or say on a talk show.

I later found out that the segment was a catalyst for one top airline executive who was watching the show that morning.

Knodt argued that my "conclusion that consumers should shop airlines themselves to ensure the lowest fare is like instructing your three-year-old to jump in the water and hopefully swim."

He said that my survey was unfair, and he argued that a travel agent in Boston couldn't be expected to know the lowest fare between Miami and San Francisco.

What? "But isn't that your job? Isn't that what you're supposed to do?" asked co-host Nancy Snyderman.

"Well," Knodt responded, looking at me, "he's smarter than the average consumer and knows all the flights and routes."

"Wait," I interrupted. "Let's look at the facts. All I did was call thirty travel agents at random. These were cold calls. An even playing field. And I asked them what the lowest fare was between two cities. How smart do you have to be to ask that question?"

The entire segment headed south. I then explained not only my survey but the results from two similar price-challenge surveys by independent, nonprofit, consumer research groups in Washington, DC, and San Francisco.

In the San Francisco survey, of thirty agencies surveyed by the "Bay Area Consumers' Checkbook," only two agents were consistently able to find the lowest prices. In a similar survey of 100 DC-area travel agents, most failed the price challenge.

For ASTA to say that consumers who seek out low air fares on their own are like three-year-olds about to drown is an insult to most travelers. I argued that anyone who had a telephone and a little extra time could often achieve substantial savings by being a good comparison shopper.

So, what is ASTA's grievance with me? In correspondence to travel editors at various newspapers, Knodt argued as follows:

- Consumers don't normally call travel agents in Chicago to ask them the lowest air fare between San Francisco and New York. They would normally call a travel agent in either San Francisco or New York. But that's exactly what I did, thirty out of thirty travel agents failed the price challenge.

- Because I possess more travel and price knowledge than the average consumer, the test was unfairly weighted. I accept the compliment, but I called agents and airlines and posed the same question in the same manner that any consumer would. I merely explained my travel itinerary and asked for the lowest air fare. You don't need any extra knowledge or special travel experience to ask that simple question.

- "Left alone with the virtual morass of ever-changing air fares," ASTA's Knodt claimed, "consumers can waste valuable time as they are left sinking in the ocean of fares, schedules, and carriers to choose from." My response: Armed with nothing other than the toll-free numbers of the airlines, it took me only twenty minutes to get the lowest prices for each pair of cities, and, in the San Francisco-to-DC example, I saved more than $800. I think that was time very well spent.

In a follow-up piece, I said that, in an ideal world, travelers should be able to find a travel agent who will consistently get them the lowest fare and the best deal. But in the real world, this does not often happen, and here is why:

- Travel agents work on a commission basis for airlines, cruise lines, hotels, and rental car companies. When a travel agent offers a customer a lower fare, that agent must be willing to accept a lower commission. What's the incentive to do that? Your continued business. Conclusion: If you can find an agent who will do that, use that agent. If not, do the agent's work yourself.

RESERVATION COMPUTER BIAS

At that time, the U.S. Department of Transportation (DOT) was conducting a sweeping investigation into the relationship between travel agents and the computer reservation systems supplied by individual airlines. Were the proprietary computers placing undue influence on the travel agents to favor particular airlines?

As part of its in-depth review, the DOT was looking closely at:

- *Override commissions.* Most travel agents then operated on an average commission of 10 percent. An airline ticket bought from a travel agent for $400 gave the agent $40 profit. But there were also override commissions, and few agents disclosed them to travelers. Some airlines paid as much as 23 percent commission to agents who steered business to them. One cruise line recently offered 20 percent commission to agents. That's a significant incentive. But how does that benefit consumers? More often than not, it doesn't. The powerful economics of override commissions often mean that some travel agents will feel pressure to book you on the flight or cruise, or at the hotel, where they make the highest commission.

- *Secret software.* Some large travel agencies had created their own "secret software" to indicate the suppliers that paid override commissions. Their computers displayed these airlines, hotels, and cruise lines first on the lists that scrolled through agents' screens.

And then came the whammy. A few months after the *Good Morning America* segment ran, Delta Airlines fired the first shot—a big one—below the waterline of most travel agencies. Delta announced commission caps. And, within days, almost every airline matched Delta's cuts. The travel agency business would never be the same. (Later, I found out that tapes of the original and subsequent *Good Morning America* segments were shown to Ron Allen, then head of Delta Airlines. He told me in an interview that the *Good Morning America* pieces served as major catalysts in his making that commission decision.)

One of the holdouts on the commission cuts was TWA. It misjudged travel agents' real power when it kept its commission rate at a flat 10 percent. ASTA also misjudged its members' power when it announced that it would boycott airlines that cut commissions.

Six months later, the numbers were unavoidable and sent a major wakeup call to the entire travel industry. Who had the real power? YOU DID!

How much new business came over to TWA when it kept the 10 percent commission? None. How much business did the other airlines lose when they cut their commissions? None.

Why? The relationship between consumers and travel agents had changed. Air travelers are loyal to the frequent flyer programs where they are members. They no longer ask travel agents for airline advice. They TELL the agents which airline they want to fly on. Period.

With no strong commission structure to financially protect them, many travel agents went out of business.

The ones who survived—indeed, the ones who succeeded—became much better travel agents in the process. These agents understand that their financial well-being no longer comes from a ticket transaction. It grows by providing service and up-to-date information on *everything*, not simply what time a plane leaves and arrives.

As a result, many travel agents began to specialize, focusing on particular market niches. We are now seeing travel agents who are experts on specific destinations or experiences. They specialize in cruise ships, East Africa, barge trips, travel for the handicapped, and so on.

Today, we consult travel agents the way we seek medical help. We don't see a podiatrist if our arm hurts us, and many of us now consult more than one travel agent.

For their part, travel agents are moving quickly into a service fee mode. Many charge between $20 and $100 (or more) for finding us great experiences, and yes, even great deals. And those agents deserve every penny they are charging.

Commission caps made travel agents proactive and service-oriented instead of transaction-oriented. For smart travelers and smart travel agents alike, it was—and continues to be—a win-win situation.

One caution: Secret override commissions still exist between airlines and travel agents. When shopping for a travel agent, you owe it to yourself to ask the agent to reveal whether he or she has any override commission or "pre-ferred supplier" relationship with any airline, cruise ship, or hotel. It lets the agent know—or serves as a reminder—that you expect him or her to work for you first.

A FINAL NOTE ABOUT TRAVEL AGENTS

The changing role of travel agents, particularly in relation to consumers, has been nothing less than dramatic, not only because of the speed at which this change has happened, but because of its impact.

No one understands that better than Matthew Upchurch, who runs Virtuoso, a consortium of expert travel agents around the world. Upchurch not only tells other travel agents how to survive, he shows them how to succeed by pointing them back in time.

Upchurch puts it all in proper perspective when he says that to understand the function and the service of a travel agent, "We've gone back to the future.

"A lot of people forget that, prior to deregulation and prior to the advent of sophisticated airline computer reser-vations systems, the majority of airline tickets were actually processed by the airlines and not by travel agents."

He reminds us: "And there used to be a lot fewer agents in this country. The process was fairly simple. There used to be four airfares: day coach, night coach, day first class, and night first class. And it was a regulated environment. And if you flew from New York to London, whether it was on BOAC, or Pan Am, or a lot of those airlines that aren't around anymore, you paid the same fare, regardless of what airline you flew."

So why did people go to an agent? In those days, it was very easy to go directly to an airline and book a flight. Up-church argues that you went to agents because of their ex-

pertise, their service, and their knowledge beyond just booking that particular ticket.

But, in the early 1970s the airlines introduced their CRS
(computer reservations systems), and, in 1978, deregulation
hit. Suddenly there was an explosion of mergers and a complexity of airfares. "Imagine the next thing that happens,"
Upchurch suggests. "Take all the airlines, which are not exactly known for their labor relations and their treatment of
their employees—and all of a sudden they talk among themselves, and they come to the same conclusion. 'We've created these computer systems but if we put them in front of
our own people and ask that staff to take phone calls both
from consumers and from agents, we're going to have to hire
hundreds, if not thousands, of these people. And, God forbid
that they want health insurance. God forbid that they want a
pension plan. And God forbid they sue us for carpal tunnel
syndrome or God knows what, and unionize, and walk out
on us. Gee, maybe we should take these computers and turn
around and GIVE them to travel agents. And here's the best
part: And then we can tell them what we're going to pay
them without any problem. And they won't have collective
bargaining, and they don't get health benefits or a pension.'

"It was brilliant," says Upchurch. "And it easily became
one of the . . . largest outsourcings of labor in the history of
the country."

Indeed, compared to having the airlines process tickets
by themselves, enlisting the travel agent community was a
much less expensive way of handling ticket distribution.
The airlines had effective outsourced labor, using their new
technology.

"It created an artificial monopoly," Upchurch argues,
"with information and fares and rates, for almost twenty-
seven years."

Then the technology caught up.

Enter the Internet.

So then what happened? The airlines started introducing direct booking via the Internet. The technology was available to the public, and the public seized it. The airlines were quick to create a direct booking mechanism, and, when coupled with commission cuts, travel agents found themselves in deep trouble.

Or were they?

Initially, virtually everyone predicted the demise of all travel agents. But it didn't happen.

Upchurch knows why. "People thought they could just go out and, with the Internet, do all their own booking themselves. For commodity purchases, like an airplane seat on Southwest, they could indeed do it. But for just about everything else, they soon found out they needed help—not in the physical booking of a trip, but in the details, in the information they needed."

And so, we've come full circle.

More people *are* booking direct, but even more people are traveling, so the numbers have gone higher for travel agents. Ten thousand baby boomers are turning age fifty-five EVERY DAY in this country, and they all want to travel—or travel *more.*

"Boomers also are the most traveled, best educated, most connected group of consumers in the history of mankind," Upchurch reports.

"This group is a tough audience," he says, "and travel is at the top of their list. Times have definitely changed. The World War II generation and the Depression Era generation . . . saw travel as a luxury. The Boomers see travel as a God-given right."

In satisfying that desire, they want added value. The good news for all of us is that travel agents have come to realize that they have to provide that added value in order to stay in business.

Today's travelers don't want to "talk to some airline person . . . they don't trust," Upchurch warns. "They just want to talk to somebody who cares. What's amazing to me is that, in one of the presidential primary debates, one of the questions that was asked was: 'What are you going to do about airline service?' This was in a presidential debate! Now if I were an industry, I'd say, 'By golly, we have a problem.'" Indeed, there has been a problem. "So what are travel agents selling?" Upchurch asks. "We're selling information, relationships, and connections."

But, in that environment, Upchurch has learned that the travel industry continues to make a mistake. It tries to sell travel based on the price rather than on the perceived merit or the experience of the trip.

He calls it "the NBA courtside-seat syndrome." "The same person that will sit there and pound down to the last dime on some sale of something—in fact, you would have thought that they didn't have two nickels to rub together— will stop at nothing to pay $1,000 a ticket for NBA courtside seats. Because they want that experience. Because it's not the money. It's the perceived value of the experience. And that's what travel is all about," Upchurch reports.

"Today, consumers are overwhelmed with information," says Upchurch. "In fact, one of my favorite quotes is that 'in a world of limitless opportunities and limitless information, the only scarcity will be human attention.' If a travel agent can be an aggregator—somebody who can filter the information that someone trusts—then that is the travel agent I want. . . . The new travel agent engages . . . customers in a dialogue about what their aspirations are. And that information gets shared. So, . . . all of a sudden, we know that there are

500 people in the United States, . . . customers of our members, who've always wanted to go dog sledding. And then the travel agent can make that happen, as a specialist in dog sledding.

"But the most interesting development," says Upchurch, is that the airlines have felt, for a long time, that they *own* travel agents. After all, they provided the agents [with] their computer systems. And they made those agents perform— sell their particular airline—to *keep* that computer system."

Do the airlines own the agents?

Upchurch says it just isn't so. "A long time ago, the Boston Consulting Group did a study for the airlines to try to determine that airline-travel agent relationship. What's amazing," Upchurch laughs, "is that the airlines would go out and pay a consulting company—God knows how many millions of dollars—to tell them the most obvious. Who is going to decide the fate of travel agents? The customer, not the airlines. But, the airlines had seen us as something that they created, as an extension of their distribution system."

That was then. This is now. Savvy travel agents are embracing a collaborative model of doing business, of getting to know their customers, of focusing less on the actual ticket transaction—its speed, accuracy, convenience, and price— and more on understanding the experiential needs of their customers.

Yes, there are still people who like using ATMs instead of dealing with tellers at banks. But travel is more sophisticated. "Ten years ago, somebody could walk into an agency and say 'I want to go to South Africa.' And they probably would consider the agent an expert on South Africa if [he or she] just even knew the country of Namibia existed and could point to it on the map. Today, that person calls the agent on the phone, and if you haven't been there in the last twelve months, if you don't have personal contacts, if you don't know the elephant migration patterns, you're not an expert."

The travel agency-customer relationship is a combination of collaborative and expertise models. It's similar to how people now deal with their doctors. "We're no different," Upchurch argues. "In the old days, you'd go to your doctor and whatever he said you took as gospel. . . . Now, people go and research stuff and walk into their doctors' offices and say, 'Well, what about this drug, or what about this alternative means of treatment?' They want to be connected with somebody who's a professional to help validate the information they've already researched on their own."

I DON'T HATE TRAVEL AGENTS, BUT I DO HATE E-TICKETS

Before I tell you about e-tickets, let me tell you a little about my mother. She has cornered the market on rotary phones, manual typewriters, and carbon paper. She doesn't understand fax machines, cell phones, or pagers. The Internet isn't another planet to her—it's another galaxy!

But my mother and I agree on one thing: we hate e-tickets.

Since 1995, airlines have been offering, promoting, and, in some cases, virtually FORCING US to use electronic tickets (e-tickets).

When they were first introduced by United Airlines, the official spin was that the airlines were giving us electronic tickets as a big present.

A present? An e-ticket, we were told, would give us the opportunity for "seamless" travel. We could make a reservation and then, with no paper ticket or document in our hand, we could simply show up at the airport, go right to the gate, show a piece of photo I.D., and board our flight.

Indeed, in principle, you could—and you can—do this with an e-ticket.

But let's examine the e-ticket more closely.

The real reason the airlines love e-tickets has nothing to do with their passengers or with seamless travel. It has much more to do with lowering the airlines' ticket distribution costs.

By some estimates, the cost of processing an e-ticket runs about 22 cents. A paper ticket costs an airline closer to $4.00 or $5.00.

Have the airlines lowered their costs? Indeed they have. In fact, since they started e-tickets, airlines have continued to close more and more city ticket offices. In some cities, when ticket counter agents leave their jobs, they are not replaced.

Some travelers actually fear that, in the not too distant future, we will arrive at the airport to confront nothing more than an airline version of an ATM machine. There will be NO human contact!

Ask the airlines about e-tickets and they will boast that their own surveys show that more than 70 percent of their customers *like* e-tickets. Besides, they claim, you can't LOSE an e-ticket.

What the airlines WON'T tell you is that they have pre-programmed their computers to automatically issue e-tickets unless the passenger demands a traditional paper ticket. They have also incentivized the ticket transaction by offering passengers mileage bonuses or even fare discounts if they book online and purchase an e-ticket.

So why do I hate e-tickets? Forgetting for the moment that customer service has been decreased in the process, I'm even more worried that e-tickets, by their very definition, immediately limit our options and, in some cases, remove them entirely.

Let me explain.

Unless you have a propensity for losing your tickets—at which point I might actually suggest you DO use e-tickets—the e-ticket is NOT your friend.

Here's a recent example. I was flying with two friends from Washington DC, to Los Angeles on an early morning American flight. I was holding a paper ticket. My friends had been electronically ticketed.

On the way to the airport, they called me a dinosaur because of my allegiance to the paper ticket.

"It's just one more piece of paper to carry," one of them said. "One more thing to lose."

Again, I made my argument that unless you lose your tickets often, there was still nothing to recommend the e-ticket.

When we arrived at the airport, we were confronted with bad news. The American flight was delayed. Our 767 would not be leaving for at least four hours.

I didn't jump on the ever-growing line of disgruntled fliers waiting to rebook. I ran to the nearest phone, called the toll-free number for American, and asked to be put on the next available flight, which was, in this case, a United 747.

I simply walked over to the United gate, where the plane was about to leave, showed my paper ticket, and away I went. My friends were last seen on that American Airlines line. Why? They had to stay there to turn their e-ticket into the paper ticket they should have had in the first place!

There's another down side to the e-ticket. If you change your flights frequently, or you have a sudden change of plans, you may be at a distinct disadvantage with an e-ticket. Not in terms of rebooking, but in terms of REMEMBERING.

Example: You're booked on a round-trip e-ticket from Miami to Boston. You fly your original segment from Miami to Boston. But when you arrive in Boston, your itinerary changes. Instead of returning to Miami, you have to fly to New Orleans and then return to New York. So you buy an additional ticket to New Orleans and then to New York.

With a paper ticket, you have a physical reminder that you never used that first return portion of your ticket back to Miami. And that return portion CAN be used. It has value.

However, with an e-ticket, a majority of fliers tend to forget they never used that return portion. The airline keeps the revenue, and you lose not only the money but the option of using that ticket.

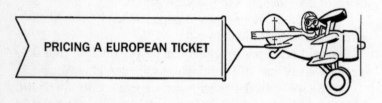

PRICING A EUROPEAN TICKET

There have always been charter operators and airlines that have dumped unsold tickets on the "bucket shop" market—another name for discount travel agencies in Europe. And a few airlines (Aeroflot, for example) continue to sell under-the-counter tickets.

But, for most travelers, there are no published discount airfares in Europe. Passengers flying between European cities pay an astonishing average of 73 percent more for their tickets than passengers flying between American cities that are the same distances apart.

The high prices have continued because European airlines have shared an unwritten agreement to keep fares high. Now, however, a few cracks have appeared in the European airfare wall. Deregulation has finally caught up with Europe, and a number of low-fare startup airlines have been the catalysts.

Years after the European Court of Justice ruled that the fare fixing practiced by most European airlines was illegal, there are now competitive airfares within the Continent.

The revision started when the British government reluctantly allowed British Midland, an independent airline, to compete on free-market terms with then government-owned British Airways between London's Heathrow Airport and Glasgow, Scotland.

Prices on the route dropped, in-flight service improved, and passengers were offered schedule flexibility at a reasonable price.

Soon after British Midland got into the act, KLM began offering one-way fares as low as $49 (U.S.) between Amsterdam and London. British Airways matched the fares. Again, passengers were happy, traffic increased, and the airlines made money.

Shortly after the European Court's decision, Air France proposed Europe-wide fare cuts of as much as 34 percent. More recently, a fare battle erupted over the Irish Sea. Ryanair discounted its fares between London and Ireland, prompting British Airways and Aer Lingus to cut their prices as well.

Now, Easyjet, Virgin Express, and Go are operating as low-cost, low-fare intra-Europe carriers.

Not only have fares dropped, but smaller nations' flag carriers—Icelandair, Royal Jordanian, and Air India—are now undercutting fares of some of the bigger airlines on long-haul intercontinental routes.

A coach seat on a U.S. carrier (or on Air France, for that matter) between New York and Paris runs $888 for a round trip. Icelandair sells the same seat for $665.

And, thanks to the Internet, American travelers can buy a number of deals in the United States before they leave home. Europebyair (www.europebyair.com) offers a flight pass deal: unlimited flights within Europe for a fifteen-day period for $699. A twenty-one day pass costs $899. You can book as many flights as you want within that period. The pass is accepted on sixteen airlines for 130 destinations in twenty-seven countries.

Remember that liberalized routes and the authority to cut fares don't automatically lead to lower prices and better service.

But demand does. Which brings me to a different way to find cheap tickets: the ethnic route.

A hidden discount world can be found among ethnic travel agents operating within ethnic communities in the United States.

Want a cheap flight to Korea from Los Angeles? Head down to Koreatown and buy the ticket from just about any Korean travel agent. In New York, Kosfo Travel sells, for $840, a ticket to Seoul that normally prices at $1,350.

Heading for Argentina? Check out Holdy Tours in San Francisco. A normal $1,300 round trip to Buenos Aires goes for just $530.

The same is true for tickets purchased for flights from the United States to India, Pakistan, Brazil, Ireland, Israel, China, and South Africa. Even Japan, not known as a discount destination, suddenly becomes one if you go through an ethnic agent/discounter. A normal $950 ticket from Los Angeles to Tokyo suddenly costs $650 if you buy it from Kintetsu International in Los Angeles.

SPLIT TICKETS

A weak currency may be a friend that makes a split ticket worthwhile. Split ticketing, or currency differential ticketing, is totally legal, and if you're flying first class, business class, or full-fare coach, the savings can be substantial.

Here's how it works. You purchase two separate one-way tickets instead of a round-trip ticket. You buy your outbound ticket in the United States and pay in dollars, and you buy a ticket for a one-way ticket flight back to the United States from the foreign destination, and pay in local currency.

Always check the fare (in local currency) of your return flight first, to determine whether the saving will, in fact, be significant. Many times, the difference is huge.

The cost of a one-way business-class ticket on Alitalia from New York to Milan is $2,553. But the Milan-to-New York business-class ticket, paid for in lira, totals out at $1,181. The split ticketing saves $1,372!

From Los Angeles to Bangkok, a round-trip business-class ticket on Thai Airways would run you $3,040 if purchased in the United States. Instead, buy a one-way ticket from LAX for $1,520 and buy your return ticket in Bangkok for $1,002. You'll save $518.

From New York to Paris, Air France will charge you $5,972 for a round-trip business-class ticket. Instead, buy the one-way flight for $2,986, pay for the return in French francs (equal to $2,102 U.S.), and save $884.

If you must fly frequently between two international destinations, you can maximize yours savings by purchasing a one-way ticket from the United States to that destination. When you arrive there, buy a round-trip ticket for your trip home and your next return overseas.

"INEXPENSIVE" DOESN'T JUST MEAN THE BACK OF THE BUS

Yes, it's even possible to get discounted first-class and business-class seats. The bucket shops and British newspapers advertise them.

Once again, if you can construct routings that take advantage of currency fluctuations and other marketing inconsistencies, you can get serious discounts in the front of the cabin.

If you're in Hong Kong and want to fly business class to London, Cathay Pacfic sells that ticket for $5,683. But if you're flying from Seoul to London (via Hong Kong), Cathay will put you on the *same flight* to London for just $3,584. So how do you take advantage of this lower fare without flying hundreds of extra miles out of your way?

Smart travel agents will book the Seoul-Hong Kong-London flight for you, and will then cancel the Seoul-Hong Kong portion. You simply throw away the first coupon and board the plane in Hong Kong.

Because these are NOT restricted tickets, you don't run the risk of being denied boarding. They are the full-fare business-class tickets on that route.

Officially, Cathay states that "we may not honor your ticket if the first flight coupon for international travel has not been used and you commence your journey at any stopover."

That's theoretically true, but as long as (1) the first coupon is pulled by you, (2) the original reservation is canceled, and (3) the onward reservations are intact (that's where your travel agent comes in), you're in excellent shape. Remember, travel agents can't and don't advertise this service, but, in Asia, they all do it. It is an unwritten and unspoken daily practice.

The worst that could happen? On rare occasions, you might be challenged and made to pay the difference. Again, it is NOT illegal, but the airlines frown on it.

THE COMMON RATED PLOY

Go beyond split tickets between the United States and foreign countries; look at some of the split ticketing *between* foreign countries. For example, many airlines charge the same fare from the United Kingdom to their main headquarters airport and to various other destinations reached by changing planes at that main airport. When that happens, these destinations are called "common rated." And free stopovers are often allowed.

Let's say you're traveling to the South Pacific. If you're headed to Christchurch, in New Zealand, that city is common-rated with Auckland, the main airport where Air New Zealand is headquartered. How does this work for you? If you book a cheap flight to Auckland and then want to fly to Christchurch, you're getting ripped off. Instead, book your flight to Christchurch and get a free stopover in Auckland.

Another example. If you're flying from London to Malaysia, don't book a nonstop from London to Kuala Lumpur. Book the ticket as London to Penang, or Langkawi, or another Malaysian destination, and get essentially a free stopover in Kuala Lumpur. (Singapore Airlines common-rates Penang and Kuala Lumpur with its own main airport at Changi, in Singapore, so the same booking principle would apply.)

THROW IN A HOTEL EVEN IF YOU HAVE NO NEED FOR ONE

On the surface, this tactic makes no sense at all, until you begin to understand how large blocks of airline seats are presold to tour operators who also control similar numbers of hotel rooms.

In the United States, getting an inexpensive ticket to Hawaii seems impossible, until you throw in a hotel room.

Large discount operators, like Pleasant Hawaiian, book huge blocks of seats on flights between West Coast cities and

Honolulu and Maui. They offer those seats as part of heavily discounted land packages—for example, six days in Honolulu, *with hotel,* for $498. A similar deal in Maui goes for $565.

If you're trying to get to Hawaii at the last minute and the cheapest round-trip ticket is $1,400, book the Pleasant Hawaiian deal, with the hotel package, even if you know you won't use the room. It's still a better deal.

The tour operator won't love having an empty room, but you're reimbursing some of the revenue spent for a seat that would otherwise go empty.

The same tactic can save you money on a number of other long-haul flights. For example, Qantas may sell you its cheapest Los Angeles-to-Sydney coach ticket for $1,299, but Qantas Vacations, its own subsidiary, has a deal for airfare AND hotel for $999.

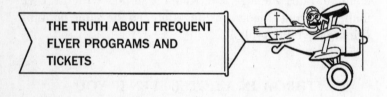

THE TRUTH ABOUT FREQUENT
FLYER PROGRAMS AND
TICKETS

In the airline marketing business, it's called a "pledge of allegiance": loyalty to a particular airline because of membership in its frequent flyer program.

We have become a nation of mileage junkies. And we will do just about anything to earn those miles.

I have friends who will fly extra flights or extra segments, or will completely reroute themselves, so they can earn enough miles or segments to qualify for "free" tickets.

But the real questions are:

- Now that you've earned all those miles, what chances do you have of redeeming them?
- Perhaps more important: How much did it really cost you to earn those miles, presuming you really can redeem them?

The numbers are nothing less than staggering. Since they began, in 1981, airline mileage programs— and, later, hotel frequent flyer/stay programs—have become some of the most popular marketing ideas ever created.

How popular? Let's look at some numbers.

More than 61 million Americans are members of at least one airline or hotel frequent flyer/stay program. (United Airlines boasts that more than 38 million people have enrolled in its Mileage Plus program alone.)

And there are more programs than ever. Because of the increased competition for market share among the airlines and hotels, it's now easier than ever to earn frequent flyer miles or hotel points.

Add some new marketing partners, and it's now possible to earn mileage for everything short of breathing. You can get miles for buying flowers, refinancing your home, buying stock, and exercising at health clubs. At some Las Vegas casinos, you even get mileage for playing slot machines! And, in Volusia County, Florida, most recently in the news because of the post-Election Day voter recounts, you can even get mileage by handling corpses. (I'm serious. Funeral directors can get frequent flyer miles by shipping occupied coffins on Delta Air Lines.)

OK. So much for the good news. Virtually everyone is out there accumulating miles. In fact, according to most estimates, more than 47 percent of all mileage earned today is earned on the ground. You don't have to fly to get miles.

As a result, there are some ten TRILLION miles in frequent flyer accounts. And, as airline traffic has hit an all-time high, frequent flyer mileage has jumped an estimated 30 percent—much of it earned by people who aren't even frequent flyers.

There can be no doubt that the frequent flyer program is one of the cleverest marketing strategies ever devised. But to get us to join and then obsessively earn those miles, the airlines have also had to get us to embrace the notion that we will actually be rewarded for our loyalty to one airline.

And that, sadly, has created a false sense of entitlement among thousands of passengers. Miles have become the global currency of frequent flyers. We look at our mileage statements as often as our bank accounts. In our conversations with other passengers, we try to one-up each other with the number of miles we've earned. And when we earn the miles, we actually think we can redeem them.

Q: How do you redeem those miles?

A: Not easily.

Airlines are reluctant to displace revenue passengers and give away free tickets, even though these programs were designed to reward us for our loyalty to a particular airline. Promises were attached to having millions and millions of miles in our accounts. We gave these companies our pledge of allegiance.

What did we get in return? Want to go to Des Moines on a Wednesday? No problem. Want to cash in those hard-earned frequent flyer miles to take that dream trip to Hawaii? Forget it.

The same response applies to upgrades, only the situation is actually worse. Want to use your mileage to upgrade that inexpensive coach ticket to first class on that Des

Moines flight? Even that might now be a problem. At Northwest, no matter how many miles you've earned, if you bought your seat at an already discounted rate, you're last in line for an upgrade. At United, last-minute Internet fares, or tickets bought through an online discounter are usually not upgradeable.

Want to book a room in Buffalo in February? No problem. Want to cash in your frequent stay points for that Arizona spa during the same month? FUGGEDDABOUDDIT.

Recently, I realized that I had accumulated enough miles to qualify for a free ticket to Hawaii on United Airlines.

I followed the airline's instructions and called to make a reservation between New York and Honolulu. I thought I would fly over for about five days—five months later, in late March. On the other end of the line, the United Airlines reservation agent started to laugh.

"You're flying on an award ticket?" she asked. "Won't happen," she said. "Every flight is already sold out."

For March? Five months from now?

Sure enough; she checked. From March 1 through March 31, not a single seat was available.

Then she checked April. Nothing. Then May, June, July, and August. Still booked solid.

"Couldn't I fly standby?" I asked.

"No, sir," she said. "You are not allowed to fly standby on a frequent flyer ticket."

After I stayed "holding" on the phone for twenty-two minutes (I timed it), she found one flight, with one seat available, on September 16 (a Saturday), leaving from New York's LaGuardia and stopping in Chicago and Los Angeles before landing in Honolulu.

And a return flight five days later? No luck again. The earliest date I could get was September 25, nine days later.

I grabbed it.

Did I really want to go to Hawaii on September 16 for nine days? No; but there was a method to my madness. The goal here was to get a paper domestic award ticket in my hands, even if the dates were wrong.

I hung up the phone from the frequent flyer desk and then called the normal reservations number at United. I repeated my New York-Honolulu request without mentioning that I was flying on a free ticket.

For laughs, I thought I'd mention I wanted to go on March 1.

"How many will be traveling?" the agent asked me, without hesitation.

For more laughs, I said "Eight."

She didn't laugh. She booked the reservation.

And, just to make sure this wasn't some computer snafu, I called United twice again, and each time, picked another date: one in late March and another in mid-April. I was easily able to reserve four seats on the late March flight, and three seats on the mid-April departure. (I later canceled all three phony reservations.)

In each case, the transactions took less than four minutes. On the first call, no "free" seats were available for nearly seven months.

On the second, third, and fourth calls, only revenue seats were available on virtually any flight I wanted.

My reservations experiences made me a member of a growing group of passengers who come face-to-face with the less-than-friendly skies of yield management and capacity control, the methods airlines use to restrict discount or free tickets on every flight in their schedule.

And what happened on March 1? I simply went to the airport with my paper tickets. I showed them to the agent and explained that I would like to fly out to Hawaii earlier than stated on the ticket.

I showed up for the exact flight on the same itinerary printed on the paper ticket. The only things different were the dates. Guess what? There were plenty of seats on my flight. The agent pulled the coupons, issued a boarding pass, and I was on.

The reality: The airline cannot initially issue a standby ticket on a frequent flyer award. But once a paper ticket is issued, and as long as you don't change the cities on the ticket, if there's space on the flights, you're on.

The airlines won't tell you this. But I just did.

As long as you're flexible and do a little advance homework (calling the airlines to find out if revenue space is available on your desired flights), you'll be fine. (Suggestion: Always book the first flight out of any city on your original award ticket).

These airline practices—failing to disclose, or responding with misleading information—continue to be high on the list of passengers' complaints filed directly with the carriers or with the U.S. Department of Transportation, along with complaints about lost baggage, delays, deceptive airline flight labeling, and, last but not least, deceptive airline advertisements.

In the United-to-Hawaii case, I got lucky. I figured a way around the blockade the airline erects to make it virtually impossible to redeem miles for desired flights on desired routes.

The situation looks like it can only get worse.

The annual 10-K reports the airlines file with the Securities and Exchange Commission (SEC) reveal even more disturbing figures.

Want to guess how many unredeemed travel awards there are at Northwest? According to the airline's filing with the SEC, there are more than 6.5 million. United says more than 7 million unredeemed awards are in its system. USAir has more than 5.9 million awards waiting to be redeemed.

Will they ever be redeemed?

Some, yes; mostly, no. Throughout the industry, it is estimated that 75 percent of all frequent flyer miles are never redeemed, go unused, or expire.

Consider the wild story of the "pudding man."

When I say that some people will do anything for mileage, I'm not kidding. Meet David Phillips.

In 1999, while he was grocery shopping, Phillips happened on a special mileage promotion offered by a manufacturer and the airlines. The deal: Buy ten Healthy Choice products and get 500 miles—or 1,000 miles for purchases made before June 1999.

It didn't seem like such a great deal until he got to the pudding section of the store. And then he saw them: small Healthy Choice chocolate fudge pudding cups at only 25 cents apiece. He quickly did the math. If he just spent $62.50, he got 25,000 miles. That's one *very* cheap coach ticket!

He ran home, told his wife of his discovery, and then headed to the bank. Within hours, Phillips was transformed from a mild-mannered civil engineer at the University of California at Davis into . . . PUDDING MAN!

Phillips did some more math and realized that if he moved fast, he could accumulate enough miles to fly halfway to the moon.

In short order, Phillips raced around to every supermarket chain in the Sacramento area, wiping them out of Healthy Choice pudding. And, in just a few days, he had spent $3,000 on 12,150 cups of pudding. And that translated into an accumulation of 1.25 million miles!

And what did he do with all the pudding? He donated most of it to charity (after taking a healthy tax writeoff).

And Phillips didn't stop at $3,000 for 1.25 million miles. He was now addicted. And when a group of Latin American airlines offered anyone a million miles if they bought something called a Latin Pass and flew all ten airlines in a specified time period, he ran to the airport.

OK, so what did Phillips do with all the miles? Like the rest of us, when he went to redeem them, he ran into problems. Capacity controls, blackout dates. When last I checked, he was a man sitting in Sacramento with a whole lot of miles, but no place to go.

The problem is compounded when you realize that the airlines not only award miles to travelers, but they sell them to marketing partners such as Healthy Choice, or Hilton, or Starwood, or Citibank, which, in turn, offer promotions like the pudding deal.

Airlines are reluctant to reveal exact deals, but, on average, the partner companies are paying about two cents a mile. From the airlines' point of view, even if the miles ARE redeemed, that outcome can be more profitable than selling some tickets and operating the actual flights!

Even if you're short on miles, the airlines are there to help. Are you just shy of enough miles to get that free trip? United Airlines and American Express will sell you miles at $25 per 1,000.

What's happening? The airlines now see their mileage programs as profit centers rather than loyalty programs—the role initially envisioned. And the airlines are striking so many deals with other marketing partners that the real value of the frequent flyer programs is becoming steadily diluted.

The airlines know that these free-mileage seats are prepaid out of loyalty, but with new players like Priceline.com, the airlines are apparently thinking that if they can get money for seats, they'll take it instead of giving the seats away. As a result, *free* comes in last.

To make matters worse, in the past few years, many airlines like American and United, added about twenty more blackout dates within the calendar year (that's twenty more dates on which frequent flyers can't redeem miles) and tightened their capacity controls.

All the news isn't bad. Currently, frequent flyer redemption is running at about 12 million free tickets a year. That sounds like a lot but, spread out over all the airlines, the number is quite small.

Here's the real problem. Under deregulation, no airline is required, by any law, to disclose how many discount seats it has available on any flight. (By contrast, if a car dealer advertises a car at a specific price, state law requires the dealer to list how many cars are available at that price.) There are also no requirements to let anyone know how many award seats are available on planes. As a result, a lot of unhappy frequent flyers who have earned those miles can't seem to use them.

Is there a way around this?

The answer, believe it or not, is *Yes.* If the airlines suddenly change the rules in the middle of the game, you may have some legal recourse. Recently, American Airlines settled a twelve-year legal battle and two class-action lawsuits involving changes it made in its AAdvantage program. In 1988, American had been accused of changing the terms of its mileage program without prior notification, thereby making it more difficult to book flights using mileage awards.

A second lawsuit challenged American's second attempt—in 1995—to increase, from 20,000 to 25,000, the number of miles needed to earn a free domestic coach ticket.

Under the settlement terms, American, without admitting any liability, agreed to give about 5 million members of its mileage program either 5,000 air miles or certificates good for $75 discounts on future flights.

Short of legal action against the airlines, here are five suggestions for redeeming your well-deserved free flights:

1. Think alternate airports. Not just JFK, but Newark, Stewart, or Islip in New York; Midway instead of O'Hare; Colorado Springs instead of Denver.

2. Be flexible on your departure times.

3. Make airline code share partnerships work for you. For example, want to use frequent flyer miles on Virgin Atlantic? Well, if Virgin says it has no award seats available, then call its code share (and mileage partner): Continental.

   Recently, when this happened, the passenger was told that Continental didn't have award seats, but could process the passenger's ticket and get him a seat on Virgin! (Remember, it's the same plane, but different availability and inventory.)

4. Never take a "no" from someone who is not empowered to give you a "yes" in the first place. Always ask to speak to a supervisor if the airline won't let you redeem miles. At each airline reservation center, there is a supervisor who has the responsibility—and the power—to unblock computer locks and release an award seat to you. All you really need to do is—gently, but firmly— remind the airline that its frequent flyer program was started to reward your loyalty to that airline. In many cases, that's when the seats get released!

5. Beat the airlines at their own game, playing by their rules. Always ask for a paper ticket for your award ticket, and remember my United/Hawaii story: when the airline laughs at you and says there are no seats available until the next millennium, no problem. Take the flight number you want—in that next millennium, and then get it paper-ticketed.

   Next, call the airline's reservations number and ask whether there are paid available seats on a flight you want to take in three weeks. If there are, then take your mileage ticket—that paper ticket—to the airport on the day you really wanted to fly. Remember, a frequent-flyer mile is a contingent liability the airline would love to unload, but not at the expense of a paying passenger. If there are still seats available on the day you get to the airport, you will be boarded, at no additional cost. Or put on standby for the next flight.

Remember, as long as there's space on that plane, I have never been denied boarding by doing this. You just have to be a little bold, a little flexible, and trust in the thought that saying no to you on the phone is a whole lot easier than saying no to you in person.

ANOTHER LITTLE-KNOWN MILEAGE TICKET GAME

Let's say (1) you want to fly from Los Angeles to New York and back, using a frequent flyer award, and (2) the airline says you can actually go when you want to go. Be creative. Under current airline rules, you can route yourself on that transcontinental itinerary in a way that maximizes your ticket. You can make stopovers and see friends, business associates, and family along the way.

What the airlines won't tell you is that, on most award tickets, you are allowed one stopover en route, either going or coming.

They also won't tell you about a little-known rule.

First, you get the free and uncontested stopover. Next, you can connect as many times as you want along the route, as long as you are not stopping over for more than four hours. But suppose your flight into a connection is the last flight of the day (or night). The last-flight-in/first-flight-out rule applies: You can stay the night in a connecting city if the flight you came in on was the last to arrive, and the flight you have to leave on is the next plane in the morning. Many business travelers use this sequence and avoid paying for an extra flight.

But let's say you don't want to risk anything. You want to travel knowing that everything along the way is confirmed.

Don't want to risk the unofficial standby game? Then check out something called WebMiles.

What's the attraction of WebMiles? Quite simply, with this offer, the miles you earn result in unrestricted free tickets, redeemable on any airline and any flight. The claim is: as long as there is a seat on the plane, WebMiles will get you on it.

How does it work? For starters, WebMiles does not work with airline frequent flyer programs. The miles you earn are used to actually purchase tickets from the airlines. Consumers earn these premium miles or "WebMiles rewards" in much the same way other affinity programs are run—by purchasing through online and offline partners, participating in surveys, referring friends and family, and using the Web-Miles MasterCard. Consumers earn one WebMiles reward per dollar spent on the MasterCard, and multiple miles if the Mastercard is used with a network partner. In addition to free round-trip airline tickets, WebMiles offers discounted travel starting with as few as 8,000 WebMiles rewards.

Specifically, WebMiles manufactures WebMiles rewards and then sells them to WebMiles Partners, who distribute the miles to consumers as rewards. When you're ready to redeem those miles for a ticket, WebMiles uses a travel partner, Maritz Travel, to provide the free or discounted tickets. This business model functions independently of any airline.

How do you join? Register at www.Webmiles.com. Members can get dollars off travel with as few as 8,000 miles. Member with 15,000 WebMiles can get $200 off any air fare—often, enough to fly free on many domestic routes. And, similar to frequent flyer programs, individuals who accumulate 25,000 miles will receive a free round-trip ticket of their choice.

The only limitation for free round-trip tickets is a 14-day advance notice. WebMiles claims it also does not enforce Saturday night stays. There's an added bonus. The miles earned translate into a purchased fare ticket, so you actually earn miles for flying the reward ticket!

No matter when or how you use your frequent flyer tickets, it's important for you to know, especially if they are "free" tickets issued by the airlines, what they really cost you, or your company, to earn.

Airlines intentionally keep annual redemption levels to about 8 percent of the available mileage eligible for redemption.

Want to get angry?

Let's talk about what that "free" award ticket cost you, assuming you ARE able to redeem it.

With 47 percent of all mileage being earned on the ground, and with most miles being awarded at a rate of one mile per dollar spent, you can soon discover why these programs are so wildly profitable for the airlines.

The minimum mileage needed for a free domestic coach ticket is 25,000 miles. That means that most people spent at least $11,750 (in real dollars) on goods and services, and the rest on real airline miles to get to that first eligible tier.

Conservatively, let's say that the other 13,250 miles were earned in the air, and a minimum of $2,000 in airline ticket costs was spent to earn those miles.

At a bare minimum, someone spent $13,750 to earn one free domestic coach ticket.

That's one very expensive coach ticket.

Now, get ready to get . . . angrier.

Each airline has to carry these unredeemed miles on its books as a contingent liability, and that liability has to be given a realistic dollar value. The airline also factors in the incremental costs of processing a frequent flyer award ticket, plus the relative costs of food and beverage, fuel, insurance, security, and all the other items that go into processing your ticket, redeeming your award, and putting you in that "free" seat.

It's all based on incremental cost. Example: Let's say a plane ticket sells for $500, but because the plane is going to fly anyway, the marginal (or incremental) cost of carrying one more passenger—slightly more fuel, and perhaps a pathetic Bistro meal—is not even close to that figure.

Many airlines, like American, value their unredeemed mileage at 40 cents per 1,000 miles. Now, let's do the math. Considering that 25,000 first-tier eligibility for that one coach ticket, the airline estimates its real costs to redeem your mileage, issue you that ticket, and fly you on your "free" flight at a whopping . . . $10!

OK, so now you know how many miles are out there—and, more or less, how many unredeemed awards.

But how can you redeem those miles in a way that is meaningful to you—a way that let you go where you want to go, when you want to go there?

Perhaps you want to forget about free tickets and use the mileage for something else.

A number of new programs can help you spend your miles, or hotel points, on things *other than* airline seats or hotel rooms.

And for once, miles may be getting more valuable.

America Online (AOL) and American Airlines will let you turn your miles into money. AOL AAdvantage, for example, will let you buy nonflying stuff such as free AOL time, books and magazines, and CDs. Want a new Palm Pilot VII? It will cost you 78,500 miles.

Another company, milepoint.com, will allow online shoppers to trade airline miles for discounts on name-brand electronics, gifts, luggage, and books, at more than 100 retailers. (Ironically, the chairman of the milepoint.com board is Robert Crandall, a former head of American Airlines, which introduced the mileage programs nearly twenty years ago.) But don't get too excited; the discounts aren't that great. Each mile is valued at just two cents. If you want a $500 discount from milepoint.com, you'll have to part with 25,000 miles. (The discounts are all relative. On what price is the discount based? Full retail value rather than the cost to midpoint.com?)

A company called milespree.com is aimed at people who already make purchases on the Web. Register, and you earn a bonus of 8,000 miles, about one-third of the miles necessary for a free ticket. When you buy something at any of 400 dot.com retailers, you earn milespree miles. For 25,000 miles, you get a free domestic coach ticket. The good news about milespree is that if you make your reservations for that free ticket thirty days in advance, there are no blackout dates. (Milespree actually purchases the ticket. It's not an award ticket.)

Looking for other ways to "dump" your miles creatively?

Most airlines offer complete travel packages (airfare, hotel, rental car) for mileage. American offers about 300 such programs. Others offer deals that combine mileage and nominal cash payments to get opera tickets, fifty-yard-line seats at football games, or cruise-ship holidays.

To be competitive, many hotel programs offer "double dipping." You get points AND miles for staying at particular hotels in selected cities. (Another word of caution here. The mileage deals and bonuses specify certain hotels, and the rates may vary. Always check whether your deal covers the hotel's full asking price.)

Lodging chains offer some interesting ways to spend your points. DaysInn has "INNcentives." You earn points for your stays there, and you can convert them into certificates of deposit for a college fund for your children.

Starwood has an extensive redemption program for merchandise as well as experiences.

In the Big Apple, guests of the Sheraton New York Hotel & Towers can trade in their Starwood Preferred Guest (SPG) points for anything from a dinner cruise around Manhattan to a pair of tickets to a Broadway show. At New York City's Essex House, romantics can take a free hour-long horse-drawn carriage ride through Central Park. In Arizona, one of the favorite Starwood redemptions can be found at the legendary Phoenician Hotel in Scottsdale. Guests can exchange points for last-minute spa treatments or, even better, for a dinner for two at the exclusive Chef's Table in Mary Elaine's kitchen. Outrigger canoe rides at the Sheraton Moana-Surfrider in Waikiki can also be booked using points.

SPG members earn two Starpoints (Gold- and Platinum-level members earn three Starpoints) for every dollar spent at any Westin, Sheraton, St. Regis, The Luxury Collection, Four Points, and W. In this program, virtually all charges are eligible, including room rates, food and beverage charges, laundry and dry cleaning fees, telephone calls, and in-room faxes, movies, and video games.

Marriott's alliance with SkyMall Inc. allows Marriott Rewards members to redeem Marriott Rewards points for merchandise and gift certificates during the holidays. Redemption opportunities start at only 18,000 points. And then there is the Priority Plus deal offered by Bass Hotels (Holiday Inns, Intercontinental hotels). If you didn't know any better and were judging only from their program, you might think you're not staying at a Holiday Inn but at the hotel shopping network!

The chain has an extensive sixty-six page catalog of goodies available for redemption: everything from redeeming your points and creating an incredible vacation package, to turning the points into a whopping shopping spree, using retail certificates for Best Buy, Sears, Target, and so on. Want to be a fighter pilot? Redeem points and you're in the cockpit. Always had your heart set on that chain saw at Target or Sears? Again, redeem points. The Priority Plus program even lets you redeem points for things that are NOT in the catalog. How? They research your request, assign a dollar value/point value, and, if you have enough points, it's yours.

Some credit cards have deals too. If you redeem 120,000 American Express Membership Miles, you get to drive a race car at Walt Disney World. Want an electric golf cart? Fork over 1,550,000 points.

Why are these programs becoming so popular? One of the reasons is the basic math. Don't be seduced by the prospect of mileage, or even more mileage, unless you can answer whether your miles or points were worth earning in the first place. (Did you fly a flight because you were going to fly it anyway, or to earn the mileage? Was that impulse purchase influenced by the promise of mileage?) Once you're ready to redeem your miles or points, what's the most financially efficient way to get the best bang out of your miles?

Cashing in 25,000 miles for an airline ticket you could buy for $250 isn't a good idea. But if the ticket would cost you $2,000 to buy, converting miles into money suddenly becomes attractive, especially when it's so hard to get a free ticket to Hawaii. Whether you redeem your miles (or points) for airline seats, hotel rooms, merchandise, or money, always try to remember that if you're earning these miles and points for purchases you'd be making anyway, that's a big bonus. If you're purchasing because you hope to earn miles, more often than not you're costing yourself money.

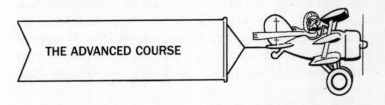

THE ADVANCED COURSE

How do you beat the airlines at their own game, playing by THEIR rules? For most of us, understanding airline rules, fares, and disclaimers is tantamount to translating Sanskrit.

But not for a man I'll call "Dr. Tom." He knows all about the talmudic complexities of hidden airline rules, fares, tariffs, and which little known exclusions benefit him.

Dr. Tom flew over 400,000 miles last year, and he did it—to put it mildly—creatively. The airlines hate Dr. Tom. But you have to give him credit. He has figured out their game.

When I first met him—on a plane, not surprisingly—he explained his ethos and his methodology: To find the best fares, it pays to be vigilant and curious.

"Today, I wanted to go to Washington, DC, so I checked routes from San Francisco to BWI—Baltimore. Then I began to see that all the other carriers were starting to match the price, not just at BWI, but at Reagan National and Dulles. I used Baltimore to get me where I wanted to go in DC." And he does it all on his home computer.

"It is easy to pay full fare, it is easy to trust a travel agent, it is easy if you are depending on corporate funding. But there are people who pay full price, and then there are people who have a great deal of sensitivity. And the airlines recognize this. The airlines have two different distinct markets: the business market and the dispensable-income leisure market."

Tom is a business market traveler who acts like a dispensable-income leisure flyer. And it works. "My desire is to minimize my costs. To get from point A to point B for less."

Dr. Tom started learning on the Internet. He goes to travel Web sites, like Travelocity and Expedia, as well as the sites run directly by the airlines themselves (ua.com, aa.com, nwa.com).

"First, I look at the official fares posted. Are they coterminus? [Meaning: Does the fare apply to all the airports that service that area? One example: Is a trip to JFK, LaGuardia, or Newark common rated?] Then I look at alternate airports. And then, once I find a fare I like, I educate myself about the rules of that fare."

Dr. Tom is a whiz on Expedia. He goes right to the airline fare list. He fills in his origin and destination cities, and his screen then displays coach-class fares in ascending order.

"Then it gets interesting," he chuckles, "because when you look at that list you will be asked an option, called a fare basis. And that will tell you when the fare is available, as well as blackout dates and routing cities."

The routing cities are key for Dr. Tom. They tell him the different ways he can use that fare not only to maximize the distance he flies (and thus, the mileage he earns) but also to take advantage of any free stopovers in other cities that he can legally manipulate.

"For example, if I want to fly from Los Angeles to Buffalo, I may be able to go through Dallas to New Mexico on the return trip if I fly American. But, on Northwest, I may be able to go through other cities. I find the alternatives to construct the trip to maximize frequent flyer points."

After Dr. Tom has the route he wants, he then goes after "inventory." He checks minimum stay requirements, and, of course, advance booking restrictions. When he finds the lowest fare that allows him to route his trip creatively, he's ready to rumble. On one recent weekend, he flew first class on ten Continental flights—five in each direction—and his total airfare was *$198*.

But another game he plays truly maximizes his deals and allows him "phantom" stopovers. As a business traveler, he would normally have to pay ten times as much for the privilege of stopping overnight en route to anywhere. But not Dr. Tom. In the airline business, he's known as Dr. Stopover.

First, here's how it's officially supposed to work. You're flying from Washington, DC, to San Francisco, but you want to stop and visit your favorite uncle in Minneapolis. Such a visit would constitute a stopover in Minneapolis. Some fares allow free stopovers; others allow stopovers for an additional fee. But most fares do not allow stopovers at all.

So how do you create that free stopover? Many travelers think that by simply booking a flight that coincidentally stops in Minneapolis, the problem is solved. They can book a connecting flight for the next day.

But it doesn't work that way. There's something called *the four-hour rule*. If you do not take off from your intermediate point (Minneapolis) within four hours, you have made a stopover. And if your fare doesn't permit one, you're going to be hit with a huge additional full-coach fare to continue your journey.

And let's say that you don't want your uncle to just race out to the airport, have a hot dog with you while you race between planes, and leave.

You really want to stay over, but you don't want to pay for it. Enter the phantom stopover.

How does it work? The four-hour rule applies, provided that there actually is a connecting flight departing within four hours.

Dr. Tom books, to Minneapolis, the next-to-last flight of the day that connects with a San Francisco flight. Then he intentionally misses that flight. He is then forced to take the last flight, which has no onward connection that night. (He also understands the standby rules. If he shows up within two hours of the scheduled departure time of a flight on which he holds space, the airline will fly him standby on its next available flight.) And he gets to spend the night in Minneapolis at no extra charge.

Internationally, there is a twenty-four-hour rule. "Sometimes I buy a ticket from L.A. [on a flight] that stops in Miami before going on to Europe," he boasts. "This means that I can legally stay in Miami for twenty-four hours with no extra cost, and take a flight the next day."

The standby rules also work on flights where he doesn't want to make ANY stopovers.

"Let's say I find a fare I like, but there is not a ticket for the time I want to go. But there *is* an available flight that I know I can't make. I will buy that flight anyway, knowing that I will not make that flight, because once I have bought the ticket, the airline cannot change the cost of that ticket." When he gets to the airport, he gets to fly on the flight he wanted in the first place, but at the lower fare.

He also researches certain routing rules. A number of airlines have maximum transfer rules: no more than four transfers on any one itinerary. Tom books tickets for those flights where he needs to make a total of (surprise!) four transfers!

You would think Dr. Tom never uses a travel agent. Wrong. "A good travel agent is worth the payments in commission or service charges, because [the agency's] computers can get you the inventory information you need to construct these routes and fares," he says.

FIGHTING THE BACK-TO-BACK WAR—AND WINNING

Dr. Tom has mastered the art of connections, reroutings, and maximized mileage—not to mention flying standby. I have embraced the concept of the back-to-back ticket.

A few years ago, for a *Today Show* segment, I was asked to do a piece on the five questions I am asked most.

One of the questions, a no-brainer, was THE question I was asked the most: How does someone get a discount seat without having to adhere to the dreaded Saturday-night stay requirement?

My suggestion was the back-to-back ticket. Let's say you want to fly to New York from Los Angeles in three weeks, on a Tuesday, but you need to return three days later, on a Friday. Although you're booking your flight and paying for it three weeks in advance, which would normally qualify you for an advance-reservation discount, you don't get that discount because you're not staying over a Saturday night. Result: A full-fare coach ticket that could be as high as $2,000.

Now, using the same scenario, call the airline and make your reservation for the Tuesday flight three weeks from now, but set your return date for some time a month later. Your fare could drop as low as $249 round trip. Then, hang up the phone. A few minutes later, call the airline again and make a second reservation, this time for a flight leaving New York for Los Angeles on the Friday three weeks from now, returning some time a month later. Another $249 fare. For just 25 percent of what the airline wanted to charge you for one fare, you now have TWO round trips to New York. If you plan properly, you will get to use both trips, and get double the mileage.

Officially—and in reality—you will have satisfied the Saturday-night stay requirements for both tickets.

Gotta love it!

And everyone watching the show DID love it, with one major exception. American Airlines went ballistic. In a caustic three-page letter to the head of NBC, the airline charged that I was violating the law, perpetrating a fraud, and misleading NBC's viewers. The letter insinuated that American would take further action if I did not cease and desist talking about back-to-back tickets: "Back-to-back ticketing is a breach of a passenger's contract with American Airlines."

American claimed that "passengers on American who attempt to use back-to-back tickets may be denied boarding, may have the remainder of their ticket confiscated, and may be assessed a charge, which will be no less than the difference between the fare paid and the lowest fare applicable to the passenger's actual itinerary."

I'm not a lawyer, but I have a basic understanding of contracts. If I buy an airline ticket and use only the first portion of the ticket, should I be penalized if I don't use the second half? No. But if I use the second portion and don't change anything, shouldn't the airline honor that ticket? Denying me boarding on a ticket I purchased in my name, for a flight on the date originally specified, and with flight coupons used in proper order, could be considered a breach of contract by the airline.

That's what American Airlines was—and still is—threatening to do to passengers who use back-to-back ticketing.

A back-to-back ticket allows me to officially comply with each required Saturday-night stay. I am purchasing two separate tickets with different itineraries and using them in order. Simple as that. American claims that the Saturday-night stay requirement "is necessary to ensure that these fares are generally used by leisure travelers. Without the ability to enforce this condition, it simply would not be practical for airlines to offer these attractive low fares to consumers."

Perhaps this is true. However, my responsibility is not to ensure financial feasibility for airlines, but to offer consumers practical advice on how to get the best deals within ticketing requirements set by the airlines. I will not stop encouraging consumers to beat airlines, hotels, cruise lines, and rental-car companies at their own game, playing by the companies' own rules.

This was the gist of my response to American's letter, and it only served to make the airline angrier.

At that point, it was suggested that I fly to American's headquarters in Texas and meet with the top officials.

It was, to say the least, a less than happy meeting.

After some basic pleasantries, the head of American public relations, holding my letter, pointed it at me. "If you don't cease promoting these kinds of tickets, we will have to take further action."

"Really?" I said. "And what would that be? Would that be to deny me a bag of pretzels on what used to be a meal flight?"

"Not funny," he responded. "If you don't cease to write and report about this, we won't be able to offer these fares to our customers."

"If you don't want to offer these fares, then don't offer them," I countered. "Remember, I don't work for you."

"OK," he said, sounding more serious. "If we discover that you are flying on a back-to-back ticket, we will remove you from the aircraft, deny you boarding, and make you pay a full fare ticket to reboard the plane."

"If you find out?" I laughed. "Get out your pens and paper." I then told them the flight numbers and dates of the next five back-to-back itineraries on which I was scheduled.

"But let me warn you that I would view your actions as a serious breach of contract and would litigate accordingly and strenuously. I am flying on a ticket I purchased myself, under my own name, on the dates and times specified on that ticket. I am conforming—to the letter—to the contract of carriage. I will also alert other members of the media to the same flight numbers and dates."

Also, I added, I would be using two different airlines. One back-to-back ticket in one direction would be on American; the other, on United.

"But that's a horse of a different color," argued the American official.

"Really?" I responded. "The way I see it, we have two horses in the same race, and they're both winners."

In short order, I received support from a number of consumer reports, including Joe Brancatelli, who likened my case to a six-pack of Coca-Cola. In his widely read biztravel.com Internet column, he wrote that if he bought a six-pack of Coca-Cola and drank only three bottles, would the Coca-Cola police come and arrest him?

The upshot of my meeting at American: I continued to fly back-to-back tickets, I was never denied boarding, and the Coca-Cola police were never sighted.

Indeed, if you want to play the back-to-back game, my advice is: Protect yourself by buying two tickets on different airlines. In the Los Angeles-to-New York model, buy your Los Angeles-to-New York round trip on American, and your New York-to-Los Angeles round trip on United.

You'll get the same low discount fares, and mileage on BOTH carriers! And the best deal is: Even if you choose to return later on each ticket, you can still use the return portion of each ticket by paying the $75 rebooking fee per ticket. It remains a great deal.

I am not advocating cheating.

All I have done—and continue to do—is report on a long-standing loophole in airline rules that benefits consumers. If any airline wants to eliminate that loophole, or the Saturday-night stay requirement, that's the airline's prerogative. I will certainly encourage consumers to abide by any new ticket restrictions, or, where possible, to benefit from them.

THE PROBLEM WITH HIDDEN-CITY TICKETS

As much as I am an advocate of back-to-back tickets, I must caution you about hidden-city tickets.

First, an explanation.

A practice that is a breach of the passenger-airline contract is the hidden-city ticket. Let's say you need to get to Dallas from San Francisco, but there no discount tickets are available. However, an airline is offering a discount fare on its San Francisco-to-Austin flight, which happens to connect in Dallas. You buy the Austin round trip and get off in Dallas.

Under the airlines' official "conditions of carriage," this practice violates a tariff when the passenger attempts to return from Dallas. By not using the Dallas-to-Austin portion of the ticket, the passenger disobeys the condition that states: "Flight coupons of a ticket will be honored only in the order in which they are issued in the ticket booklet."

Most airline computers are programmed to cancel reservations if a passenger does not check in for any portion of the reserved journey. Thus, a passenger using a hidden-city ticket runs the risk of being caught on the return flight.

Is it illegal? No. But when the passenger violates that tariff, the airline reserves the right to deny boarding to that passenger, void the remainder of the ticket, and charge full coach fare for the return flight to San Francisco.

Ironically, there's an exception, and it happens with first-class tickets! Remember, first-class tickets are full fare, and they carry no restrictions as to when you use them or when you fly each segment.

Consider this bizarre fare example: Want a first-class ticket between Los Angeles and Green Bay, Wisconsin? No problem. American Airlines will sell you a ticket for about $2,100 and will also let you know that your itinerary will be a nonstop flight between Los Angeles and Chicago, and then a connecting flight to Green Bay. Call the same airline and ask what a first-class ticket costs for just a simple round trip between Los Angeles and Chicago, and the fare is more than $3,000! Is this ludicrous or what?

The moral of this story: If you want to fly first class to Chicago, book a first-class ticket to Green Bay and get off in Chicago. You are not flying on a discount ticket, so the airline would either honor your reservation at a later date (should you actually decide you want or need to go to Green Bay), or simply pull the Chicago and Green Bay coupons. You can then make a new reservation and fly home from Chicago for almost $1,000 less than if you had bought a straight Los Angeles-to-Chicago ticket.

What's the reason for this? Airlines like American know the real breakdown when Chicago is the destination. O'Hare is one of America's biggest hub airports, but fewer than 20 percent of the people who fly to Chicago want to go there.

Those who DO want to fly to Chicago, especially in first class, are business travelers who HAVE to go. Translation: The airline thinks it can get away with charging a higher fare. And, for the most part, it gets away with it.

Still, remember that with the exception of these first-class hidden-city tickets, you run a serious risk of being denied boarding on your return flight. My advice: Don't do it.

In back-to-back ticketing, the situation is different. Passengers are flying, in their own names, on the date, flight, and time listed on the ticket, and are using the coupons in the order they appear in the booklet. They have not sold or bartered their ticket, or changed or altered any reservation. They have followed the terms and conditions printed on each ticket.

In recent years, virtually every session of Congress has seen at least one bill introduced that is specifically geared toward battling airlines' back-to-back and hidden-city ticketing restrictions. And at each session, the bill dies in committee.

The most interesting of those bills was introduced late in 2000 by Nevada Congressman Jim Gibbons. The legislation—called the "Consumer Airline Ticket Transfer Act" (CATT)—would direct the U.S. Secretary of Transportation to issue regulations prohibiting airlines from penalizing passengers who use hidden-city tickets. It would also stop airlines from penalizing passengers who do back-to-back tickets.

A very interesting part of Gibbons' proposed legislation would allow consumers to transfer their tickets to another customer without penalty. (After all, if I buy a theater ticket in advance and then can't go to the play, no one stops me from giving that ticket to a friend.)

The Aviation Consumer Right-to-Know Act, introduced in 2000 by Representative Peter DeFazio of Oregon, would directly permit purchase of back-to-back and hidden-city tickets without jeopardy.

Not surprisingly, the airline lobby is fighting both bills, and if recent history is any indication, both may die.

Which brings things full circle. For the moment, I do not advocate the use of hidden-city tickets, but I wholeheartedly endorse back-to-back ticketing.

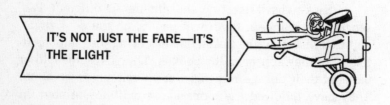

IT'S NOT JUST THE FARE—IT'S THE FLIGHT

Remember that Northwest late-night flight between Detroit and Washington, DC? It is one of dozens of flights that I call "secret flights."

These flights are on scheduled airlines. They are published in regular flight itineraries, but few people know they exist. They are either nonstop flights or direct flights that make one stop but do not require a change of planes. And, more often than not, these are flights that are never full, offer better service, and often are less expensive.

In the United States, where skies have been deregulated, there are few surprises. Still, there are some relatively secret flights. Savvy travelers know—and, in some cases, live by— these secret flights.

And why do the airlines operate these little-known flights?

Some of them are simply positioning flights. The airline needs to get a particular aircraft from point A to point B so it can fly a better-known route between point B and point C. The A-B route thus constitutes the secret flight.

Or, the airline has been granted something known as "fifth freedom" rights by a host country. Besides having permission to land there, even for refueling purposes, it is allowed to embark and disembark point-to-point passengers.

In the United States, where skies have been deregulated, any airline can fly virtually any route, so there are few surprises. Still, there are some relatively secret flights.

If you're flying between Los Angeles and San Diego, you'd expect United, American, and Delta to handle the route. Indeed, these three airlines operate the majority of the flights between these two southern California cities. And, in a majority of cases, the airlines operate small commuter aircraft. United, however, has some positioning flights that use Boeing 737s for the twenty-minute trip.

What I call the secret transcontinental red-eye flights are another variation. No, I'm not talking about the red-eye flights that are nonstop. Indeed, American, United, and TWA have nonstop late-night flights between Los Angeles and New York. Most leave about 10:00 P.M. and land at JFK just in time for you to get stuck in heavily congested rush-hour traffic into Manhattan. The regular red-eye flights are a bad deal for another reason. Because they leave at 10:00 P.M., they don't give travelers enough time to have a leisurely dinner in Los Angeles. They must rush to the airport in time to get stuck in New York.

Instead, virtually all the U.S. airlines have secret red-eye flights from Los Angeles. They leave shortly before midnight, and they connect in the individual airlines' hub cities. American, for example, has a flight that leaves at 11:55 P.M., connects in Chicago, and lands at LaGuardia at 10:00 A.M. the next morning. The cab ride from LaGuardia is shorter, faster, and less expensive because all the rush-hour traffic has already entered the city. United has a similar flight. Delta has a late flight connecting in Atlanta.

Northwest also has secret red-eyes from Los Angeles through Detroit, Memphis, or Minneapolis. Midwest Express departs Los Angeles at 11:30 P.M., flying through Milwaukee.

The international routes between cities outside the United States make secret flights really shine. Flying from Manchester to Bombay? One would think the airline choice would be British Airways or Air India. My secret choice: Singapore Airlines' Flight 327, a 747-400 flight with superb service. Singapore Airlines' Flight 334 also flies from Paris to Manchester with a 747.

Between Los Angeles and Tokyo, there are regular Northwest, United, and Japan Air Lines flights. But a long-standing international secret flight on this route belongs to Varig's Flight 836. The Brazilian carrier flies nonstop between Los Angeles and Japan.

Thinking of traveling from New York's JFK to Frankfurt, or from Newark Airport (in New Jersey) to Amsterdam? Again, you can take advantage of Singapore Airlines' secret flights: Flights 25 and 23, respectively. Four days a week, Royal Jordanian's Flight 262 flies from JFK to Amsterdam on an Airbus 310. If you're heading to Europe from the Midwest, Royal Jordanian's Flight 264 can take you from Chicago to Shannon, Ireland.

Singapore Airlines seems to fly everyone else's route. What happens if you're flying between Singapore and London? That's the time to try Emirates Air's Flight 67. It terminates at London, but, en route, stops in Dubai for some serious duty-free shopping.

How about Los Angeles to London, or to Frankfurt? Most people don't know that Air New Zealand flies the route—

often, for as low as $349 round trip. (Or $599 round trip between Los Angeles and Fiji.)

On the Hong Kong-to-Bangkok route, most travelers will choose either Cathay Pacific or Thai Airways. But Gulf Air's Flight 153 is nonstop on its Airbus 340 series. British Airways can fly you between Hong Kong and Manila. So can Swissair.

A number of secret flights into Central and South America start in the United States. In fact, the least expensive flights to Central America are operated by LTU International—a German carrier that flies out of Miami. Want to go to Costa Rica? For $259, from November through April each year, LTU operates flights that start in Germany, bring tourists to Florida, and, after a short stop, head to San José. The Santiago-Buenos Aires route is loaded with secret flights. LanChile or Aerolineas Argentinas aren't alone as they crisscross the skies above the two cities. Lufthansa goes from Santiago to Buenos Aires (en route to Frankfurt) once a day, and Air France's Flight 416 flies directly to Buenos Aires four times a week.

It would be logical to expect that a Rome-to-Madrid route would be flown by either Alitalia or Iberia. But Thai Airways' Flight 942, or Aerolinas Argentinas' Flight 111 also will get you there. If you're headed from Bangkok to Rome, a great secret flight is Flight 15 on Qantas.

The routes, and the "secret" airlines that fly them, indicate that no great air-traffic jam is involved. SAS may have more flights between Copenhagen and Malaga than British Airways, which may have only one per day. Lufthansa has many more flights between Hamburg and Leipzig than SAS.

Any of these flights can change seasonally.

Finding hidden airlines on unusual routes is not only fun but can save you money. Remember, some of the secret flights on these routes offer lower promotional or bucket-shop fares, and because so many of them have U.S. partners in their frequent flyer programs, there's an additional incentive to fly them.

With a little planning, you can get better service, a more comfortable plane, and cheaper fares. That's a secret that should be shared.

COURIER FLIGHTS—OVERRATED?

I have a friend who always flew for free. She would check with certain companies, pack only carry-on bags, and go to the airport. Twenty-four hours later, she was in Istanbul, Hong Kong, London, or Cairo.

Once a month I'd get a postcard from Sydney, Rio, or Bangkok.

She flew for a courier service, and as long as she was somewhat flexible with her time, the price was more than right. It was zero.

The trade-off: She had to fly when the service wanted her to fly, and she returned, often with no notice, when the service wanted her to return. Still, it was a great way to see the world for free, in short bursts of time.

Over the years, thousands of budget travelers have taken advantage of courier flights. But I'm sorry to report that there are few courier bargains left. So many people discovered the deals (you flew for free because it was cheaper for the courier services to buy you a cheap ticket and use your international check-in baggage allowance than it was for them to pay international cargo/air freight bills), that the courier services realized they could make money by selling the tickets. Soon, the total savings were reduced to 75 percent and then to 50 percent.

Some bargains can still be found, but many online offers for discount airline tickets match or beat the courier fares and offer far more options for travelers. Don't jump at courier fares only because you like the concept of discount travel. These days, a courier fare from New York to Paris runs about $550, so you can do better on your own, and get to take YOUR OWN bags!

WHEN YOU ABSOLUTELY HAVE TO FLY (BEREAVEMENT FARES)

This is advice about flying the sympathetic and not-so-sympathetic skies. These days, when someone dies, you can get killed financially when you try to get a last-minute compassion or "bereavement" fare so that you can pay your respects to the recently departed.

In theory, bereavement fares are deeply discounted fares supposedly offered by airlines at a time of medical emergency. I say "supposedly" because each airline differs not only in its rules but in how it applies those rules. No airline is *required* to offer these fares; some do it as a courtesy, not because of any government regulation.

Even on the airlines that offer these fares, the definition of terms often changes. What constitutes eligibility for a bereavement fare? On some airlines, a bereavement fare applies only when a member of your *immediate family* dies.

But who constitutes "immediate family"?

No one seems to know. For example, United Airlines says: (1) it will offer a bereavement fare only when a death has occurred, and, (2) immediate family means parents and children; grandparents and grandchildren; natural, step-, and adopted children; and half-relations.

And what's the discount on the fare? United will only say that it will handle each case on an individual basis.

In the recent past, American Airlines has said it will give immediate and extended family members, as a bereavement fare, a 50 percent discount off the minimum fare offered. Continental Airlines waives the 14-day advance-purchase requirement and includes just about anyone in the family—nephews, nieces, uncles, aunts, and in-laws.

Northwest expands its discount to include medical emergency. Its fare takes 70 percent off the full coach fare. TWA, Delta, USAir, and Southwest each have different rules and deals. They range from "Yes" or "No" to "Sometimes" or "Maybe."

Each airline will ask for some documentation, or a contact name at a hospital or funeral home, to verify the reason for emergency travel.

The discounts offered may occur after the fact and not at the time of booking or payment. On some airlines, what you get is a discount against future flights, and that could kill your wallet.

In effect, traveling at the last minute and asking for a discount because of someone's illness or death may only obligate you to fly the airline again.

So, in a time of emergency, what can you do to get a real bereavement fare? The same thing you do when you book your regular flights.

Consider this story. A few years ago, a friend of mine called—in a panic. Her forty-one-year-old cousin, who was apparently in good health, had collapsed and died of a heart attack.

Burial was to be near her cousin's family home in New Jersey, and the man's wife and daughter wished to fly with the body. They had called United Airlines and, after explaining the circumstances, asked for the lowest fare to Newark from Los Angeles.

Could the airline waive its advance-purchase fare? they asked.

The United reservations agent told the widow that because the airline had no published bereavement fare, the lowest possible price she could quote her was $1,176, the full coach round-trip fare.

I called the reservations agent for her, and the agent repeated the same information to me.

"Clearly," I said, "you must have some policy on these situations."

"No," she replied, "we have no published fare and she doesn't qualify for an advance-purchase ticket. Besides," she added, "there are no discount fares available for the flights to Newark."

"But are there *seats* available for that flight?" I asked.

"Yes," she said. "But not at that fare."

"If there are seats available for the flight," I replied, "then surely someone in your office has the authority to override the computer and sell these folks a cheaper seat."

It took another ten minutes before I convinced her that she could, in fact, override her computer, waive the advance-purchase restrictions, and give the two family members a reasonable fare. I told her that not only would the family provide a copy of the death certificate, but the mortuary had informed me the body would be accompanying them on the same flight (in the cargo hold). "How's that for proof?"

Finally, she relented. The $1,176 per-person fare was dropped to $418.

It is true that United does not have a published bereavement fare. The airline continues to deal with these requests on a case-by-case basis. Translation: There are no guarantees that, in a time of emergency, you'll get a bereavement fare, or, even if you do, that it will be compassionately priced.

The airlines are not always to blame. Northwest Airlines saw the death rate suddenly soar in southern California during Easter and Christmas vacation periods. One American Airlines agent told me, "We actually had calls from people saying their grandmother died and the funeral will be on December 25 in St. Thomas." Whoops!

Ultimately, determination of the fare rests with the street-level discretion of individual reservationists or ticket counter agents.

And if handled properly, it can do wonders for an airline's public relations.

Recently, an advertising executive from San Francisco— a visitor to Hawaii—approached the American Airlines ticket counter at the Honolulu airport. He had flown from San Francisco to Honolulu and was scheduled to fly back to San Francisco on a discounted and highly restricted ticket.

"I was wondering," he asked the American agent, "if I could change my return flight to Los Angeles instead."

The agent told him that she could, in fact, change his ticket, but the difference in fares would be substantial. "I could waive the additional fare," she then advised him, "if there is a hardship involved."

"I don't think so," the executive said with a shrug. "It's just that my daughter called me last night and asked if I could come to her eighteenth birthday party, and she lives in Los Angeles."

"That's the reason?" the agent asked.

"Afraid so," he said, resignedly.

The agent quickly scanned seat availability for the Los Angeles flight. There were plenty of empty seats. She looked up from her computer screen, smiled, and winked. "That's a hardship," she said, as she rewrote his ticket at no additional charge. "Have a nice flight."

Great, true story. But don't count on that kind of response.

Remember: Even if the airline DOES have a bereavement fare and WANTS to offer it, you can often do better by purchasing a last-minute ticket on the Internet. After all, you're distressed; why shouldn't you also purchase distressed inventory?

Finally, if you don't want to be a fare casualty, you must do some comparison shopping before accepting an airline's offer of a bereavement fare at a time of loss. If the worst happens, this is the best time to cash in some of your frequent flyer miles. And, assuming you can actually redeem them, that's the ultimate sign of an airline's compassion!

2

At the Airport

**OK, NOW. YOU'RE PACKED.
YOU'VE GOT YOUR PAPER TICKET,
YOUR DOCUMENTS. SO, GET READY,
GET SET . . .**

DON'T GO!!!

That's right: Don't leave home yet. You need to make one final call. And most of us regularly *do* make a final call before leaving our home or office to go to an airport.

We call the airline, indicate our flight number, and ask whether the flight is on time.

"Yes," we are told, "the flight is leaving on time."

Wrong. When we get to the airport, we discover that the flight has been delayed for four hours. In fact, the plane isn't even on the ground. How did that information snafu happen?

It happened because you didn't word your question in the right way.

When you ask whether the flight is on time, the airline agent can interpret the question as: "Is the flight scheduled to leave on time?" Or, if you're calling to confirm an incoming flight, the interpretation might be: "The flight is scheduled to arrive on time."

Are we really interested in the airline's INTENTIONS? Think about it. The *Titanic* was SCHEDULED to arrive on time.

It all boils down to the words you use when you ask the question. Instead of just asking whether the flight is leaving on time, go one step further. Let's say you're booked on Flight 505, from Los Angeles to Boston. It's supposed to depart at 11:00 A.M.

When you call, ask the on-time question the following way: "I'm on Flight 505 from Los Angeles to Boston. Could you please punch up 'FLIFO' [airline jargon for internal flight information] and tell me the aircraft NUMBER assigned to my flight?"

Pause.

"Yes," will come the answer. "The aircraft number is 82."

OK, almost there. "Now, could you tell me the status of aircraft number 82?"

Pause.

"Sir, aircraft number 82 is in Bangladesh."

Bingo! You now know that although Flight 505 is SCHEDULED to leave on time, it has no possible chance of even ARRIVING on time at the airport, much less leaving on time for Boston.

Understanding airline schedules means understanding the "cycle" of aircraft. Believe it or not, there are still some folks who believe that their aircraft has been sitting on the ground, waiting for them, for hours or even for days. Instead, as any airline executive will tell you, schedules are all about utilization of aircraft.

An airplane on the ground earns the airline no money. The key is to schedule aircraft to be in the air as much as possible, and, depending on the aircraft type, to carry a maximum number of revenue passengers.

Thus, the cycle. It is not unusual for the flight from Los Angeles to Boston to take off from Los Angeles, land in Boston, turn and fly to San Francisco, and, in less than two hours, become the San Francisco-to-London flight. Two hours after its arrival in London, it is flown to New York, and, ninety minutes later, it turns and heads back to Los Angeles. And that, as an example, is a plane's cycle.

James Gleick, who wrote the excellent book *Faster: The Acceleration of Just About Everything,* called the cycle the "paradox of efficiency."

He tracked American Airlines aircraft number 241, an MD-80 that started its cycle by flying from Phoenix to Dallas, then to Richmond and Norfolk, back to Dallas, and then to Calgary—in one day. The next day, the aircraft flew back to Dallas, then to Los Angeles, and then to Austin, Texas. On day three, it went from Austin to San José, Dallas, Nashville, Chicago, and Denver. And so on.

Gleick tracked the MD-80's high-use cycle for an entire week. "Its ramblings are not random," he reported. "They are precisely charted by computers. The goal is a schedule of maximal efficiency."

But if one glitch develops in that cycle, a slight delay explodes exponentially.

And suddenly, a flight to Boston is, for all practical purposes, nonexistent.

That's why you need information on your aircraft number, not just your flight number.

And now, before ever leaving your home or office, before ever confronting the chaos of the airport, you have enough information to plan your options.

Well, not yet—not until you understand the power of something called Rule 240.

The airlines are not exactly eager to share Rule 240 with you. (Recently, it was amended to something called Rule 120.20. More on that later.)

You must remember this rule, because the airlines will NEVER volunteer it to you.

Rule 240 (or Rule 120.20) is actually old jargon for a policy that no longer exists. It referred to a Civil Aeronautics Board (CAB) requirement; in those days when the government actually provided the perception that it actually controlled and regulated the airlines, the carriers actually had to tell the board exactly what it would offer passengers if they delayed them, cancelled their flights. It covered everything from free phone calls home, rooms, meal vouchers. That was then. The airlines are no longer forced to tell the U.S. what they will provide, but they do have to tell YOU if you ask. In fact, and most people don't know this, but it's actually part of the "contract of carriage" between the carrier and the traveler.

So, what does Rule 240 do for you? In its broadest interpretation, Rule 240 deals only with the airlines' minimum responsibilities to you. If you read that contract of carriage, it simply says the airline must deliver you to your destination within two hours of your scheduled flight time. If it can't, it must put you on another carrier at no additional cost, even if it means an upgrade into first class.

So how—or when—does Rule 240 kick in?

The airlines will 240 you only in the event of mechanical delays or delays that are completely the "fault" of the airline, like misconnections or cancellations. They won't do it for weather delays, acts of God, riots, wars, or labor problems.

And it only works in the United States.

Again, the airlines aren't exactly racing to tell you about this rule. This is the one rule that gives you, with one or two exceptions, immediate options in the event of a delay or cancellation of your flight.

But you have to ask for it. NO ONE at the airline will just offer it.

In the airline business, virtually everyone knows it simply as "240." This is what it says. In the event of the specified "flight irregularity"—if Rule 240 is invoked—the airline must endorse your ticket and put you on the next available flight; not just its own next available flight, but THE next available flight.

(That's one of the main reasons I love paper tickets!)

So, in this scenario, you found out real-time information about the status of your flight because you asked for the status of your AIRCRAFT.

And now, armed with this information, you have the weapon you need to take back your options and actually travel from Los Angeles to Boston.

So, let's go back to your telephone conversation with the airline agent.

"Now that we've established that there is absolutely no way my flight is leaving on time," you tell the agent, "I'd like you to 240 me."

And then, before you even leave for the airport, you're truly protected (unless there is a weather problem). And you've saved a lot of time you'd otherwise lose waiting for a flight that isn't leaving, or waiting on line for so long that you miss one that IS leaving.

OK, NOW you can go to the airport.

But wait. HOW you go to the airport also makes a difference.

First, have SOMEONE ELSE drive you. Have a friend take you, or call or hail a cab. Do ANYTHING necessary so as not to take your own car to the airport.

Then, embrace a contrarian view during heavy "push" times at the airport. At most major airports in the United States, the heavy "banks" of flight departures are usually between 6:00 and 9:00 in the morning, and 4:00 and 7:00 in the afternoon and early evening.

The key here is to avoid automobile gridlock at the airports. When you are heading to an airport that has divided upper/lower departure/arrival levels, go against the flow. During the high-push times for departures, avoid the departures level altogether. Instead, head for the lower arrivals level. It will be empty. Pull up; no crowd, no waiting. Rent a baggage cart, go inside, and take the elevator upstairs. At some airports, you could easily save up to fifteen minutes of precious time. If people are meeting you at your destination, have them reverse the process as well. When you land, head downstairs, grab your bags from the carousel, and then take the elevator or escalator upstairs where they can meet you at the then uncrowded departures level.

OK, you're now at the airport, you've got your bags. Now what do you do?

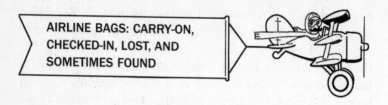

AIRLINE BAGS: CARRY-ON,
CHECKED-IN, LOST, AND
SOMETIMES FOUND

Airline baggage is one of my favorite topics. If you're like me, you embrace the somewhat cynical philosophy that there are only two kinds of airline luggage: carry-on, and *LOST.*

I try to carry on as much as possible. Most of the airlines, of course, don't like this. Why? It all gets down to a definition of what actually constitutes a carry-on bag. And sometimes, it borders on the ridiculous.

The U.S. Department of Transportation reports that the airlines lose or mishandle 7,000 bags every day. And even though the airlines claim they are trying to do a better job, many passengers will do everything they can to *not* check their luggage.

They will schlepp it, roll it, push it, even hide it—anything to ensure that it goes onto the plane, at their sides. And it doesn't matter that it might be an unconventional piece of luggage.

There are some extreme examples. What do the following items have in common: An eight-foot totem pole, a large industrial vacuum cleaner, a refrigerator, and a BMW transmission?

These are all items that passengers have attempted—successfully—to take on airplanes as carry-on baggage.

"There are people out there who will try to bring just about anything on the plane," says Debbie Sculley, a Delta airlines ticket-counter agent in Los Angeles. "Tires, fenders, drive shafts [car items seem particularly popular], everything short of the kitchen sink." (Kitchen sink? More on the kitchen sink later.)

But as absurd as the carry-on situation has become from the airlines' perspective, it has become equally bizarre from the passengers' point of view. Most major airlines seem to be doing everything they can to stop passengers from carrying their belongings onto the plane. At certain airports, carry-on baggage rules are enforced with nothing less than a Draconian spirit.

Consider this absurd but true example: I was in Atlanta, on my way to board a Delta flight to Orlando. I carried with me two small black briefcases. Each contained a computer. As I neared the gate, I stopped at a news kiosk and bought two newspapers and a bag of gummy bears. The clerk asked if I wanted a bag for them. I said yes, and she put them in a white plastic bag. I then headed for the gate.

When they called my flight, I dutifully stood in line to board. But when I approached the gate agent who was pulling tickets, he pointed to my bags.

"Those yours?" he asked. I nodded. "Sorry, you can't board the flight. You've got too many bags."

Too many bags? Two small briefcases, and a third, thin plastic bag with a *New York Times,* a *USA Today,* and a package of gummy bears?

I'm the first one to understand the difference between portable and transportable. I know that just because a piece of luggage has two wheels on it doesn't mean it belongs in the passenger cabin.

But this was going too far. "You can't be serious," I laughed.

He didn't laugh. "You either check one of those bags or you don't board."

He was declaring the gummy bears as an illegal *third* carry-on bag!

He was serious. And he was being ridiculous. I decided to take him at his word.

"All right," I countered. "Since these other bags contain computers, I want to check this bag," I said, pointing to the open plastic bag.

"I can't do that," he said.

"So what do you suggest I do?" I asked.

"You pack that plastic bag inside one of your other bags or you can't board the flight."

"OK," I said, trying to suppress a laugh, "but let me ask you a question of logic. Let's say I do that. And then I board the plane. What do you think is the first thing I'm going to do when I get on the plane? I'm going to unpack the bag. Now, can you tell me what you've accomplished here, other than holding up the boarding process?"

He wouldn't answer. So, I packed the two newspapers in the bag, along with the gummy bears, and in the process promised about six people behind me in line that I would share the candy with them once on board.

The gummy bears didn't last long.

But my anger about the incident remains. Why? The underlying problem is that there is no universal agreement on what is and isn't a carry-on. Looking to the government for help? Forget it.

The Federal Aviation Administration doesn't provide a definition. FAA rules only require that cabin baggage be properly stowed, either under the seat in front of you, or in the overhead compartment.

Not surprisingly, flight attendants hate the situation. The Association of Flight Attendants (AFA) has been lobbying hard for an industry standard definition—an FAA rule—for carry-on baggage. "It's tough," says AFA president Patricia Friend. "We end up in the middle, trying to tell people that there's no room for it in the cabin and it's going to have to be taken off the plane. And that creates a conflict."

The flight attendants are not alone. Another group calling for a federal standard carry-on bag policy is the Luggage and Leather Goods Manufacturers of America. The LLGMA has also started a nationwide effort to have passengers "think small."

SO WHAT *IS* A CARRY-ON BAG?

It depends on the airline, the airport, and the kind of plane you're flying. What is acceptable to one airline is barred by another. And it's gotten downright nasty out there. In 1998, United Airlines tried to limit the number of carry-on bags brought onto its planes by installing restrictive "templates" at security checkpoints. The airline soon enlarged them (even small garment bags were being stuck at the templates), but they proved singularly unpopular.

"We think the templates are a cheap trick," charges Gordon Bethune, the CEO of Continental Airlines. "The reasons why some airlines want to use templates is that it takes the confrontation away from them [and directs it] to a third party—the security guard at the checkpoints. These airlines would like to have a law to take away the rights of the consumers to carry their underwear with them when they fly, and most people don't like to be separated from their underwear."

Continental thought it had gone a long way toward solving the carry-on problem: It spent $15 million on installing bigger overhead bins on its planes. Even the large roll-on bags now fit inside them.

However, at two airports where Continental shared gate space with United, passengers were apparently being separated from their underwear and denied boarding with their carry-on bags, which didn't fit United's templates.

Continental got angry and sued United. In the antitrust lawsuit, filed in the U.S. District Court for the Eastern District of Virginia, Continental claimed that United was trying to limit competition by requiring Continental's passengers to conform to United's standards in order to board Continental planes.

"In their quest to prevent customers from carrying their bags on board, airlines like United are thwarting our ability to compete on the basis of offering a superior product," Continental claimed. Shortly before going to trial, United settled out of court with Continental.

In the meantime, it gets worse for passengers who interline—who fly, for example, on a Continental flight from Newark to Atlanta and then change to a Delta flight to Salt Lake City. With the carriers' different rules, passengers could easily have trouble on their connecting Delta flight.

Templates or no templates, the continuing problem is that there is no standard for carry-on bags. Is a purse a bag? Is a laptop computer? On some airlines, each counts as a bag.

Other airlines make a class distinction: Both American and Northwest allow business-class and first-class passengers a more liberal carry-on amount. Of all the major airlines, Continental appears to have the least restrictive and most flexible carry-on policy. The airline officially allows up to three (and sometimes more) carry-on bags per passenger, depending on how full a particular flight is.

Thankfully, at least for the moment, I haven't found an airline that counts overcoats, umbrellas, canes, or small cameras as additional carry-on bags.

Although enforcement is spotty at best, here are some of the airlines' current rules (coach class only). American allows two carry-ons; Northwest allows one bag plus one purse, briefcase, or laptop computer; Southwest, United, Delta, and US Airways each allow two bags as carry-ons.

But again, the dimensions vary by airlines. Many carriers put a limit on carry-ons: 9 inches by 22 inches by 14 inches.

Carry-On Confusion: Sizing Up the Rules

Airline	Size Limit	Comments
Alaska	10 x 17 x 24"	Size limit is for both bags combined.
America West	Not listed	When space is limited, it may be necessary to limit carry-on bags to one per customer.
American	9 x 13 x 23"	Total of three checked/carry-on bags permitted. Bags limited to 62,55 and 45 linear inches.
Continental	Not listed	Total of three checked/carry-on bags permitted. Bags limited to 62,55 and 45 linear inches.
Delta	9 x 14 x 22"	A purse is exempt. Restrictions may apply on certain flights.
Northwest	9 x 14 x 22"	Official carry-on limit is one bag, but exempts purses, briefcases, and laptop computers.
Southwest	10 x 16 x 24"	Purses of reasonable size and food for on-board consumption are also permitted.
TWA	10 x 16 x 24"	Trans World One passengers allowed three pieces of carry-on luggage.
United	9 x 14 x 22"	A small purse is exempt. On full flights, you may be asked to check one of your bags.
USAirways	10 x 16 x 21" 8 x 16 x 24"	Handbags are exempt. Carry-ons may be restricted due to a lack of space. Limits each bag to separate sizes.

Notes: All airlines exempt coats, canes, umbrellas, and reading materials. Some also exempt child seats and baby strollers. Most also restrict a carry-on bag to 45 linear inches (length × height × width).

Source: Based on a chart entitled "Carry-On Confusion: Sizing Up the Rules" from The Brancatelli File at biztravel.com. Copyright © 2000 by biztravel.com. All rights reserved. Adapted by permission of biztravel.com. Source of carry-on size information from the Web sites of the listed airlines.

American shaves that by an inch: 9 inches by 23 inches by 13 inches, which can sometimes be a problem if the bag has wheels and the wheels stick out more than an inch from the bag itself. Southwest and TWA allow slightly larger bags: 10 inches by 16 inches by 24 inches.

Remember the reference to the kitchen sink? Believe it or not, I found an airline that will actually let you board with one of those—that's right, a kitchen sink—as a carry-on.

Just for laughs, I went to a hardware store and bought a double porcelain sink. I took it to LAX, put it on a luggage cart, got it through the security machines, and yes, got it onto a plane as a carry-on!

The airline? A then new carrier, Legend Airlines, based at Love Field in Dallas, was offering 56 (all) first-class seats on its DC-9 aircraft flying from Dallas to Washington, Los Angeles, and Las Vegas. "We designed the overheads so that each passenger literally has his or her own bin," says Allan McArtor, Legend's CEO, and a former administrator of the FAA.

"Whether you're a mom with kids, carrying a stroller and a child seat, or you're going on vacation and have a lot of extra gear, or you're a business passenger who needs that extra computer, we'll make room for you," he says. In addition to the bins, the airline offers extra-large closet space on board.

"Our policy," says McArtor, "is that if you can carry them to the gate, you can bring them on the airplane. Do we have a template for bags at Legend Airlines? It's the aircraft door. If you can bring it through the airplane door, you can bring it on."

Sound good? Shortly after I did the interview with McArtor, the airline, hit by high fuel prices and head-to-head competition with American, suspended operations.

So you might want to forget the kitchen sink for a while. Instead, here are my sure fire tips for surviving the carry-on chaos:

1. Try to be among the first passengers to board the plane (before all the bins fill up).

2. Use carry-on bags that will satisfy the dimensions of the most restrictive airline on your route.

3. Pack for weight, not just for size. If you can't lift your bag, do not expect the flight attendants to lift it for you, once you're on the plane.

4. Never ask at the counter if your bag is approvable as a carry-on. Only do that at the gate. The counter people will, more often than not, tell you your bag must be checked. The gate people are the best arbiters. If the flight isn't full, they're more likely to let you on with your bag. If the flight is full, they will gate-check it. The good news there is: (1) you know it made your flight and (2) last bag on, first bag off! Be sure to pack at least one of your bags well enough so that, in case you're forced to check it, you can easily do so.

An important note to remember if your connecting flight requires you to switch airlines midtrip. The SECOND carrier is responsible for your luggage. Believe it or not, this applies even if the switch wasn't planned and was caused by a flight cancellation. For example, you're flying from Washington to Chicago on United, but St. Louis is your destination so you must switch to TWA in Chicago. Even though your original ticket may have been issued by United, TWA assumes responsibility, in Chicago, for getting your bags to St. Louis.

The subject of checking bags brings up another sore spot: the dreaded excess baggage charges.

Consider this scenario. A friend of mine took a flight on Lufthansa from Los Angeles to Budapest. The plane made one stop—in Frankfurt—and my friend changed planes for his journey to Hungary.

When he had checked in for the outbound flight in Los Angeles, he had two large suitcases and one carry-on bag. The suitcases were full of clothes and gifts for friends in Hungary. The carry-on bag contained documents for a business meeting in Budapest. The two suitcases were checked through to Budapest.

Two weeks later, as he was preparing to leave Hungary, he had less baggage than when he arrived. The gifts had been presented, and most of the business documents had been left for his colleagues. He packed his empty carry-on bag inside one of his two suitcases.

But when he arrived at the Budapest airport for his return flight to Los Angeles on Lufthansa, officials told him he was overweight and would have to pay excess-baggage charges—a whopping $254.

Even though it was a Lufthansa flight, the Lufthansa agent actually worked for Malev, the Hungarian national airline, which handles all ground operations for Lufthansa in Hungary. The agent was not in an understanding mood. My friend had no choice: either he paid or his bags stayed in Hungary.

Excess baggage charges are among the biggest airline ripoffs—the few areas of modern travel where no standardized international rules exist.

Overweight tariffs are applied—or not applied—depending on when you fly, who you are, and the mood of the airline counter agent. It is a capricious, unfriendly, and immensely profitable side business for many airlines, and, more often than not, the unwitting passengers victimized by the charges are left—literally—holding either the bag or an empty wallet.

Airlines can—and do—charge outrageous amounts for excess baggage, especially overseas. The problem stems from the fact that different countries and international tariffs dictate the baggage rules in each place you fly.

In the United States, the Civil Aeronautics Board (CAB; it was deregulated out of business in 1978) did something to protect American passengers. It initiated the "piece" system.

On domestic flights, each passenger is usually allowed to check two pieces of luggage and take one carry-on. Generally, each bag can weigh up to 70 pounds. The two bags must not exceed, respectively, 120 inches and 106 inches in total dimensions. (The carry-on, which can weigh up to 70 pounds on some airlines, theoretically must fit underneath the seat.)

Since 1977, that CAB rule has also applied to international flights arriving in or departing from the United States, regardless of the carrier.

But once you leave the United States, you can generally forget the 70-pound allowance per bag. And you had better start jettisoning some of your stuff or preparing to pay for it. In most other parts of the world, bags are weighed. Passengers are permitted to carry forty-four pounds (total) in economy class and sixty-six pounds in first class.

For baggage over that amount, you will be charged 1 percent of the regular coach or first-class ticket price per overweight kilo (2.2 pounds). For example, a coach passenger flying between London and Johannesburg, and carrying three bags (including one carry-on), each weighing 70 pounds, could be charged about $1,200 for being 166 pounds overweight. Another person, flying between London and Los Angeles and bringing on board the exact same number of pieces and weight of luggage, carries it all for free under the U.S. piece system.

If you have foreign stopovers en route to your final destination, some airlines will charge you excess baggage rates at each stop along the way.

Authorities at Moscow's Sheremetyevo Airport are notorious for not only extracting huge excess-baggage charges from departing passengers, but also demanding that the fees be paid in hard currency.

To be fair, some airlines do seem to have a legitimate excess-baggage problem. Philippine Airlines is regularly plagued with dozens of passengers checking in large, heavy cardboard boxes on their U.S. flights to Manila.

American, which flies an extensive route system in South America, has suffered from excess-baggage problems. It is not unusual for the airline to institute a bag cutoff rule, especially during holiday periods. Generally, American never tells passengers about the cutoff until they arrive at the ticket counter with their bags. Under that rule, excess bags just aren't carried on the flights. If you're flying to the Caribbean during Thanksgiving, no big problem. But at any time within ten days of Christmas, you'd be better off mailing your bags. At that time of the year, a lot of folks come up to Miami to do their shopping, and the return flights are jammed with bags.

So, always call first and make sure there is no baggage moratorium on your flight. If you get to the airport and then find out there IS a cutoff, at the very best, you'll be charged excess baggage, your bags may not make your flight, and, worse, the airline is then not liable to deliver your bags once they DO arrive.

A few airlines have tried variations of normal excess-baggage formulas. But nothing seems to work. As a result, the excess-baggage problem—and airline-by-airline confusion—continues, with no easy solution.

WHAT CAN YOU DO?

With all due respect to airline security (or the lack thereof), I often look for a fellow business traveler who understands my predicament (because he or she has been there before), and appeal to him or her to check my bag on the plane as if it were theirs. I am traveling on the same plane, so the obvious security fears are alleviated.

If you're traveling with your family, remember that each of your kids has the same baggage allowance you do. Use it.

Also consider the aircraft type and whether your bags will actually make it on the flight with you. A fully booked 747 has the capacity to carry all passengers' bags. But a fully booked commuter flight on United Express or American Eagle? Forget it. On the last ten booked commuter flights I've taken, the airlines are batting ten for ten—they've delayed at least one of my bags every time, because the planes simply couldn't hold all the passengers' bags. Suggestion: Don't check ANY bags on commuter flights. Instead, walk them to the gate and have them gate-checked. It really works! (Gate-checked bags go into a different compartment in the plane and have a better chance of making the flight.)

You can avoid the problem altogether. Consider FedExing your bags ahead of you. FedEx and other courier services offer discounts for two- and three-day delivery (just send the bags out that far ahead). Virtual Bellhop will do the same thing. Think that's too expensive? How valuable is your time to you or to your business? On average, you will be spending between 60 and 90 minutes checking luggage in for a flight and then, upon your arrival, waiting for your bags to show up on the pick-up carousel (assuming they were actually on the same flight with you!).

Depending on the time of day you arrive, that extra waiting time may be the difference between getting from the airport to your destination in a reasonable time, or getting stuck in rush-hour traffic. There's also a schlepp factor—lifting your bags, renting a cart, schlepping the bags to and from ground transportation, and so on. Suddenly, sending your bags by courier seems like the *least* costly way to go!

WHEN YOU ABSOLUTELY HAVE
TO CHECK YOUR BAGS

Remember, with more airlines forcing us to check our bags, that means more airlines are now losing more bags. (Ironically, Delta and United, the two airlines that started putting baggage sizers at security checkpoints to limit carry-on bags, have seen their complaint percentages zoom. Delta's have nearly doubled, and complaints against United have more than doubled, in the most recent report issued by the U.S. Department of Transportation.)

When an airline loses your bag, you're known as one of the "PAWOBS"—"passengers without bags." You've seen them wandering aimlessly near baggage carousels at airports, waiting without hope for the luggage that never seems to arrive.

So, how do you avoid being a PAWOB or at least lessen your chances?

Let's start with the bags themselves. First, there's a great deal of difference between portable and transportable. Just because your bag has wheels on it doesn't mean it belongs inside the airline cabin.

Second, realize that baggage conveyor belts are not your friends. They will eat, mangle, and otherwise destroy anything left dangling on the outside of a bag. Translation: Straps, hooks, and even identification tags stand an excellent chance of being yanked from your bag.

Advice: Clean up your bag before you get to the airport. Take anything—and everything—off the bag that can be pulled, caught, or hooked.

The luggage ID tags the airlines give you are purely ornamental and are almost begging to be stripped from your luggage. Instead, buy some heavy-duty ID tags and put two on each bag. Attach them to different parts of the bag, and not necessarily on the handle. (If the handle breaks, the tag slips off.)

What about the destination tags the airlines put on the bags? How these tags are labeled and how you—and others—read them make a big difference as to whether they reach your destination—or, for that matter, ANY destination.

Most destination tags today are bar-coded and well labeled. If they are generated by machine, they most likely will include your last name, the originating as well as the connecting flights, and the three-letter code of the city that is your ultimate destination.

But not always. It is your responsibility to understand the three-letter code of your destination city BEFORE you get to the airport. When you make your reservation, ask for that code, write it down, and keep that slip in your wallet. Why?

If the proper code isn't on your bag, it can be lost forever. Here's an example of what happens a lot more than the airlines want to admit.

Going to Los Angeles? Putting LOS on your bag tag won't get it anywhere near Los Angeles, or even California. In airline jargon, LOS sends your bag directly to Lagos, Nigeria! Given the current state of airport security—or lack of it—in Lagos, you can kiss your bag a big goodbye.

LAX gets your bag to Los Angeles.

The same warning applies with LON instead of LHR (Heathrow) or LGW (Gatwick) if you're headed to London. Otherwise, your bags could end up at the wrong airport in London—or, worse, in London, Ontario, Canada!

It's not just where the bags are going—it's where YOU are going.

BTM isn't Baltimore. It's Butte, Montana. (BWI is Baltimore.) Planning a vacation in Mazatlán, Mexico? Make sure the tags don't read MAZ. If they do, your baggage could get a

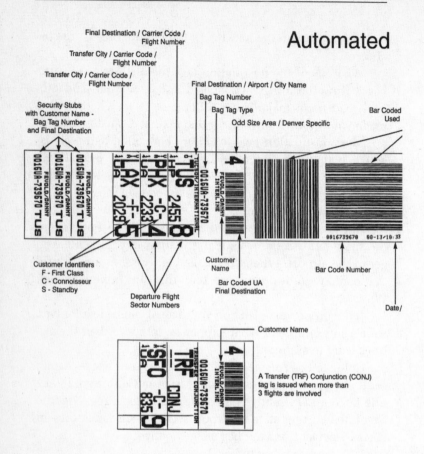

long rest in Mayagüez, Puerto Rico. MZT is the correct Mazatlán tag. Going to Kansas City? If your bags say KAN, you're in trouble. They'll land in Kano, Nigeria. The correct code for Kansas City is MCI. ALB is Albany, not Albuquerque.

Sometimes, even if the codes are correct, you can be in trouble if they're not written clearly. For example, IND is the correct code for Indianapolis, Indiana, but if it's misread as IMD, it may be a while before you see your bags. Their

Baggage Tag (United Airlines)

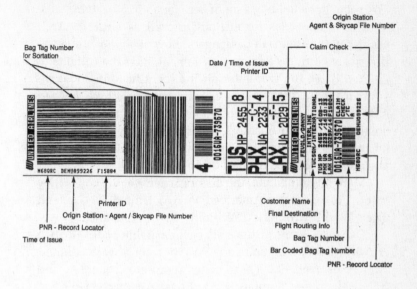

Origin Station
Agent & Skycap File Number

Claim Check

Date / Time of Issue
Printer ID

Bag Tag Number
for Sortation

Printer ID
Origin Station - Agent / Skycap File Number
PNR - Record Locator
Time of Issue

Customer Name
Final Destination
Flight Routing Info
Bag Tag Number
Bar Coded Bag Tag Number
PNR - Record Locator

destination would be Imonda in Papua New Guinea. There's an equally big difference between JSI and JSL. JSL lands you in Atlantic City, JSI in Skiathos, Greece.

Some mistagged-luggage stories are legendary. Some years ago, a gate agent mistakenly tagged all the bags of a charter group headed for Mazatlán with SIN (Mazatlán is in the Mexican state of Sinaloa). When the group arrived in Mexico, there were no bags. A few days later, Pan AM stations around the world received a frantic telex from a confused employee in Singapore. "Is anyone looking for about 60 bags?" he asked. "We seem to be holding a lot of bags for a Mr. Mazatlán."

There are codes for airlines as well as airports. And, each year, thousands of passengers show up at the wrong airline ticket counters and may, as a result, miss their flights.

You'll see the two-letter airline identification codes on your airline ticket as well as your luggage tags, if you have to change planes or airlines en route to your destination. In the competitive travel business, airlines fight for these letters. Once an airline gets a code it wants, it fights to the death—and sometimes even beyond death—to keep it.

More often than not, the major carriers get the codes they want. For example, American is AA, United is UA, and Trans World Airlines is TW. (Pretty easy to remember.)

Overseas, some airlines also get desirable codes (British Airways is BA, Air France is AF), but not always. Finnair isn't FI or even FN. Those codes represent Icelandair and SFO Helicopters. Finnair is AY. Royal Air Maroc isn't RA, RM, or even AM. RA is Royal Nepal Airlines, RM is Wings West, and AM is the code for AeroMexico.

And since most airlines code-share these days, the confusion only gets worse. Pay attention to your ticket as well as your bag tags.

If at all possible, try to get bag tag stubs with the UPC bar code. Ask to have the stubs pasted or stapled inside your ticket jacket. Without them, you're as lost as your bags if the luggage is MIA at your destination.

Always double-check what the skycap or counter agent puts on your bags. It's even more important when your itinerary demands making a connecting flight on the same airline—or worse, interlining among different airlines. Be aware that not every airline has an interlining agreement with other airlines.

For example, you can fly from San Francisco to Chicago on United, transfer there to a Delta flight to Atlanta, and your bags will connect. But if you fly Southwest to St. Louis and then want to connect with TWA to Los Angeles, your bags will NOT interline. Southwest only will connect bags within its own system, so you'll need to get your bags in St. Louis and then check them in all over again with TWA. If you have a short connection time (less than sixty minutes on the schedule), your bags may not make the connecting flight. Always ask whether the airlines you'll be taking have an interline agreement if your itinerary requires a connection, in another city, between two different carriers.

Next comes the hard part. You need to determine the real as well as the emotional value of the contents of your bags.

The good news: Recently, the liability limits for damaging or losing your bag were raised to $2,500, but that figure needs to be put in perspective. Most travelers don't realize that the $2,500 figure is based on "per incident," not per bag, and on depreciated value. And there are numerous exclusions for what the airline will *not* cover, including jewelry, furs, and negotiable financial instruments.

For example, United Airlines claims it "won't be responsible for loss or damage to: fragile items, spoilage of perishables, loss/damage/delay of money, jewelry, cameras, electronic/video/photographic equipment, computer equipment, heirlooms, antiques, artwork, silverware, precious metals, negotiable papers/securities, commercial effects, valuable papers or other irreplaceable items."

Translation: You'll never see anywhere near $2,500 if the airline loses your bags.

On international flights, the risk is even worse.

Liability for loss, delay, or damage to baggage is limited to approximately $9.07 per pound ($20 per kilogram) for checked baggage and $400 per passenger for unchecked baggage. Translation (using an internationally recognized word): You get *bubkus.*

An additional problem has to do with how much your bags weigh. Remember that forty-four-pound allowance in coach?

You may notice that, on an international flight, the counter agent usually weighs your bags, and writes their weight on your ticket, as well as on the airline's copy of the ticket, before handing you your boarding pass. Enter the forty-four-pound limit and international liability.

If the agent actually writes down the total weight, be prepared for virtually nothing if the airline loses your bags.

It all has something to do with the Warsaw Treaty—definitely not a Polish joke—which established the $9.07-per-pound liability on international flights. In a decision handed down in a recent court case, that liability applies only if the airline confirms what your bag actually weighs at the time you check in. It can't assume your bag weighed only forty-four pounds—or anything at all.

This rule emerged from a case in which a Silver Spring, Maryland, family—14 persons—flew on American Airlines to Santo Domingo for a wedding. The Cruz family had checked twenty-eight suitcases. The airline lost five of the bags. A sixth arrived late and was damaged AND empty.

Normally, the family would have been severely limited in its recovery. But when the family checked in, the airline forgot to note the weight of the bags.

When the family filed a claim, the airline simply estimated the weight of each bag at 100 pounds, and offered to settle the case for $4,535. The family refused. Then the airline raised its offer to $7,500. Mrs. Cruz then retained the services of a lawyer. Ironically, she already worked for the lawyer, as his cleaning lady.

He sued the airline.

A lower court dismissed the case and called the omission of the weight a technicality. But a three-judge circuit court panel reversed the lower court's decision, and not only reinstated the suit but allowed Mrs. Cruz's request to certify it as a class action. What does this mean?

Judges are now more inclined to go after airlines when they abuse passengers. A suggested reason: Judges, as passengers, have also been abused by the same airlines.

You don't have to file a class action suit if the airline loses your bag. But you do need to pay attention. On an international flight, did the counter agent write down the weight of your bags? If you have to file a claim, that detail can significantly affect the settlement you'll receive. You'll also have to provide receipts and dates of purchase for anything lost.

There's a little-known tactic you can use when checking in your bags, but it only works on domestic flights. The airlines don't like to publicize this (in fact, they *don't* publicize it) and would prefer to have you *not* know about something called "excess valuation."

Here's how excess valuation works. For a charge that averages $1 to $2 per $100 of coverage (up to $5,000 of coverage, over and above the standard $2,500 limit), the airline essentially insures the bag. You must request this extra insurance at the ticket counters. Skycaps can't accommodate you. Not all companies offer excess valuation, and yes, there are some exclusions here, too. But if you have the option and harbor any doubts about your bag's arrival, *buy the coverage.* It's an excellent incentive for the airline to get your bag to your destination.

So, is your bag worth at least $50 to make sure it arrives on time and in good shape? In many cases, it's worth a multiple of that.

One essential piece of advice: Assume that if the airline loses your bag, your luggage tags will also be missing. Think of traveling as sending your bags to a bad summer camp. Identify everything twice, or even three or four times. Put two ID tags on the outside of each bag; put another two, in visible areas, on the inside of each bag. And *never* put anything other than your name and your phone number on the tags.

Why? Clever airport crooks look for bag tags with a person's home address plainly listed. These criminals aren't looking to steal the bags. They're looking to unload your entire house! You're traveling, and you're advertising that fact simply by being at the airport. A bag tag with your home address on it is an open invitation to burglars while you're out of town.

Another helpful tip when you're traveling internationally. A number of airports have services that shrink-wrap your bags in thick plastic, for a nominal charge. This is a great idea, for one obvious reason. At your destination, if your bag has been opened during the trip, you'll know it immediately.

What happens if you've done all your homework and the airline still manages to lose your luggage? What are your rights? And what can you expect the airline to do until it finds the bag—or worse, if it doesn't?

The answers to these questions vary wildly among airlines and depend on an unspoken caste system: How much you paid for your ticket, what class of service you're flying, where the loss occurred, and your status in that airline's frequent flyer program.

Some airlines, like Swissair, offer an immediate debit card, like a Visa card. The airline preloads it with a specific dollar amount and allows you to buy essentials—clothing, toiletries, and so forth.

Northwest has announced a "compensation program" to help ease the pain if the airline delays your bags. (It's not really a compensation program; it gives you vouchers that allow you discounts on a sliding scale starting at $25.)

But compensation in the form of a voucher is not really compensation; it obligates passengers to spend even more money. To use the voucher, they must fly the airline that delayed their bags. It's nothing more than a nominal discount on a future flight.

Yes, it's better than nothing, but let's put this sequence in perspective. The airline emerges in a good position. It can use the vouchers as a sort of reverse incentive to encourage its baggage handlers to do a better job—to make sure passengers and their bags arrive at the same time and at the same destination.

In the United States, most airlines insist that lost, damaged, or delayed property must be reported within twenty-four hours, and a claim must be made, in writing, within forty-five days. The full description and value of the missing property must be listed. If you need to make interim purchases, United also insists that it "may consider up to a 50 percent reimbursement of the necessities purchased, taking into account your ability to use the new items in the future."

Over at TWA, if your bag is still missing after twenty-four hours, the airline says it will offer you "$35 per day, for a maximum of 3 days—or a total of $105. This is for passengers not arriving at their permanent residence, and original purchase receipts must be presented to the arrival station where the loss occurred."

What if the airline doesn't lose your baggage, and your luggage actually arrives at the same time, and at the same airport, as you do? Are you home free?

Not necessarily. Here's one final tip. Most people don't realize that a majority of airline baggage thieves do not steal the bags themselves. They take individual contents from those bags. And when you're at that baggage carousel waiting for your luggage, you're so happy to see it appear that you don't check to see if everything is still there. Shrink wrapping eliminates that worry. Remember, once you get home and discover a loss, it's only your word against the airline's—a disadvantage when you try to reclaim the value of your lost goods.

Common Sense Rule 101: If you pack valuables, you're asking for trouble. "Valuable" may describe your prescription medicines, extra eyeglasses, or important phone numbers.

What kind of bags are you using? Expensive Louis Vuitton bags are a screaming advertisement for disappearance. Buy the sturdiest, and, yes, sometimes even the ugliest bags. Make sure of their construction. Bolted is better than stitched, especially at corner seams.

If you're buying a bag with wheels, check its center of gravity. Some bags with wheels not only are unsturdy, they can injure you, or others!

Hardsided suitcases often fare worse than softsided ones.

How do I know this? I tested five of the top suitcases in an unusual way: I took all five, still in their original shipping containers, to Hawaii.

There, I opened each one and did some unusual packing. Inside each bag I placed an orange, a banana, an apple, and a coconut. Then I closed the bag.

And then, one by one, with the aid of some friends at the Honolulu Zoo, I placed each bag inside the elephant cage.

Forget the commercials showing a gorilla and some bags. This was the real thing! Hardsided bags lasted an average of one minute before being shredded—literally—by the hungry pachyderms. The bag that won this bizarre durability test was a soft-sided garment bag constructed of bulletproof nylon. There's a lesson there.

Make an inventory of the items packed in each bag. It helps the airlines if they must try to find your luggage. And, it helps you later, if you have to file a claim.

Many people worry about look-alike bags being taken mistakenly. It happens all the time, but there's an easy way to prevent this. Tie a bright-colored ribbon on the handle, or use some day-glo tape on the side of the bag. Remember, being stylish here doesn't count; retrieving your bag does.

When you arrive at the airport, if your luggage doesn't come off the plane, contact someone immediately. Baggage is often loaded into different compartments of an aircraft, based on destinations or connecting flights. If it is improperly loaded, it continues on. So you need to move quickly to make sure other compartments are checked before the plane continues its journey.

Let's say that you've done all the right things and the airline still manages to lose your bag.

And worse: It NEVER comes back. The U.S. airlines are quick to claim that 97 percent of all lost bags are reunited with their owners within twenty-four hours. What about the remaining three percent? The airlines also boast that half of those are reunited with their owners within seventy-two hours.

Even if you believe the airlines' robust claims, it's time to forget the percentages and look at the real numbers they represent. The remaining 1.5 percent—the bags that are lost and never found—translates to a staggering 435,000 bags! And where do THEY go? With the exception of some bags that are victims of outright theft, they head for the foothills of the Appalachian Mountains and the small town of Scottsboro, Alabama—an unlikely destination that has now become the depot for all lost luggage.

And within a few days, the bags—and their contents—are on display, and for sale, at the huge Unclaimed Baggage Center.

This tiny northeastern Alabama town has become the top tourist destination in the state. More than a million visitors came in 2000, from every U.S. state and from forty foreign countries.

And for good reason. Some serious bargains can be found in Scottsboro.

The Center was started thirty years ago, when it bought lost bags from Eastern Airlines, National Airlines, and, for a while, Air Florida.

What began as a small warehouse dealing with three airlines has now grown into a huge operation, and its airline list has greatly expanded. In fact, 115 people now work at two huge locations: (1) the main retail space in Scottsboro (30,000 square feet) and (2) a "clearance center" in Boaz, Alabama, about fifty miles away (17,000 square feet). Here's how it works. When an airline loses a bag and a passenger files a claim, the airline tries to find that luggage. But, after ninety days, if the airline is unable to match a bag with a passenger, it pays the claim. (The current baggage liability limit for the airlines is $2,500, but hardly anyone ever gets paid the full amount. The airlines exclude many items from coverage, and those it includes are covered based on depreciated value.)

After the claim is paid, the airline officially owns the bag. And then the bag and its contents are sold, sight unseen, to the Center.

Because of contractual agreements with the airlines, the Center's owners (as well as the airlines) refuse to discuss the nature of their arrangement with the carriers, or how much they actually pay for the lost bags. "All I can tell you is that our trucks go all over the country picking up these bags." The Center's staff separates and catalogs about one million items a year.

On any given day, about 6,000 new "things" are put on sale. The list includes just about anything you can imagine.

There are some obvious items—about 60 percent of the store is given over to clothing—but there's also fine jewelry, cameras, golf clubs, skis, electronics—a veritable Wal-Mart of lost airline bags.

Not surprisingly, there are some big surprises when the bags are opened. In recent years, staffers have discovered a camera from the space shuttle (it was returned to NASA), rare Egyptian artifacts (they weren't returned; they were auctioned at Christie's in New York). Windsurfing boards, kayaks, and boogie boards line the walls of the store. (Question for the airlines: How do you lose a kayak?)

Separate display cases are dedicated to Barbie dolls, designer sunglasses, watches, and portable CD players.

But don't forget the full suit of armor ($1,000.00), the $23,000 5.8-carat diamond solitaire ring, or the original $8,000 Versace runway dress—with the price tag attached, which sold for $500. Jewelry shoppers, take note. At any given time, the Center has thirty wedding bands and twenty diamond rings for sale.

And there are even more bizarre items: an airplane wing, a coffin, and a constant parade of dentures (they go to the clearance center or get thrown out). The most popular item these days? Palm Pilots, which, like all the other stuff at the Center, typically sell for about 30 percent of their original retail price.

Hundreds of brand-new items are for sale, still with their original price tag. People often shop for new clothes, and other things, before taking a trip or while they are enjoying their destination.

Indeed, on my most recent visit to Scottsboro, I bought a brand new Mizuno baseball mitt, which retails at $160, for $40; a new pair of pants ($16), and a slightly used large metal suitcase, which normally retails for $825, for just $30.

Every so often, someone goes to Scottsboro and gets the biggest surprise. Not long ago, a man from Atlanta traveled to the Alabama store, looking for a birthday present for his wife. At the warehouse, he found a pair of ski boots. They seemed to be his wife's size, and he thought she would like the color. He was right. She loved the boots and the color. Then she looked at the inside of one boot and saw the initials of her maiden name. You guessed it. She had lost the exact same boots on her honeymoon!

So much stuff comes into Scottsboro, the Center now has special sales: in March, a scuba sale; on July 4, sporting goods; on Labor Day weekend (and I'm not kidding), an art sale. The big daddy—on the first Saturday in November—is the ski sale. Each year, a few hundred people show up the night before and camp out in the parking lot, waiting for the store to open.

In case you can't make it to Scottsboro in person, don't worry. The Center's Web site is www.unclaimedbaggage.com.

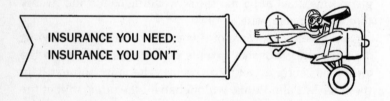

INSURANCE YOU NEED:
INSURANCE YOU DON'T

Let's assume you've got your baggage under control.

Should you insure your TRIP? Or your life?

One of the most overrated—and overpriced—things you can do is purchase flight insurance.

All insurance is based on actuarial tables, so let's apply one here to prove the point.

The U.S. death rate attributable to airline crashes is just .01 per BILLION passenger miles. A British survey has shown that flying is 176 times SAFER THAN WALKING!

Flight accident insurance is truly beneficial only to the company selling the policies. But there is other insurance you absolutely HAVE to have. Let's start with the trip itself.

We'll assume that you've negotiated the maze of tour-brochure language; you've satisfied yourself that the terms described are in sync with your expectations; you've narrowed down the destination, the tour operator, the length of the trip, the extras, the amenities, and the cost. Now comes the most important part: paying for your trip.

We'll assume that you've budgeted well and can afford the package price. Now comes a crucial moment: What amount/percentage should you pay, and when should you pay it? Are you protected financially in case you must cancel the tour or, in a more dreaded scenario, the tour operator goes out of business before your scheduled departure date?

To protect your money in the event that you can't make the trip, buy cancellation insurance, which is sold by most travel agents. The policies are specific in what they will and won't cover, so read the various clauses, exclusions, and conditions before you sign and buy.

The cost of most of these policies is minimal; just be sure the policy you buy will cover you if you have to cancel the trip for *any* legitimate emergency reason, not just an illness to yourself. A close relative or a coworker may get sick, forcing you to cancel your vacation and help out. Ask, before you buy the policy, whether you will be covered if the tour is canceled because of low subscriber numbers or natural disasters (hurricanes, floods, or earthquakes). These policies are standard and are suggested as basic common-sense protection.

What if the tour operator simply goes out of business? Can you protect your investment against that possibility? Yes, but not in the form of an insurance policy. Instead, do some homework about the tour operator or travel agent *before* you hand over any money. In the past, I've written about the need to pay for your trip with a credit card instead of with cash or a check. But many tour operators will not accept credit cards for payment. (Most travel agents will.)

Many travelers, especially those signing up for package tours or charters, pay with cash. When they are told their money is safe because it's being put into an "escrow account," they think it's *really* safe. Not necessarily.

In the travel business, "escrow" is a secure-sounding buzzword that means nothing. Not only do individual travelers sometimes get burned, but so do their travel agents. Just because your money is placed in escrow, does that mean it is a true escrow account? Is it legitimately being held by the bank under proper regulations and guidelines until after the trip is completed, or does the bank have a very cozy relationship with the tour operator?

Unfortunately, the latter can often be a rhetorical question. A number of states (including Florida, New York, Ohio, and California) have consumer protection laws requiring tour operators to post bonds, or to use escrow accounts to protect passengers' money, but the protection offered is minimal.

Indeed, until recently, these "escrow" accounts were no different from any other bank account, and now-defunct tour operators were dipping into the accounts to pay the bills for previous trips. When the cycle finally caught up to them, all the money was gone, and thousands of travelers who had already paid for their trips never got the money or what it was supposed to buy.

Don't assume that only poorly capitalized, heavily leveraged newcomers to the tour operator business can be risky. Recently, a 25-year-old tour company—a specialist in trips to the Caribbean, Bermuda, and Mexico—abruptly went out of business and stranded passengers in hotels in the Bahamas and Bermuda.

Specific U.S. Department of Transportation regulations govern tour operators and charter flights. But few travel agents follow the regulations, or even know about them, and you may be subjected to a costly lesson.

Here's how to protect yourself when paying for a package tour and/or a charter flight, whether you pay directly or through an agent. First, ask whether the tour operator is a member of USTOA (United States Tour Operators Association). If it is, then it is covered by a $1 million bond that the company cannot access. That money is used solely for reimbursing consumer deposits and payments resulting from bankruptcy or insolvency. Even if the operator is a member of the USTOA, have your travel agent check the operator's relationship with its "escrow" bank. Does the bank actually exist? If so, what is it doing with the escrow account? Who really controls the account? Is it a true escrow?

To protect yourself when you're paying by check, list the tour operator *and* the bank escrow account as payees, and, on the memo portion of the check, write the scheduled dates of departure and return. This protects you against the operator's using your funds to pay for someone else's trip.

You should never leave home without comprehensive travel medical insurance. Every year, more than 200,000 Americans get sick overseas. Their illnesses may range from a cold or a stomach virus to a full-blown heart attack. Malaria, hepatitis, and typhoid are often the culprits—or, they get hit by a bus!

Whatever health insurance you carry, it probably does not cover you outside the fifty United States. If your insurance does cover you overseas, don't expect it to reimburse you for anything other than emergency treatment expenses.

Most insurance policies do not cover emergency medical evacuation, often the greatest expense when an ill U.S. citizen needs to be brought home.

Travel medical insurance can be purchased through most travel agents or directly from many insurance companies. If you lack this protection, a medical emergency overseas could easily get you into serious financial trouble. Besides ruining your vacation, it could eliminate your entire nest egg, your retirement account, and even your house.

Think I'm exaggerating? Recently, I boarded a Cairo-to-London flight. Occupying two rows of four first-class seats was a 58-year-old American traveler, lying flat on a stretcher. He had slipped off a curb on the streets near the pyramids, and had broken his hip. On the plane with him: a nurse. He was in pain and had been sedated. The evacuation costs—which involved taking him to a hospital, stabilizing and treating him, and taking him to the airport and placing him on a commercial aircraft back to London and then on to the United States—were more than $120,000.

Some corporate or personal health plans cover you when you're outside the United States, but most don't. Those that do are restricted in what they will and won't pay for. Check the limits and restrictions before you leave town. Don't wait to discover those limits in an emergency.

Often, travelers get confused about their coverage. Travel medical insurance is not trip cancellation insurance. The latter is important and useful, especially if your scheduled trip involves a large, nonrefundable deposit. Cancellation insurance covers you if you are unable to make the trip, or if the carrier (tour operator, airline, cruise line) ceases to operate before your planned departure or return date. The policy also kicks in if sudden illness, death, or injury strikes you or a member of your family.

Trip cancellation insurance does *not* cover the medical bills incurred because of that illness or injury. Invest in a comprehensive travel medical insurance policy that not only covers any medical treatment needed on your trip, but, in a serious medical emergency, pays to evacuate you from the area and bring you home.

Buy the policy before you go. Most policies offer coverage for up to fourteen days. (Some can be extended.) Premiums range from $29 to more than $70 per trip; annual policies are also available. The premium might seem high for such a short period, but the coverage is a bargain if you ever need it.

Various policies are offered; read the fine print. For example, one offers medical evacuation but the evacuation decision is wholly the insurer's. Another policy offers evacuation, but only to the nearest facility where adequate treatment (in the insurer's opinion again) is available.

What you really need is a policy that allows your own doctor direct input into any medical decisions. Some travelers already may have coverage but don't know it. Holders of the American Express Platinum card may now have one very good reason to justify the card's stiff annual membership fee. The card offers "travel emergency assistance," including medical evacuation by air ambulance, at no cost to the cardholder.

A key term to look for in the fine print: *guaranteed payments.* If you think getting proper emergency treatment is tough in this country, try getting it abroad without money up front. Shop for a policy that doesn't make you—or the care providers—wait for payment.

A key word to avoid: *reimbursement.* Some policies provide payment only after the fact. You are solely responsible for payment. Blue Cross, for example, will not pay in advance, and must preapprove all payments made by the patient and later submitted for reimbursement. When I called to check specifics, a spokesman first said, "If you have a Blue Cross policy and you're covered here, then you're covered abroad."

What about medical evacuation? "If you need to be evacuated, we'll take you wherever you need to go." That was their position.

Sounded great. But when I called again, to reconfirm the specific wording of their policies, I got a slightly different answer: "We will pay for all medically necessary treatment." And what does that mean? Who makes that decision? "We need the treating physician to get in touch with us immediately to make that determination," said the spokesman. (Your personal physician needs to be firmly in the communications loop between the doctor on location and the insurance provider, to help make the proper decision—not for the insurer, but for you).

Under the American Express program, all medical emergency services must be arranged by the emergency assistance officials in advance. Amex is very clear that "no claims for reimbursement will be accepted."

One of the best medical insurance programs is offered by International SOS Assistance (ISOS), one of the largest personal and travel assistance companies in the world. For $55, travelers can purchase an ISOS membership for a trip lasting up to fourteen days. This is money well spent. The package includes a worldwide medical evacuation provision.

In a typical one-month period, ISOS repatriated a man with severe abdominal pain from Portugal back to the United States; evacuated, from Mexico to Houston, a scuba diver suffering from decompression sickness; and transported a traveler from Siberia to Helsinki for an emergency appendectomy.

My favorite program, MEDJET, is located in, of all places, Birmingham, Alabama. MEDJET does a great job of providing emergency medical evacuation and treatment. For $175 per person per year, MEDJET does the best job for one very important reason. The fine-print disclaimers that you'll find in other policies are virtually eliminated.

For example, on some policies, the determination of when, how, and—most importantly—WHERE you are evacuated TO is determined by the insurance provider, based on where it thinks the closest available treatment is located.

I don't have to tell you, but I will anyway, that these decisions—in this age of the HMO mentality—are often based on cost versus common sense. If you hemorrhage in Nairobi and your insurance company thinks the closest treatment is in Uganda, that's where you're flown. Considerations of the quality of the blood supply or the capabilities of the doctors in Uganda may not come into play.

MEDJET officials consult directly with your own primary care physician in the United States, and, based on that consultation, will usually send one of their medically equipped jets, complete with EMT personnel, to bring you back HOME.

That's a big difference.

Last but not least, if you get sick overseas, do the same thing you would do at home: Call your doctor. Many times, you can be treated over the phone. If the problem is more serious, don't wait for the hotel doctor. Head straight for the largest local medical center. It's very important to get all records of your treatment—not just for reimbursement, but to allow your own doctor to track what worked or didn't work if the problem continues when you get home.

No matter where you're going, or how, don't assume that you'll have adequate medical treatment available or that you'll be properly covered by your insurance plan. Many travelers on cruise ships assume that because the ship's doctor is featured in the line's brochure, the cruise cost includes free medical care on board. With virtually no exceptions, a ship's doctor is another on-board service that is available to passengers for a fee, as is the photographer or the beautician. Buy comprehensive travel medical insurance that has emergency evacuation provisions.

MEANWHILE, BACK AT
THE AIRPORT

You've made the right calls. You've protected yourself with appropriate insurance. Your flight is not only on time, but you made it to the airport in one piece.

You've got your paper ticket. You've handled your bags.

And now comes a pivotal move: Do everything in your power to avoid the ticket counter.

Why? In the process of travel, the key is to minimize the number of points of abuse. Every time you give someone an opportunity to validate his or her job, you run the risk of additional abuse.

You are empowered to go straight to the gate.

So go there. But—not yet!

First, check the departure board. It is not your friend. Like the original "on time" phone call you made, the departure board often lists a *scheduled* departure time, not a real one.

More important, check the arrivals board. If you know your departure gate, check the arrivals board for the same gate. Is there actually a plane at that gate? If so, you have at least an initial indication of whether your flight is still on time.

Either way, keep moving; head at least in the direction of your departure gate.

The reason: If you keep moving, you lessen the risk of airport crime.

Most people don't associate airports with crime. They associate airports with travel. After all, if you plan correctly, an airport isn't someplace you go *to.* You go *through* it to get somewhere else.

The very real problem of airport crime is often overlooked by the people who most need to know about it: travelers.

If you don't familiarize yourself with some of the various scams criminals use to rip off travelers at airports, you can easily become a victim. I'm not talking about violent crime—homicide, robbery, or rape. Most airport crime is limited to crimes against property: pickpocketing, luggage theft, and automobile break-ins.

But, in almost EVERY case, travelers are unwitting accomplices to actual crimes.

How? Most airport criminals count on travelers' good will, or their nervousness at being in unfamiliar surroundings.

It might surprise you to learn that these airport crooks almost always work in pairs. With few exceptions, they practice what police call crimes of "distraction."

Their tactic is to get you to focus on something else. They will almost always approach a victim and ask a question, or make him or her look in another direction. Or they will delay the victim so that a crime can occur.

Working in pairs, airport criminals usually target folks traveling alone. Here are some of the typical distractions aimed at permanently separating you from your luggage:

- *The phone booth question.* You're standing at an airport pay phone, making a call. Your bag is on the floor, alongside your right foot. Suddenly, from the left, a person walks up to you and asks you a question that requires directions. While you are responding, trying to help, the second criminal walks by and lifts your bag.

By the time you are finished helping the accomplice, your bag is gone.

• *The money trick.* You're standing in line, waiting to check in for a flight. Alongside you is the luggage that you intend to check into the baggage hold, and you're holding your purse or briefcase. Someone approaches you and points to an area of the airport floor, about eight feet away, where three or four dollar bills are visible. "Excuse me," the person asks, still pointing to that spot, "did you drop this money?" Your first instinct might be to put down your briefcase or purse, walk the two or three steps over to the money, bend down, and pick it up. And the minute you do that, the second criminal whisks away your briefcase or purse. The criminal will walk quickly away, holding it at chest level in front of him or her, so that it is not visible from behind.

• *The mustard trick.* You're in line at a ticket counter, a gate, or an airport restaurant or snack shop. Again, you're holding your briefcase or purse. Someone behind you quietly squirts mustard or mayonnaise on the upper part of your back—usually near your left or right shoulder, where you can see it if someone points it out to you. And that's exactly the intent. The first criminal approaches you, tells you that something has been spilled along your shoulder, and offers to help clean it up. Coincidentally, the crook just happens to have a supply of napkins. And your first instinct? You drop your briefcase or purse, and the rest is history. While your attention is focused on cleaning up the mess created by the first criminal, the second is long gone with your briefcase or purse.

• *Auto thefts and break-ins.* The crime suppression advice is the same at airports as on city streets. Park in well-lighted lots, and don't wait until you get to the airport to lock any valuable items in your trunk. Someone could be watching.

- *Conveyor belt tactics.* Crimes that require distraction often occur where travelers are least likely to suspect criminals: security checkpoints at airports.

    You're in line to go through the X-ray machine. You've just placed your most valuable possessions—your carry-on bags—on the conveyor belt, when someone steps in line ahead of you. This criminal is armed—not with a gun, but with every piece of metal he or she can find. Inevitably, the audio alarm sounds; he or she is stopped and told to empty all pockets. Of course, not all the pockets are emptied. The heavy-metal-jacket man walks through a second time, and again the alarm sounds. By the time the security guard deems the person free of metal, his partner—who went through the metal detector minutes before—has stolen your bags.

    Never place your bags on the conveyor belt unless you are absolutely sure that (1) you have first placed any of your own metal objects in that separate tray, and (2) your carry-on bags do NOT precede you. The object of this race is to get through the detector before your bags come through the X-ray scanners.

What makes these criminals hard to catch? The person who initially distracts you—with inane questions, money on the floor, mustard, or heavy metal—is never the person who steals. Unless someone actually witnesses the theft and/or detains the thief, there is no evidence against the distracter, and that person cannot be arrested.

Some of the scams border on genius. Here's one scenario.

A limousine pulled up to the curb and discharged a man, his wife, and their child in front of the airline terminal.

The driver unloaded expensive Louis Vuitton luggage from the trunk. The family entered the terminal and the wife then went to the bathroom. Moments later, a man rushed up to the husband and said, "Excuse me, sir, but did your wife just go to the bathroom?"

"Yes, she did," he replied.

"Well, I think she had an accident and fell down," said the man.

The husband instructed his son to wait there and watch the baggage as he ran toward the bathroom. As soon as the husband was out of sight, a van pulled up outside and another man approached the child.

"Are you flying out today?" he asked.

The child nodded affirmatively.

"OK," the man said. "I'll load your bags up."

He then proceeded to put all the Vuitton bags in the back of the van, closed the door, and drove off.

When the husband and wife returned, they discovered only their son. The bags were never recovered.

The key is to remain in actual physical contact with your bags. When you're standing at a pay phone, place your bag firmly between your legs.

When you're sitting near a departure gate, try to keep your leg or foot resting on your bag. (It's easy to doze momentarily while waiting for a flight, and that's when luggage can disappear.)

Always put an ID tag on the outside and the inside of your bag. Luggage thieves will quickly rip off any outside tags, but the inside tags may help you recover something if your luggage is stolen.

When you fill in your ID tags, never write down your home address. Yes, you're going out of town, but why advertise it?

Always use your office address, or simply list a phone number. Some airport criminals have no intention of stealing your bags at the airport. They actually want you to leave town, on time, *with* your bags. They're after a much bigger prize: your house. Police statistics report all break-ins as home burglaries, but many are initiated as airport crimes in which the homeowners or residents were unwitting participants.

Whether you're headed to a gate or the VIP lounge (assuming you're a member), another important principle applies: It's not just the flight, it's the SEAT.

Not long ago, the airlines eliminated advance boarding passes. Too many no-shows. But although they didn't eliminate advance seat assignments, they did restrict the number of seats they will allocate in advance for any one flight.

On many airlines, the cap on prior seat assignments runs at about 60 percent of the total number of seats available on a flight.

This is an arbitrary figure and can often be overridden by phoning savvy reservations agents.

Which seat do *you* want? Most folks will tell you to get the exit row or a bulkhead seat. Each has its positives and negatives.

But, on virtually every aircraft in the air, there are other secret coach seats that the airlines will never tell you about. These seats can actually be better than business-class or even first-class seats, in terms of comfort, privacy, or ease of movement.

The airlines tend to make these seats part of the 40 percent they do not allocate in advance.

To protect yourself, you can always ask for an exit row or bulkhead seat. But then plan on getting to the airport in time to get one of the secret seats.

Before I get to secret seats, let me address the totally overrated concept of window seats. Their only benefit comes on a late-night red-eye flight when you want to lean up against the window. What other possible benefit is there with a window seat?

First, what are you going to look at for six hours? A window seat limits your options. You're essentially trapped for the entire duration of the flight, unless you want to inconvenience your fellow passengers by crawling over them to get to a lavatory.

You can forget about being first off the plane. And, if you're last on, you face another uncomfortable and awkward moment as you climb over your seatmates.

Sitting in an aisle seat requires only two cautions:

1. You run the risk of severe bruising by rogue beverage carts in the aisles.

2. When the plane lands and the captain turns off the seat belt sign, you need to immediately jump up and grab the latch of the overhead bin directly above you. Items DO shift in flight, and if you aren't first to open the bin, you'll be first to be hit with stuff flying out of it.

Now, back to secret seats. Some statistics: 700,000 airline seats go unsold every day. Besides the aspects of unearned revenue, airlines hold back the secret seats until they absolutely have to sell them—or until you walk up and ask for one!

Here are just a few of them:

If you'll be flying on an American Airlines 767, there are two secret seats on domestic flights. 17H and 17J. On international flights, these two seats, located across from the galley and actually curtained off as a special section, are designated as "crew rest" seats.

However, on domestic flights, they can be sold as revenue seats. They are also special coach seats: they recline further, they have foot rests, and they give you more space in front because they have their own bulkhead.

If you're flying on an American 757, there isn't a special secret section for you, but there are secret coach seats. Ask for either seat 10A or 10F. These are window seats on either the left or right side of the aircraft.

What makes them so special? Nothing, except that on these planes there is no seat 9A or 9F. Result: You're in a window seat, but you're not trapped. And because there's no seat in front of you, there's no tray table to impale your stomach. You have unlimited legroom, and if you need to get up during the flight, you don't have to crawl or climb to the right or left. Instead, you simply get up and move FORWARD.

A similar situation applies on Delta's and United's 757s, but the seat numbers can be different.

Look for seat 20A on Delta's 757s or seat 8A on United's 757s.

On Northwest's 757s, look for seat 16F or 15E.

If you're about to board a USAir 737-200, look for seat 11A or 11F. Again, like the 757s, there is no seat 10A or 10F. Result: Serious legroom.

Flying on a United 767—Model 200, and lucky enough to be in business class? Ask for either seat 10A or 10F. These are single business-class aisle seats, with petite desk areas on their sides. Very cool.

Overseas, there are also secret seats, and they might really surprise you.

On Swissair MD-11s, you want seat 21A, B, or C.

On British Airways 747s, the real surprise seats are at the back of the plane, and they're center seats at that.

Am I nuts? No. Read on.

The seats you want on those 747s are 51J or 52J on the right side of the widebody, or 51B or 52C on the left side. Why? Because of the curvature of the plane toward the rear, there are only two seats in each of these side rows: an aisle seat and a middle seat. There is NO window seat. The result: You have extra room for your legs (you can stretch out almost sideways) and more room for your carry-on bags!

Remember, virtually every aircraft type has them. So, when you make your reservations, always ask the agent what aircraft type will be serving as your flight. A DC-9 is different from an MD80; a 757 is completely different from a 767 in the configuration of its seats and aisles.

You can also ask for, and get, seat charts from just about every airline. They are either printed in the airlines' schedule books or visible on their Web sites. The Official Airline Guide Schedules also feature pages and pages of seat charts for each airline and aircraft type.

Now, let's say you can't get a secret seat. Your scenario is even worse: when you get to the gate, you discover that the only seats left are center seats, and passengers are already boarding the plane. Are you out of luck? Not necessarily.

Exhibiting your best behavior, go to the gate agent and ask, "Could you possibly tell me whether there are any two people flying in coach with the same last name?"

Chances are excellent that at least one couple on the plane is sitting, for example, in seats 15A and 15C, desperately hoping that NO ONE will take that middle seat. And that is precisely the seat you want. Ask the agent at the gate—as long as they only have center seats left—if you could have 15B.

Then, when you get to that row, chances are also excellent that the couple will offer to switch with you, and you will get either the aisle seat or the window seat. (Caution: There's always the possibility that the two people in row 15 already hate each other, or always ask for the seats they're in, and do not want to switch. Still, I'll take my chances.)

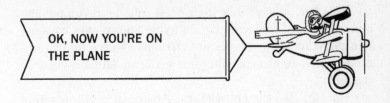

OK, NOW YOU'RE ON
THE PLANE

Let's presume you got the seat you want. Don't get too comfortable. The plane hasn't pushed back yet.

Every time I'm sitting on a plane that hasn't reversed back from the jetway, I'm reminded of a high school science experiment. Start with a glass of water, absolutely full. Carefully, drop by drop, continue to fill the glass. The water is then actually ABOVE the rim of the glass, held there through the concept of surface tension. Continue to add water, drop by drop, until suddenly the last drop breaks the tension. Ripples appear and water flows over the side of the glass.

The airlines have been adding those little drops of symbolic water to our schedules for years.

But there's a whole lot more than surface tension out there. And when it breaks, it explodes.

Airline scheduling—or the lack of it—makes us angry. And we have a right to be.

Most savvy travelers have come to the painful realization that airline schedules are nothing more than attempts at clever marketing on the part of the airlines, and nothing less than wishful thinking on the part of some passengers who actually believe them.

Basic math will tell you that if there are two active takeoff runways at Los Angeles International Airport, and thirty-five departures are listed in airline schedules for 8:00 A.M., thirty-three airlines are, to some extent, bending the truth if not outright lying.

Basic common sense will also tell you that if you publish a schedule that says you will be flying your planes between two slot-controlled airports and claiming a forty-minute turn-around time for each of your planes, you are either lying or in denial.

Here are two examples: (1) the American Eagle operation out of Miami, and (2) the United Shuttle in Los Angeles.

In Miami, the Eagle operation almost always resembles a chaotic refugee center. Disgruntled passengers are trying helplessly to deal with late, delayed, or canceled flights. It's bad enough that when you finally get to your aircraft, the pilot looks about age seventeen and his name is "Skippy."

On virtually any given day, the Eagle folks are competing for the title of the world's largest collection of "misconnects"—harried travelers who never have a chance at making their connecting flights.

In Los Angeles and San Francisco, the crowded United Shuttle terminals often resemble Saigon in April 1975. It's a "last flight out" panic scene. Flights are canceled, other flights are combined, passengers are bumped and swear they will never go through this ordeal again. And yet, thanks to the power of both the American and United frequent flyer programs, these same people, expecting the worst, usually return for more abuse. And they often get it.

THE FLIGHT THAT NEVER WAS

One frequent United flyer proposed this challenge to me: In a given week, if I flew five round trips between Los Angeles and San Francisco on the United Shuttle, I would be lucky if I took off and arrived on time on even one of those five trips.

And, that's presuming the flights actually weren't canceled. Guess who won the bet? The other morning I was in San Francisco and had an 8:30 breakfast meeting at an airport hotel in Los Angeles. So I booked the 6:50 A.M. United Shuttle flight from San Francisco to LAX. Of course, when I made my reservation, they asked for my phone number. (I always find this a ludicrous exercise, because no one ever calls me.)

In any case, I arrived at 6:00 A.M. at SFO, handed my ticket to the skycap, showed him my identification and my luggage, and answered all the appropriate security questions. He looked at my ticket and laughed. "Well, you picked the loser."

The loser?

"Yup," he replied. "This flight is always the loser. They seem to cancel it every morning. They already protected you on the 7:30 flight." I love the word "protected."

How was I "protected?"

When did they cancel the flight?

"Well," the United skycap shrugged, "hours ago ... maybe even last night." I went inside and was told to go to the gate to get my boarding pass.

The gate scene was Little Saigon. A few hundred people, tired and angry, had started their day by beating the sun, only to be beaten by the airline.

I gave my ticket to the gate agent. She handed it back to me. My lucky day: A center seat in coach. "Sorry, that's all we have."

"Let me ask you a question," I began. "Why did you cancel this flight? Was it weather? A mechanical?"

"Sir," she deadpanned, "the FAA canceled this flight."

I'm usually the first on my block to blame the FAA for many of the air safety problems that still confront us, but her answer made absolutely no sense.

"The FAA canceled this flight?"

"That's right."

"Excuse me, but unless I'm terribly mistaken, the only time I've ever known the FAA to cancel a flight is when they ground an entire airline, or after a plane has hit a mountain. *Then* the FAA cancels the flight. Miss, there is no way you can stand there and blame the FAA for canceling this flight. I understand you cancel this flight all the time."

This struck a chord.

"Well, actually, YOU PEOPLE made us cancel this flight."

She was changing her story, and this was getting good.

"Us?" I laughed. "How did we do this?"

"Frequent business travelers demand that we schedule an early flight, and so we do."

How that translated into blaming us escaped me. "Let me see if I'm understanding you. You're saying that we forced you to publish an unrealistic schedule, so you could then cancel the flight and make us angry?"

She saw no humor in this.

"Sir, if you keep this up, I'm going to have to call security."

"You're going to call security because you don't want to answer my question, or because you can't? Or because you know the real answer and it makes you uncomfortable? And what will I be charged with? Somehow violating the airline code of misinformation?"

Soon a supervisor appeared. He couldn't—or wouldn't—answer the question either.

But he didn't call security. He just called the flight. I boarded, sat with my knees touching my chest in my center seat and missed my meeting in Los Angeles. But I received a few hundred miles.

OK. So much for unrealistic airline schedules.

But wait. There's more. Remember the American Eagle example in Miami—or, for that matter, the United Express operation at O'Hare, or the Delta Connection out of Atlanta?

The commuter operations, in and of themselves, contribute to delays. Let's look at the numbers. Because of the old Federal Railway Labor Act, and some scope clauses of the pilot unions, the airlines have been expanding the size and frequencies of their regional subsidiaries. The regional fleets have grown in the numbers of aircraft being flown and operated. And, ironically, this has been where the most expansion has been occurring in recent years. Due to the Act and union "scope clauses" that limit the size of a regional carrier's aircraft, the regionals are severely limited in the number of people an aircraft holds.

That's a surefire recipe for delays at major airports. Why? The number of aircraft being flown has increased, but the planes are smaller in size.

Yet the same flight rules apply. Each of these smaller aircraft takes up the same amount of protected taxispace and takeoff separation when it is on the ground, and it takes the same amount of protected airspace while it is airborne.

It will also occupy a terminal gate at each airport. Some airlines argue that they can park more of the smaller planes at the gates, but I haven't seen operational proof of this. At each gate, smaller aircraft are taking up space that could be utilized by larger aircraft.

Why is this happening? The major airlines' reason: money. Pay scales are much lower at the regional, commuter level. The airlines like the smaller planes, and, quite frankly, the pilot unions like them as well. They insist that if the airlines want to fly larger planes, the pilots have to receive a substantial upgrade in pay. The result: Continued congestion at the airports.

At least one airport—San Francisco, otherwise known as the gateway to gridlock—has at least recognized this problem. Think about this statistic BEFORE flying to or from San Francisco: current figures show that one out of every four passengers flying out of SFO will not leave the gate at the scheduled departure times. At SFO, aircraft that carry fewer than thirty passengers account for a sizable 18 percent of the airport's takeoffs and landings but only 3 percent of the total passengers going to or through SFO. The airport has petitioned the FAA to limit the number of those commuter flights. The airlines, of course, are fighting the petition. Don't hold your breath.

My argument is that it all starts with fudging the schedule.

Recently, I was flying to New York from Los Angeles. American Airlines Flight 10 left LAX at 10:00 P.M. and was scheduled to arrive at New York's JFK Airport at 6:07 A.M. the next morning. But when the red-eye landed at 6:00 A.M., the pilot announced, "Will the flight attendants please prepare for an early arrival?"

Early compared to what?

Ten years ago, the same flight, departing at the same time, was scheduled to arrive in New York at 5:44 A.M. By 1980 standards, we had arrived sixteen minutes late.

Yet, officially we had arrived seven minutes early; the flight arrived ahead of the time printed on the official schedule. The real issue is truth in scheduling.

To be sure, delays in the air and on the ground are at an all-time high. Delays in the New York area, for example, have increased 45 percent in the past year, according to the FAA.

The American air-traffic control system is still suffering the effects of the air-traffic controllers' strike nineteen years ago.

But, ever since 1987, the U.S. Department of Transportation (DOT) began requiring airlines to report their on-time performance. For the past thirteen years, a flight has been considered "on time" if it departs from, or arrives at, its gate within fifteen minutes of the scheduled time.

Since the reporting rule went into effect, a number of airlines have been playing with their schedules—adding extra minutes to the official flight times.

However, because so many of the airlines have padded their flight times on the schedules, a majority of the on-time performance reports, and the final statistics, are meaningless for most travelers, and those that get reported do not reflect efficiency in air travel.

I remember an investigative report that the General Accounting Office (GAO) gave to Congress in the mid 1980s. At issue was whether the airlines had adjusted their flight schedules unrealistically, and whether on-time performance statistics reflected improved airline efficiency.

The last year when travelers got even a semblance of a realistic schedule was 1980. A flight from Washington to Chicago took two hours and fifteen minutes. The present schedule shows two hours and forty-five minutes. The airlines claim they're on time, but even the fudged times are exceeded by the airlines more often than not.

Another problem that the GAO discovered was the number of flights delayed or canceled for mechanical reasons.

Officially, mechanical problems exempt a flight from being included in on-time performance stats. It's an important exemption, because of safety considerations. On one hand, it could certainly be argued that no one really wants airlines flying broken planes just to support an on-time performance percentage.

However, the GAO investigation found that, although the DOT "monitors the number of flights excluded . . . from the data for mechanical problems, it does not verify that these flights had mechanical problems."

The most recent DOT statistics show that thousands of flights are excluded from on-time data each month because of apparent mechanical problems.

An obvious interpretation: There are a lot of phony "mechanicals." (Remember my canceled SFO-LAX United Shuttle flight?)

To be fair, there ARE real mechanicals, and let's be honest: if they are discovered during maintenance checks, we are thankful.

I am reminded of the time when President Richard Nixon flew to Moscow to meet with President Leonid Brezhnev. After the meetings in the Kremlin, Nixon was scheduled to fly to Kiev. And because of international protocol, he would be flying on Aeroflot within the Soviet Union, not on Air Force One.

U.S. officials were more than a little worried about the safety of the Aeroflot planes. But protocol was protocol. When the Moscow meetings concluded, Nixon headed for the airport, where he boarded the Russian aircraft. The rest of the plane was loaded, the doors were closed, and then the plane sat on the tarmac. And never moved.

Soon, nervous Russian officials approached the plane, and the door was opened. A high-level, embarrassed Soviet military officer walked down the aisle where the President was sitting. With the officer was a trembling Soviet Air Force colonel. Through an interpreter, the military officer addressed Nixon. "Mr. President," he stumbled nervously, "this is the colonel in charge of this flight. We have discovered this plane has broken and cannot fly. What would you want us to do with him?"

Nixon looked up and, without hesitation, responded, "Promote him."

The Soviet officer believed Nixon's answer had been improperly translated. "Mr. President, may I ask you again. This is the colonel in charge of this flight, and the plane is broken. What shall we do with him?"

Again, Nixon answered, "Promote him."

This time, the officer knew he had heard correctly, but he was still in shock.

"Mr. President, why would we want to promote him if the plane doesn't work?"

"Because," Nixon answered, in a rare moment of spontaneous humor, "the colonel discovered the plane was broken ON THE GROUND."

Yes, we should be thankful for mechanical delays, even during moments of great embarrassment.

You can believe it was a real mechanical in Moscow that day, just as it was a real mechanical at New York's LaGuardia Airport when now-defunct Eastern Airlines tried to pull a publicity stunt.

Eastern had decided to honor one of its most loyal business travelers, an insurance executive named Michael Cohen. Right before he was about to take his 2,000th trip on Eastern, the airline announced that it would award Cohen a special commemorative plaque.

The airline alerted the media for the special presentation. However, the plane—which was to fly from Miami to New York—broke down before Cohen could board, and his flight was delayed nearly three hours. To make matters worse, the embarrassed airline towed away the broken plane and replaced it with another that had been scheduled to fly to San Juan, thereby angering the Puerto Rico-bound passengers.

Mechanicals, real or otherwise, contribute to making the published airline schedules laughable.

There's an additional rub to the scheduling scam. Airlines that pad their schedules are somewhat reluctant to do so. If a flight is scheduled at two hours and forty-five minutes instead of two hours and fifteen minutes, pilots have to be paid based on the scheduled time.

Commercial pilots are limited, by FAA rules, to a certain number of flight hours per month. Some airlines are finding that the public relations gains they might be enjoying by an-nouncing improved on-time performance are being out-weighed by a shortage of flight crew members toward the end of each month. Ironically, flight cancellations can result.

Finally, there's the problem of language. The next time you are advised to "Prepare for an early arrival," you might want to remind the offending airline that our clocks are set ahead only once a year.

In the most recent report on flight operations in the United States, the DOT found that, of 5,527,884 flight opera-tions:

154,311 flights were canceled;

1,091,584 flights departed late;

1,320,591 flights arrived late.

One in four flights either left late or arrived late. Not good.

If the airlines are truly concerned about air rage among passengers, they need to address the underlying causes of many of these problems.

Phony cancellations are among the main ingredients for air rage.

My unanswered questions to the top management of American, United, and Delta are:

- Whatever happened to honesty and basic common sense?

- Why do you not instill in your ground staff the ability, as well as the confidence, to tell the truth and to use basic intuition and discretion in dealing with your cus-tomers?

- Who told a United gate agent that it was official policy to lie—to say that the FAA canceled the flight?

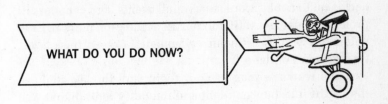

WHAT DO YOU DO NOW?

You already know why I hate e-tickets. A delay or a cancellation only compounds the problem if you're not holding a paper ticket.

But if you get to the airport and your flight is delayed BEFORE you board, do NOT stand in line. Run, don't walk, to the nearest pay phone. Call the airline's 800 number and ask, on the phone, to have Rule 240 applied.

If you've already boarded a plane and a mechanical delay is announced, you've got to think a few things through. First, are you flying on an airline based at this airport? If you are, your best bet is to stay on the plane. Home-based planes are first in line for mechanical help.

Second, how much duty time has the flight crew logged for that shift? Did the cockpit/cabin crew start the workday on your flight, or did they join it as part of their schedule? Ask. Even an additional thirty-minute delay needed to fix a mechanical can make a crew illegal to fly. If you can get a heads-up on that information as soon as a delay is announced, you'll get a head start toward getting off that plane and being rebooked.

If your flight is operated by an airline that is NOT based at that airport, and the clock tells you it's a peak push time for scheduled flights, don't worry about the crew. Worry about YOU. You can do one of two things—or both. First, if the plane is equipped with an airphone, ask a flight attendant for the two-digit toll-free code that immediately connects you to the airline's reservation agents, and get yourself protected right away. (If you're still at the gate, most airlines will allow you to use your cell phone.) Get on the phone, then get off the plane.

This works as long as your flight isn't the last flight of the day. If it IS the last flight and the delay looks like it will cancel the flight, start the paperwork while you're still at your seat. Protect yourself with a hotel room for the night, possible meal vouchers, some phone calls, and so on.

If no acceptable flights are available, the airline must refund your money if you request it. This policy applies even if you are holding a "nonrefundable" ticket.

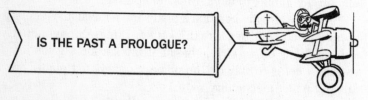

IS THE PAST A PROLOGUE?

The past two years have been nothing less than insufferable for airline passengers. The winter of 1999 and the summer of 2000 combined to form an apex of frustration and a summit for a mountain of ill will.

Just about everyone in Detroit remembers January 1999. An organizational implosion occurred at the Detroit airport when Northwest Airlines simply became paralyzed. Thousands of passengers were stranded, locked, imprisoned inside their aircraft, many for as long as nine hours.

The cruel and unusual punishment at the airport resulted in a tidal wave of anger manifested by a legislative proposal to finally create an airline passengers' bill of rights.

No less than thirteen bills were introduced in Congress to force the airlines to be legally responsible for keeping the promises they all too often make and then ignore.

Soon, the airline lobbyists were in full battle mode. They passionately argued to Congress that the airlines were in a much better position to develop, communicate, and implement a series of passenger rights, and no federal mandate was needed.

The lobbyists prevailed and, in time, the airlines published their own set of guidelines for customer care. Virtually every statement was surrounded with qualifiers and disclaimers. "Endeavor," "try," and "best efforts" were among the words used to protect the airlines.

And, not surprisingly, in June 2000, an interim report from the Inspector General of the U.S. Department of Transportation indicated that the airlines, as a whole, were not living up to their promises.

Ironically, the report was issued in the midst of the most frustrating, anger-inducing period in U.S. air travel history.

WHAT I DID LAST SUMMER

For those who traveled the unfriendly skies during the unfortunate millennium summer of 2000, conditions were almost bad enough to make them stop flying forever.

It was possibly the worst summer for delays and cancellations since air travel began.

To discover how really bad it was, I dispatched myself on an ambitious journey.

For two days, I crisscrossed the country on eight separate flights and six different airlines. My mission: To determine whether any airline would be on time. And perhaps more important: To see whether any of them would tell the truth.

To give the airlines a benefit of doubt, I flew first on a Wednesday and Thursday; these are not heavy traffic days. There was no bad weather. With one exception, which wasn't planned, I flew either to or from airlines' headquarters cities or to hub airports they solidly control.

On two days, on a journey that took forty-one hours, from early Wednesday morning until Thursday evening, I virtually lived on airplanes and at airports. Here's what happened.

On Wednesday, at 6:00 A.M., I checked in early for the first flight of the trip: Washington, DC, to Dallas-Fort Worth, on American Airlines. The weather was clear, the sun was shining, and, not surprisingly, every flight on the departure board at Washington's Reagan Airport was posted as being "on time."

Precisely at 7:35 A.M., American Flight 489 pushed back from the gate, and I was off to Dallas. It was an uneventful flight, except for one thing. I arrived in Dallas ten minutes early!

OK; that was good news. And that was the only good news that day.

I then transferred to United Airlines Flight 1604 to Chicago. The flight was scheduled to depart Dallas-Fort Worth for Chicago at 11:15 A.M. The departure board showed an on-time arrival, but when I got to the check-in counter, the agent said the departure would be a few minutes late. How late?

"It will leave at 11:30," she said. OK; so far so good. A slight delay. And the reason for the delay?

"Weather," she said.

I checked the gate. No plane. I checked the departure board again. It still said 11:15. Then I checked the arrivals board. The plane arriving from Denver for our flight to Chicago wouldn't even be landing until 11:24 A.M.

When I got to the agent at the gate, she said the delay was because of crew problems. There was no weather problem.

And, oh yes, there was no plane.

The only thing we could agree on was that the plane would be late.

But how late? It depended on where you got your information.

According to the agent, my United flight would now be leaving 23 minutes late, at 11:38.

(The lesson here: The departure board is not your friend. To be kind, it lies all the time. At best, the times listed are best case, hoped-for times, not real times. In this case, the board wasn't even close.)

A listing for another flight was downright ludicrous. A separate United aircraft coming in from Chicago was listed as landing late (at 12:30 P.M.). But the flight from Dallas to Denver—using the same gate and the same plane—was still listed as an on-time departure at 12:30!

We finally took off for Chicago an hour later, which meant, of course, that we landed late at Chicago's O'Hare Airport. To many passengers on the flight, the delay was not a surprise. They expected it.

When the plane finally landed, the departing passengers were thrust into the chaos of Terminal C.

The area was a tableau of frustration and despair. Some passengers were downright angry.

Bill Memefee, a United frequent flyer, was steaming. "I am going to Wichita right now. . . . I checked at noon today through the Internet, and United said it was running on time. Then, when I was walking to the gate, the arrivals board showed Grand Rapids inbound flight arriving at 3:47, baggage inbound, Flight 1027, which is the flight inbound from Grand Rapids going to Wichita. My flight was scheduled to leave at 3:14. But the departure board still says 'on time.' The gate agent tells me it's on time and I say it can't be. I go to check in at the Premier Mileage Plus check-in desk. The lady says it's on time, and I say it can't be; downstairs is showing 'delayed.' She checks the nose numbers and shows a pushback from Grand Rapids at 3:01 Chicago time."

"Now," he began laughing, "if you have a very fast plane that gets here in thirteen minutes, can unload baggage and everything else, then you are on time."

In reality, Memefee's flight was running about an hour late, at best. "The real problem isn't the delay," he fumed. "It's that people lie to you. Why can't they just be honest and make it real and fair? That's all I want, I don't expect any special service or anything else. I just like to know what is going on, and I think there is not another soul in this build-ing that wouldn't like the same thing."

The airlines claim that they are giving out accurate in-formation, and they blame an antiquated air traffic control system. And they blame weather. (To be fair, the weather in the early part of the 2000 summer was terrible.)

Still, the airlines argue when I suggest that, with about thirty-five planes scheduled to leave from LAX's two run-ways at 8:00 A.M., thirty-three planes are going to be late. "No," claims Air Transport Association spokesperson David Fuscus. "They're SCHEDULED to push back from the gate at 8:00 A.M., then they have to get in line and then they have to take off. That's what airline scheduling means. It doesn't mean wheels up at 8:00 A.M."

U.S. Senator Ron Wyden (D-Oregon) strongly disagrees with that "on time" definition. "I think it's particularly out-rageous for airlines to go scheduling above their capacity," he said. "If you take an ideal situation where the weather is clear, there are a maximum number of runways available, they're still scheduling beyond their capacity and that's just not right."

Wyden may have a point. Consider this: At Dallas-Fort Worth, an incredible fifty-seven planes are scheduled to take

off within ten minutes, beginning at 6:00 P.M. every day—
twenty-two more than the top capacity of the entire airport!

There are some other capacity issues, otherwise known
(in football terms) as "intentional grounding." Wyden calls
the cancellations of some flights phony. When passenger
loads don't materialize, flight cancellations due to "mechanical reasons" coincidentally show up.

"For the life of me," he argued, "I can't figure out why
the airlines are unwilling to offer their passengers the same
consumer protections that apply everywhere else in the
economy. The local movie theater doesn't arbitrarily cancel
the three o'clock showing on the weekend because they
don't have enough people who bought tickets. But the airlines have been doing that for years."

And finally, there's the flow of information. "There are
all sorts of problems about delays," said Wyden. "But the
one problem the airlines can do something about is giving
the public straight information, and the fact of the matter is:
The Inspector General of the U.S. Department of Transportation found that some airlines knew about delays four hours
before departure and yet they wouldn't tell the flying public.
That's just inexcusable."

OK, we're now in Chicago, and there are lots of delayed
flights. Passenger service counters are jammed. We're
scheduled on United Flight 255 to Denver. A 3:30 departure; the board is showing that it's "on time." We head to
the gate. It's a full flight, but somehow the agents are able to
board everyone on the huge 777 on time. And within ten
minutes of the scheduled departure, we actually push back
from the gate.

In airline terms, we're on time. In real terms, we're now
right on schedule for waiting on the tarmac. And we do, for
forty minutes.

We arrive late in Denver. Things only get worse. While we were flying there, to connect to another United flight to Seattle (a 7:30 P.M. departure), United canceled the 4:30 P.M. departure from Denver to Seattle, making some travelers very unhappy.

When we land—late—lines of travelers are everywhere. A quick look at the departure board is a depressing experience. On one screen, out of eighteen departures, only three are on time. The rest are delayed or canceled.

As expected, our 7:30 P.M. departure is moved back—twice—and we leave late for the third time in that day. Some of my fellow passengers have been flying even longer than I have that day. Many of them were rerouted to United by other airlines because their original airlines were even . . . later!

We landed in Seattle late. We had just enough time to catch a few hours' sleep before the next day's round of flights began.

Day two started at 5:00 A.M. in Seattle. Again, the weather was surprisingly perfect for our 6:15 A.M. flight on Alaska Airlines to San Francisco (SFO). And the weather had to be perfect on this leg for an on-time departure and arrival.

Miraculously, it was. This is a surprise, considering that SFO has one of the worst on-time performance ratings of major U.S. airports. The airport is plagued with fog conditions and with two runways that are too close together.

Smart travelers claim they will do anything to avoid SFO. But on this day, there were no problems. My America West flight to Phoenix was right on time. Even the gate agents were surprised. So were the passengers. I was now two for two. After landing in Phoenix, I hopped onto a Southwest flight for my short hop to Las Vegas. Would the third flight be the charm?

It was. Another on-time landing in Las Vegas. But that's where my lucky streak ended. I still had to get home to Los

Angeles. The American flight was delayed nearly three hours for a flight that lasted only forty-eight minutes.

Of the eight flights I took, four were late. The United flight to Los Angeles was delayed an hour. Folks at that departure gate weren't happy; the United flight to San Francisco was canceled.

The final score? Remember, I flew on days that weren't full-capacity days. I flew in good weather, and before the escalation of United Airlines' crew-related delays. The departure boards never told the real story, and gate agents gave inaccurate and misleading information.

The moral to this story: Keep your options open. Look at the departure boards to find the lie, and look at the arrival boards to prove it. And do a little homework before you leave for the airport.

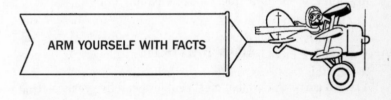

ARM YOURSELF WITH FACTS

Start with your initial reservation. Each month, the DOT publishes a list of the worst offending delayed flights—their flight number, airline, and route.

Check the weather at your destination. Based on the most recent DOT report, if you're flying between Washington's Dulles Airport and Seattle, you might want to avoid United Flight 219, which has been late more than 96 percent of the time. (The average delay is one hour.) You might want to bring a copy of *War and Peace* onto America West Flight 2882 between Phoenix and Fort Lauderdale. It's late 93 percent of the time and its average delay is 51 minutes. Another delay winner is USAir Flight 1820 between Philadelphia and Boston. That flight is late 81 percent of the time and has a 53-minute average delay. Many more flights are listed. You can easily access this information at the Aviation Consumer Protection home page (www.acap1971.org).

Among other useful on-time Web sites, check Flight Arrivals and Departures (www.thetrip.com/flightstatus). To check on weather delays, log onto the Air Traffic Control System Command Center (www.fly.faa.gov).

Remember, 200,000 flights leave airports each day. Each airport has it own way of calculating departure times. However, for purposes of record keeping, the on-time departure clock starts when the plane's doors close. This clock continues unless the pilot returns for mechanical reasons and *only* if the plane returns for mechanical reasons. If a plane pushes back from the runway and then returns to the terminal for any other reason, the clock does not stop.

HOW BAD IS IT?

A recent survey found that most people spend five years of their life waiting in lines, and six months sitting at traffic lights.

And lest you think delays are bad only in the United States, consider this: Lufthansa reports that its aircraft spent more than 5,200 hours in holding patterns over Frankfurt, Munich, and Düsseldorf in 1999.

If the average executive spends an estimated twenty-nine days a year on business travel, he or she spends a great deal of that time waiting at airports or stuck in airplanes. In fact, the average business traveler spends twenty-one days a year simply locked in transit.

Here's an even scarier statistic. In 2000 alone, delays on flights within Europe rose a whopping 30 percent. Total up the delay time caused by computer failures and air traffic controllers' and others' labor strikes, and the total would be 57 YEARS!

And if you think that's a long time, fasten your seat belts. A report by the Inspector General of the DOT found that the airlines had underestimated the amount of time lost by passengers on U.S. flights by a total of 247 YEARS! The DOT report said that 130 million minutes of extra travel time were added to airline schedules between 1988 and 1999—and that was BEFORE anyone was counting time lost because of delays.

At U.S. airports, delays are no longer seasonal. They are daily. And according to the DOT, the average "dwell time" at airports is now nearly seventy minutes—a new high.

But not only can you check your flight to see its average on-time performance (obviously, a flight that is an hour late 97 percent of the time will be late for you as well), you can also identify—system-wide—the worst times to try to leave each airport.

Some examples are obvious. Don't count on an on-time departure or arrival from O'Hare between 5:00 and 6:00 P.M. on weekdays. Washington (National) is about the same. Between 6:00 and 7:00 P.M., it's a real mess. But Dulles is actually worse; 25 percent of all flights leave there late.

At other airports, the worst times to leave might surprise you. At Denver and at Dallas–Fort Worth, the worst time to leave is between 8:00 and 9:00 P.M. New York's Kennedy Airport, which has the fewest flights of the three New York airports, also has the highest concentration of specific time-block flights. Between 6:00 and 10:00 P.M., international flights all compete for taxi and runway space.

LaGuardia Airport, also in New York, was congested beyond capacity five years ago. Yet, in 2000, airlines added 200 more flights a day, and they want to add 400 MORE. On an average day, more than 1,390 flights would then land or take off at LaGuardia.

Delays are system-related, so LaGuardia can be blamed for a lot of the mess at other airports. It is now the source of one-fourth of all U.S. flight delays. All but two of American's most delayed flights began or ended each day at LaGuardia.

The math is ridiculous. For LaGuardia to process that many flights, it has to cram in eighty-four takeoffs or landings each hour—a physical impossibility.

What can you do about delays? You can protect yourself in a number of ways.

First: Try to book the first flight of the day. If you're flying from an airline's main operation center or hub city, there's a good chance the plane is already on the ground.

If you're flying from another city, there's an equally good chance that the aircraft flew in as the last flight the evening before and is ready.

Book anything other than the first flight and your chances of a delay increase dramatically.

Second: Get a paper ticket.

Third: Know the flight schedules of the route you're on. What airline has the next flight? And the next? If you arm yourself with that information, that's one less phone call or line you have to endure. You can react quickly.

Fourth: Apply Rule 240. It's your best friend.

Fifth: Be a good reporter. Take notes that include the trail as well as the chronology of misinformation.

Sixth: Understand your own status at the airline. If you're a frequent flyer, the airline will work that much harder to keep you happy. And whether you fly seldom or often, understand that the price you pay for your ticket often will determine the care you receive if your flight is delayed or canceled.

Who's first when a flight cancels? Full-fare first-class passengers who are members of an airline's frequent flyer program. You bought a discount fare through a consolidator? Unless you know your rights, find a seat and sit in it at the terminal. You may be there a while. Many airlines—TWA, for example—will do anything they can NOT to "interline" their passengers—put them on another carrier's flight—when there is a delay. Invoke Rule 240. Insist on it. The airline will never openly volunteer that remedy. Recently, TWA made things even worse. IF you bought your ticket from a discount online broker, like Priceline.com, and the TWA flight was delayed or canceled, the airline would often make you wait six hours before invoking Rule 240.

Seventh: You may have status based on where you BOUGHT your ticket. In 2000, delays became so bad that one enterprising online travel e-tailer made a bold guarantee. Biztravel.com started offering refunds for canceled or late flights on American, Continental, US Airways, British Airways, and Air France. Registered users who booked their tickets through the Biztravel.com Web site would receive $100 if the flight was delayed more than thirty minutes, and $200 for flights arriving more than an hour behind schedule. For flights delayed more than an hour, or canceled for reasons other than mechanical problems, Biztravel.com issued a full refund, even if passengers were finally able to use the ticket. If there was ever an incentive to book online, this one was the best. (Guess what? After supposedly paying out a whopping $1.7 million in penalties under the guarantee, Biztravel.com then revised its deal sharply downward. Instead of receiving $100 for flights 30 minutes late, customers will now get $25. Flight an hour late? Instead of $200, only $50. What does that tell you? Delays are costly, and making guarantees did not incentivize any airline to do better.)

Eighth (but not least): Understand your legal rights. A number of recent court cases have been resolved firmly on the side of passengers. For years, airlines have tried to have lawsuits dismissed, based solely on the concept of deregulation. The theory is: Because states can no longer regulate airlines' pricing or scheduling, they cannot have any legal jurisdiction allowing them to enforce any state laws concerning failure to disclose, breach of contract, *et al.*

However, in recent years, the deregulation defense has stumbled. Why? Judges fly, too!

Consider the 168 very angry passengers who were stranded on the tarmac in Milwaukee for six hours on Christmas Eve 1997.

United Flight 1536, from Orange County, California, to O'Hare was diverted to Milwaukee's Mitchell Field.

Once on the ground, the passengers claimed in their lawsuit, they went without food or functioning restrooms for six hours before their flight was then canceled.

United's attorneys tried for nearly two years to quash the suit. But a Chicago Circuit Court judge let the case proceed. And United, not eager to set any sort of legal precedent by having a class action lawsuit go against an airline, settled. Each passenger got $500 in cash plus a $500 airline voucher.

In the summer of 2000, when the airline delayed or canceled thousands of flights, the legal cases against United intensified.

One particular lawsuit, still pending, sued United for breach of contract and claimed that United, during the summer of 2000, willingly sold tickets, on many of its flights, fully knowing that the airline had no intention of operating those flights.

And that's WITHOUT weather problems!

Nothing can come close to that one day, in January 1999, at the Detroit airport. It was a horrendous, cold day, but it also was ground zero in the renewed fight for passenger rights.

Improvements have been made at the Detroit airport—specifically, by Northwest—but thousands of angry passengers remain angry.

A friend of mine—a hardworking Northwest counter agent in Detroit who somehow survived the siege of January—called the other day.

"Hey, did you hear our new customer service slogan?" she asked, laughing. "We're not happy until YOU'RE not happy!"

Wait, that's no joke. WE're Not Happy!

And while no new federal legislation has been enacted, there are residual rights and tactics that passengers can invoke.

PLAYING THE BUMPING GAME

Your flight is on time but it's oversold?

Welcome to the wonderful world of bumping, otherwise known as denied boarding compensation (DBC). If you play the game right, it can pay you big dividends.

First, some history. Airline seats are a precious and perishable commodity. Airlines hate to have them empty. And the airlines' sophisticated computer systems have become more accurate in predicting the no-show factor—the 10 to 15 percent of ticketed travelers who simply don't show up for their flights.

The result: Airlines traditionally overbook their flights, sometimes as much as 20 percent, based on the time of year and past years' travel patterns.

When everyone DOES show up, the bump-and-grind games begin.

More than a million people were bumped from the top ten U.S. airlines in 2000. The math works out to about one bump for every 488 passengers.

Here are the basic rules: If an airline bumps you, the DOT requires that airline to cover the cost of your flight, as long as:

1. You are holding a confirmed reservation *and* a paid ticket.

2. You met the check-in deadline for the flight. This can get a little hairy, so be careful. Each airline has different rules, but, in general, it's not just the time you check in at the original ticket counter or check in your bags. It's the time you check in AT THE DEPARTURE GATE. For example, USAirways has a ten-minute boarding gate deadline. Northwest's is thirty minutes.

If the airline can get you out on another flight (theirs or someone else's) within an hour of your originally scheduled departure, it owes you nothing. (Translation: Not much to worry about here. I've NEVER seen that happen!)

If the airline can get you out between one and two hours of the original departure time, it must reimburse you for the cost of the one-way fare, up to $200.

But if it takes them more than two hours, you're entitled to twice the value of your one-way ticket, up to $400. Remember, these are minimum compensation figures.

There are two kinds of bumping: involuntary and voluntary. Once you know the difference, being bumped can have its finer moments.

Involuntary bumping: You are one of the last to check in, or you never bothered to get an advance seat assignment, and the plane is overbooked. Chances are good you're about to get bumped involuntarily. The airlines won't admit this, but if you're flying with only carry-on bags, you stand a better chance of getting bumped, because the airline doesn't have to find and remove your bags before the flight leaves.

Then comes the art, the dance—the finesse, if you will, of the alternative.

Voluntary bumping: Let's say you're holding a ticket for American's Chicago-to-Dallas flight, leaving at 8:00 A.M. tomorrow morning. You're going to visit your long-lost Uncle Howie. But the flight is overbooked. When you get to the gate, the airline offers you a free round trip if you volunteer to give up your seat on the 8:00 A.M. flight and fly later in the day.

Sounds good, if it's a Wednesday in early December and you're not in a rush to see Uncle Howie.

But before you jump at the free ticket and the later flight, you need to ask some important questions, or Howie will never see you.

"When is the next flight on which you can guarantee me a CONFIRMED SPACE seat?" Don't ever give up a confirmed seat for a standby seat.

Most of the time, your free ticket will be in the form of a voucher that has cash value equal to your original ticket. That sounds fair but, once again, some people will be more equal than others. Be careful when accepting that voucher. Be sure to ask, BEFORE you accept the voucher, whether it is an *unrestricted* voucher. Many vouchers have blackout dates, and some only allow standby travel.

If the wait between flights is long, ask for some other entitlement deals: meals, phone calls (after all, you don't want Uncle Howie to worry).

Now comes the fun part: upping the ante.

In the first scenario, the airline asks for volunteers who will give up their confirmed seats, for which they will be compensated.

But what if there aren't any volunteers? Get ready for an auction.

The DOT mandates the minimum an airline must compensate you when you are involuntarily bumped. But neither a minimum nor a maximum cap is applied to voluntary bumping.

Example: I was on a morning flight to New York. I was already in my seat when the announcement was made that the flight was overbooked and the airline was looking for volunteers. Anyone who volunteered would be given a travel voucher for $500 and a seat on the next flight.

Thirty people jumped up and raced for the exit door.

The airline only needed six, and yes, each got the $500 voucher.

A more rewarding example: A month later, I was on the same flight and the same announcement was made. On this flight, there must have been more experienced travelers, because NO ONE GOT UP.

And when no one volunteered, the ante was immediately raised. The voucher offer was increased to $700; still, no one moved. Then $900. When the offer was punched again to $1,200, two people got up to claim their prize. But the airline needed four. The voucher deal went to $1,350, and the last two very happy travelers collected their prize.

Some travelers have made the bumping game almost a way of life. They know, for example, that the first flights from New York to Detroit, New York to Chicago, and New York to Atlanta are always oversold. They carry full-fare tickets on those flights and have no intention of taking those flights.

They simply show up at the required times, wait for the overbooking announcement, and collect their vouchers for future flights.

And some, during particularly heavy travel times, have double- or even triple-dipped. If you're bumped from the first oversold flight and the second flight is also oversold, you get bumped again.

During one Thanksgiving holiday, a family of five was able to be bumped four times in one day. They received enough high-value vouchers to be able to take three family vacations that year.

One important note: Whether you play the bumping game by accident or by design, always assume that no matter what other flight the airline puts you on, it may not have removed you from the oversold flight completely. The airline's computers could actually list you as a no-show for your original outbound "bumped" flight and may cancel the rest of your flight itinerary. So, if you're bumped, make sure that the gate agent goes back into the computer and protects you on all subsequent flights on which you hold a reservation.

If delays are inevitable, how can you cope? A better question: How can you win?

There are remedies, and, every so often, some real value is attached to them. But you need to know the game.

As with a standby or waitlist, a caste system is applied by the airlines when something goes wrong.

If you're at the bottom of the proverbial food chain, you are about to be "stuck at the airport."

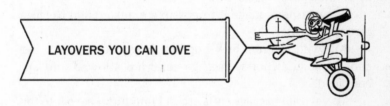

LAYOVERS YOU CAN LOVE

Until recently, being stuck was a fate only slightly worse than death.

The first time I found myself at an airport with a few hours to kill, I was confronted with these depressing choices:

1. Sit in an uncomfortable plastic chair, listen to the tin sounds of Mantovani, and make believe I was in my dentist's waiting room.

2. Sit in *another* uncomfortable plastic chair, insert quarters into a small black-and-white TV set, and watch bad soap operas.

3. Try to guess the ingredients inside the mystery hot dog sold at the combination newsstand/snack bar.

A friend once described waiting at an airport as akin to being "trapped inside a large dirty sock."

Indeed, we all have terrible airport stories, and the plots all start with logistics.

Land at Heathrow in London and, despite the long distance between your arrival gate and the immigration and customs queue, you have an excellent chance of finding a free baggage cart within 100 feet of your gate.

Land at LAX and no carts are to be found anywhere near the gates.

In Zurich, the corridors are a mile long, and carts are prohibited at the gates.

Some airports make it impossible to take rental baggage carts to the gates.

And yet, at Frankfurt, London, Hong Kong, and other equally busy airports, baggage carts are allowed and encouraged.

My favorite baggage carts are in Frankfurt. Leave it to the Germans to design the sturdiest and most versatile baggage carts I've ever seen. An ingenious design allows them to ride, without ever slipping, on any escalator. The time saved by not waiting for elevators is substantial.

But saving time at an airport means nothing if you get to your gate and realize you're going nowhere for a very long time.

An entire generation of poorly fed, overtired, and impatient travelers expects nothing more than abuse during airport layovers. Airport food is pedestrian (at best). Airport shopping is limited to overpriced items you never purchase anywhere else. Airport sleeping, while waiting for a flight, requires perfecting the painful art of slumbering in an upright position.

But now, at a growing number of airports, you can shop for things you want or need, eat food that's good (as well as nutritious), be entertained, take a shower, and even sleep in a real bed. You can have a sauna, use exercise equipment, buy a rare book, or use a fully operating temporary office, complete with a secretary, fax machines, and personal computers.

In short, many airports are trying to create a practical extension of travelers' daily life instead of a hindrance to it.

One of my favorites: At McGhee Tyson Airport in Knoxville, Tennessee, check out the wooden rocking chairs and watch everyone ELSE take off.

Slowly and surely, airports are offering some FUN to travelers forced to spend time there.

You can eat very well in one of the oyster bars at Logan International Airport in Boston. Fresh crab and salmon are always on the menu at the San Francisco Airport restaurants. At Honolulu International, you can rent a bed or buy an eight-hour package deal that gives you a bed and a shower.

On the concourse level at Mitchell Field in Milwaukee, the Renaissance Book Shop sells new, used, and rare books. This is not only one of my favorite airports (locals like to call it "Chicago's secret airport"), but one of my favorite bookstores.

At least once a year, I fly into Milwaukee and give myself at least a three-hour layover. I go to the bookstore and usually buy about fifty books. I put them on my credit card and have them shipped, at a nominal fee, to my home in California. No schlepping and no sales tax!

In Rome, the airport offers wine tastings. The new international terminal at San Francisco Airport has a 5,000-volume library and a museum of flight. At the Pittsburgh Airport, there are 100 separate stores in the Airmall.

O'Hare International Airport, in Chicago, has a "Kids on the Fly" learning and play space in Terminal 2. Developed by the Chicago Children's Museum, the 2,200-square-foot area is equipped with a build-your-own-Chicago Lego™ space, a mock cargo plane to clamber around on, and a fantasy helicopter.

A "Back Rub Hub" in terminal 3 offers chair massage sessions. (When you're facing a long wait at the airport, you might as well be depressed AND relaxed!)

Airports throughout Europe now offer comprehensive business centers. At Amsterdam's Schipol Airport, one of Europe's most negotiable airports, for about $20 an hour, you get a private office equipped with a computer and full Internet access. Schipol also has a casino.

Need a manicure? Check out Washington's Reagan National. In Denver, ask about a massage. And at McCarran Airport in Las Vegas, take advantage of a twenty-four-hour fitness center. The fully operational gym has more than 1,500 frequent flyer members. Cost: $15 per visit.

Stuck at Dallas-Fort Worth? A golf course at the southwest corner of the airport will rent clubs to anyone stranded at the airport.

If you're delayed in Portland, Seattle, Denver, San José, Minneapolis, or San Diego, the latest airport amenity is DVD rentals offered by InMotion Pictures. For about $12, you get the DVD player; the movie titles rent for as little as $2.50. Savvy travelers rent the player for their round-trip flights and select at least three movie titles. In the event of a delay, they're at least entertained.

Orlando's 15,000-acre airport is the third largest in the United States. I actually like this airport. With the recent addition of a fourth airside terminal, the airport now boasts forty-six name-brand stores, twenty-four restaurants, and a micro brewery. (Beer lovers: Show up on Wednesdays, when the freshly brewed batch is ready.)

I also like having a Hyatt hotel located within the terminal. The 446-room hotel is great for business travelers. If I'm flying in and need to stay at the hotel, I call ahead and have the bellman meet me in the baggage claim area. I get checked into my room there, while waiting for my luggage. A great time saver.

Want to shop? The Disney Store, Universal Studios store, and Discovery Store are no surprise. But there's also a Bijoux Turner store, and none of its 8,000 items costs more than $10.

Miami also has a hotel at the airport, but it is definitely NOT one of my favorites. It closely resembles an original airport hotel—an afterthought that temporarily houses stranded travelers.

But this hotel does have one upside. I'm not keen on staying there, but if you have a few extra hours at the airport, take the elevator to the eighth floor of Terminal E, and take advantage of the Miami International Airport Hotel's health club, open from 6:00 A.M. to 10:00 P.M. For just about $8, you get a dip in the outdoor pool or a run along the rooftop track.

The new Hong Kong airport has a great Cable & Wireless business center in the check-in hall. If you have enough time, check out the Oriental Massage Center on the Level 6 concourse. I especially recommend the foot massage.

In England, there's a concept of "retail therapy" at airports. A recent survey showed that because most travelers were so stressed at airports, they spent very little time shopping. Not anymore. Upscale shops at Heathrow include branches of Harrod's, Pinks, Austin Reed, and other well-known stores. An exercise room offers stationary bikes and Nautilus® equipment, along with lockers and showers. For $5 more, you can play a game of racquetball. Alternatively, just sit on the windy terrace, sip a frozen daiquiri, and watch others exercise.

In Singapore, airport officials often offer a two-hour tour of the city. If you're changing flights, they'll waive the departure tax.

Are you looking for a bolder airport layover experience? In Malaysia, at the new Kuala Lumpur International Airport at Sepang, you can do a hike along the trails in the jungle nearby.

One of Europe's most complete shopping centers is at the Frankfurt am Main airport. The 100-shop complex opens early and closes late. The stores sell everything from smoked salmon to stuffed toy bears. There are thirty restaurants, two supermarkets, antique and modern art stores, and a Harrod's, plus a pharmacy, a dry cleaner, a locksmith, and a shoemaker, a porn bookstore, a disco, the biggest airport medical clinic in the world (three doctors and a staff of fifty), and, yes, even a dentist. More than 4,000 people—none of whom has any travel plans—flock to the airport each day. If you get tired, there are excellent hotels within the airport perimeter. Using the great baggage carts the airport provides, you can check out of a hotel, walk a very short distance to the airport, and get to your gate in under nine minutes!

Are you traveling with kids? Or do you want to escape from them for a brief while?

At Denver's airport, there are cozy corners at the south end of the Jeppesen terminal (www.flydenver.com). Concourse A has a great view of the Rocky Mountains.

London's Heathrow (www.baa.co.uk) has children's play areas in each of its four terminals.

Remember the rocking chairs in Tennessee? Philadelphia's airport has them as well (www.phl.org). Look for the chairs between Terminals B and C.

At Singapore's Changi Airport (www.changi.airport .com.sg), you can go swimming, hit the hot tub, or play virtual reality games.

In Amsterdam, if shopping becomes too tiring, check out the airport Web site (www.schipol.nl) and read the list of the best places to simply sit and WATCH other planes take off.

At LAX, the best place to plane-watch is at the Encounter Restaurant, which rises seventy feet in the air at the center of the airport. Or, a free shuttle bus will take you to the nearby Hilton Hotel where, for $10, you get all-day access to the 24-hour fitness center, which has workout facilities, sauna, and steam.

Type A people (like me) who dream of 24/7 access to a T-1 line can have that, too, by checking into "Laptop Lane" (www.laptoplane.com). Currently, at thirteen airports throughout the United States, in addition to the high-speed T-1 line, you can get your own office, with a PC, printer, and fax. There are two laptop ports per cubicle, so you can use your own computer, not just theirs, to access the line.

But before you ever get to an airport, log on to www.quickaid.com—perhaps the most wide-ranging directory of airport Web sites, with links to almost 160 international airports.

Quickaid.com will also help you locate lounges, within airports, where it pays to become a member. The Wing, Cathay Pacific's first-class VIP lounge in Hong Kong, is one of the best in the world. It features a complete Elemis Day Spa, two restaurants, a long bar, relaxation rooms, shower rooms, and computer rooms with Internet access. It is not unusual for travelers to arrive at the airport four to six hours EARLY for their flights, just to take advantage of the lounge.

The same is true in London's Heathrow, where the British Airways new-arrivals lounge offers aromatherapy sessions, and the Virgin Clubhouse is by now legendary for its vast array of "pre-flight grooming" opportunities.

I may be understating the case, but I have yet to visit this lounge without consistently being *annoyed when my flight was called!* This very upscale, fun oasis in the middle of the chaos of Heathrow makes travelers *want* to go to the airport.

In design and function, the Clubhouse deliberately challenges the traditional airport waiting room in very creative ways. Imagine a facility with a sushi bar, a putting green, a music room (a sound-proofed private sitting room equipped with a state-of-the-art Linn hi-fi system and leather sofas), a ski simulator, a hydrotherapy bath, a beauty and haircutting salon, a massage room, a relaxation room, and shower rooms.

The Clubhouse has views of airport runways on two sides and from the roof. Its library has a few thousand books. My favorite machine here is the "Alpine Racer," a ski simulator featuring mounted ski poles for balance and ski steps for rapid turns. Players can choose from three courses that progress in their degrees of difficulty. "Naturalistic" elements such as fog and blizzards are simulated quite realistically.

There is a business center, with all the usual contraptions: computers, a fax, a photocopier, telephones, and access to the Internet and to international financial news services. But most everyone is playing on the ski simulator, or getting a massage, a facial, or a haircut, or eating sushi and hoping their flights will be inexorably delayed.

Travelers who have no such über-lounges use their airport layover time in other, possibly healthier and more constructive ways. A number of airline passengers landing at JFK and connecting to or from international flights make use of the airport's full-time dental facilities. You can find the airport dentist—Dr. Robert Trager—in Room 2311 in the

International Arrivals building. The staff at the dental center is multilingual and often handles dental emergencies of foreign passengers, though it's not unusual for some regular transiting passengers to visit Dr. Trager to get their teeth cleaned. (At the Frankfurt am Main airport, an excellent full-time dental clinic is also available.)

Need to get a prescription filled? A pharmacy at the Miami Airport is open from 9:00 A.M. to 5:00 P.M. every day.

At Charles de Gaulle Airport in Paris, look for one of the better delicatessens anywhere. (A word of caution: If you're buying any fish or meat or fruit to bring home, ask whether it has been approved for travel to the United States. Many items sold at the delicatessen are not approved by the U.S. Department of Agriculture and might be confiscated upon your arrival in the United States.)

No one is looking for hotels at one of the largest transit airports in the world—Dubai International Airport, in the United Arab Emirates. Most passengers have just an hour during a refueling stop, but they head immediately for the airport's 22,000-square-foot duty-free shopping complex.

Dubai is a duty-free port, and the duty-free complex offers unbelievable prices for some of the more traditional purchases: a liter of Johnnie Walker Scotch, or a carton of Marlboro cigarettes.

I remember when my first late-night flight stopped in Dubai on the way to London from Asia.

As I left my plane, aircraft from Ghana, India, Ethiopia, Germany, the Netherlands, Russia, England, and Singapore were lined up, unloading passengers.

For the most part, they weren't really there for the booze and the cigarettes. They had come for the deals on the Rolex Oysterdate, the Chanel perfume, kilos of beluga caviar, and gold sold by weight. There's a special room for Cuban cigars, and a fur shop where a mink coat sells for $1,800. Want a Mercedes or a HumVee? No problem.

The complex sells chocolates, too—about 40 tons of Tobler products per year.

Every once in a while, there's a rush on scotch whiskey. The night I was there, an airplane from LOT, the Polish airline, landed in Dubai on a flight from Delhi. The passengers rushed the store, cash in hand. An hour later, the plane was almost overweight when it roared down the runway toward Warsaw.

In just sixty minutes, the passengers had purchased fifty-eight videocassette players and seventy-eight cases of Johnnie Walker Scotch. How the plane ever lifted off the ground remains a mystery. But, for those who could forget the cramped and uncomfortable flight, Dubai was a layover to remember.

3

On the Plane

**JOINING THE UPGRADE BRIGADE,
THE AIR YOU BREATHE, AND
OTHER (UN)NECESSARY EVILS**

You're almost there. They're about to call your flight to board. Even the departure board is finally telling the truth. It's almost time to go.

But, if you're like me, you're an unofficial member of the upgrade brigade. You desperately want to fly in the front of the cabin.

And the scene, all too familiar, is repeated at virtually every airport gate around the world. It's the attack of the "lurkers." Or worse, the "demanders."

Most of us fall into the former category.

Come on, admit it: You are a lurker. Or you've been one. You want an upgrade. You go to the counter and ask. The agent tells you that no upgrades are available (you don't believe it) or says that you'll have to wait (you want to believe there's hope).

Doing your best impression of a demented cocker spaniel or a foreign refugee boat person, you hunch your body over, and you slowly shuffle, stalk, and circle the counter at the gate.

And, most of the time, you don't get an upgrade.

Trust me when I tell you that, within the United States, the upgrade is overrated.

Think about the aircraft type you're booked on. Getting bumped to first class sounds great. But if it's on an MD-80, a 727, or a 737, the first-class section will be crammed. And sitting there is tantamount to being sent to your room as a young child.

I'd much rather take three seats together in coach than fight for an upgrade on a narrow-body plane. When I'm flying, I like to have space to work and read. I'm not there for the movie or the gourmet meal. An open coach seat next to me gets a higher rating than a seat in the full first-class section.

On overseas long-haul, wide-body flights, it's another story. Usually, more seats are available for an upgrade, and more space is available once you're on board.

So stop whining about that domestic upgrade and head for the jetway.

Some passengers are "demanders."

One of my favorite stories happened at the old Stapleton Airport in Denver. A crowded United flight had been canceled, and a long line was quickly forming at the gate. An airline agent was trying to rebook everyone on the next available flight and on connecting flights.

Suddenly, out of nowhere, an angry passenger pushed his way through the line and slapped his ticket down on the counter.

"I have to be on the next flight," he announced, "and it HAS to be first class!"

The agent tried to be nice. "Sir," I've got all these people here, and I'm trying to help everyone. If you'll just bear with me and give me a few minutes, I'm sure I'll be able to help you as well."

He would hear none of this. He raised his voice, as if to make an announcement. "Do you have any idea who I am?" he bellowed.

The agent didn't miss a beat. Without hesitation, she reached down, grabbed the public address microphone from below the counter, and raised it up to her mouth.

"May I have your attention," she began. "United Airlines has a man at gate 17 who does not know who he is . . ."

The entire line of passengers broke up laughing.

The man, of course, was not amused, and stared her down.

"#$*& you," was all he could muster.

Again, the agent was smooth.

"I'm sorry," she countered calmly. "But you're going to have to stand in line for that, too." Guess what? No upgrade.

Again, the bottom line here is to comprehend the reason why you're at the airport in the first place: to go from point A to point B.

Still, if getting an upgrade is that important to you, remember these basics:

1. Dress for success. Jeans and a backpack just won't cut it.

2. Know the lingo. "Is the plane full?" immediately identifies you as a civilian. The language of the gate— "What's the load today?"—is a better way of asking that question.

3. Is your flight an originating flight and the first flight of the day, or a midday flight waiting for other connecting passengers? If it's waiting for connecting passengers, even if the flight is showing full, you stand a better chance of an upgrade because not all the passengers will connect.

4. DON'T ASK for an upgrade. That's the first sign you're an amateur. Remember, gate agents have been hardened by years of lurkers and demanders. They KNOW why you're there. Often, it's much easier NOT to talk about the upgrade but to employ the "schmooze" tactic. First, you'll always learn something about the airline or the process of travel in that conversation. Second, if the agent likes you and there's a seat available, that's when the upgrade happens. "Can I see your ticket?" the agent will ask, and the unspoken upgrade process has begun.

5. Don't be a lurker or a demander. Just get on the plane. Start by going down the jetway.

What you do next, from the moment you walk down that jetway until you take your seat, will often determine the quality of the flight you're about to take, no matter what section of the plane you're in.

If the airline is preboarding, and you're a member of the carrier's elite program, then by all means preboard. I don't have to tell you that overhead space is at a premium. First come, first stowed.

But unless you're sitting in a window seat in the back of the aircraft, there is no upside to getting on that line. Invariably, you will have to wait for everyone else to show up to fill the center and window seats next to you.

So . . . wait. And when there is no line, start down the jetway.

When you get to the aircraft door, don't turn right. Instead, turn LEFT.

Why? Because you're headed to the cockpit. No, you're not hijacking the plane; you're going to ask an important question.

"Are all the air pacs on?"

No one in that cockpit will think you're crazy. Instead, they now know that YOU know.

An air pac is part of a plane's air conditioning and circulation system. Most modern jetliners have at least two. Wide-body aircraft have three.

Jets were designed to have an almost constant flow of new air through the cabin.

Today, about half of the air is recycled; until the 1970s none of it was. And with more planes flying full, anecdotal evidence suggests that the low ventilation levels increase the chances that people will get sick.

Here's what is supposed to happen. The air enters through the plane's jet engines. It is compressed and heated by those engines. Then it enters near the cabin ceiling and is circulated through the cabin. Some is recirculated through the plane, but most is purged out through the cabin floor.

Many airlines, in an attempt to save money, don't use all their air pacs to do this. Instead, they recirculate old air continuously through the cabin and only purge that old air slowly—or, on some flights, not at all.

The money saved is significant. On one medium-size aircraft, airlines save $60,000 per year in fuel costs when they simply recirculate the air within the cabin and don't introduce new air.

The people traveling within that cabin generate dust and fibers as well as bacteria and other microorganisms. This dramatically diminishes the quality of the air, and it affects the flow of the air through the cabin. It can easily promote the spread of bacteria and disease.

Think about this: Economy-class passengers on some 737 aircraft are given eight cubic feet of recirculated air per minute. On some other airlines, first-class passengers on the upper deck of a 747 get sixty cubic feet of recirculated air per minute.

Is it therefore a big surprise if a passenger in 5B has the flu and passengers in 17A and 23C then catch the flu?

The quality of onboard air improved measurably when U.S. airlines banned smoking on their flights. Some airlines, like United, then used new HEPA filters on their flights to remove more particulates from the air. And these high-efficiency filters do reduce the level of airborne particulate contamination.

Still, unless all those air pacs are operative, the air is, at best, stagnant.

In one study conducted by the Harvard School of Public Health, flight attendants were issued special belt-clipped atmospheric monitoring devices to wear while flying.

When those monitors were analyzed, the percentages of carbon dioxide and carbon monoxide were above the lowest acceptable levels listed by OSHA (Occupational Safety and Health Administration) for most office buildings! Add the airborne aspects of altitude and pressure—and dehydration—to the mix and you have a quite unhealthy environment on most flights.

Onboard air is very dry, and thus can cause headaches or itchy skin.

But, given the quality of onboard air, some health professionals are more worried about communicable diseases.

Some airlines deal with this issue better than others. Air France only eliminated smoking on all of its flights late in 2000!

The aircraft type is another factor. Ironically, some observers think you're getting a better quality of air when you're flying on an older Boeing 727 than when you're on a new Boeing 777. In fact, some reports indicate that, on a newer plane, you have a higher likelihood of feeling dizzy or nauseated than on other, older airplanes.

After a rash of complaints from flight attendants, the two biggest operators of the 777s—United Airlines and British Airways—are investigating the air quality on those planes.

With the 777s, the air pacs may not be the problem. The altitude at which the planes normally fly could be delivering less oxygen.

Compounding the problem is the 777's size. It is so large that its air-conditioning system has been known to create different kinds of "weather" in various parts of the plane—especially variations in temperature and humidity.

How did this problem surface? Through flight attendants' complaints. In 2000, United's own flight attendants filed twenty-six reports—an unusually high number—of becoming ill on the plane.

Next, an ex-pilot and former medical examiner for Britain's Civil Aviation Authority was quoted as saying that a lack of air made him feel "slightly hallucinatory" on a flight from San Diego to London.

United has started to modify the air systems on its forty-three 777s to make the air temperature more consistent throughout the cabin during the entire length of the flight.

Ever notice that you tend to feel colder, the longer you're on a flight? Aeromedical specialists have discovered that your metabolism tends to slow during long flights.

So, practice the reverse layered look. Pack a sweater in your carry-on bag.

OK, let's recap. You've stopped at the cockpit and asked the pilots to make sure all the air pacs will be turned on. (If you're intercepted by a flight attendant en route to the cockpit, ask the flight attendant to transmit your message. On this one issue, flight attendants are actively on your side. You ALL benefit from this.)

Now, on to your seat.

Legend has it that Orville and Wilbur Wright were convinced that people who flew in flying machines would be most comfortable if they did so lying on their stomachs.

That idea made sense when flight distances were measured in hundreds of feet, not in miles.

Thankfully, most aviation pioneers decided against a horizontal, face-down experience, and made sitting the preferred flying posture. The first Ford Tri-motors, which cruised at the leisurely pace of 115 mph, offered stiff wicker cane-backed chairs, but, before long, passenger comfort became the focus of intense competition among airlines.

One French manufacturer outfitted his planes with overstuffed armchairs and lounging divans. Even the Douglas DC-2 offered its fourteen passengers upholstered contour seats, thick carpeting, and footrests.

In later years, the Boeing Stratocruisers, the Lockheed Constellations, and the DC-7s catered to passenger seat comfort. But the era of passenger comfort seemed to end when the first Boeing 707s and Douglas DC-8s were introduced.

The jet age quickly reduced standard seat distances from forty to thirty-six inches, then to thirty-four and even thirty-two inches. It was no longer comfortable to fly.

When the jumbos arrived, with ten-across seating in coach, people seemed to stop dressing up to enjoy their flights. Instead, they dressed down, hoping just to survive them.

The airline seat remains a serious problem for many passengers. Few things are less enjoyable than an uncomfortable, narrow, hard seat on a long and crowded flight.

On international runs, most carriers offer—and boast about—sleeper seats in first class. With the 747, airlines returned to promoting seats as part of their advertising campaigns.

Pan Am and American had advertised "dining in the air for four" in the upstairs lounges of their 747s. The lounges are gone now, but the seat wars continue.

The first sleeper seats were twenty-four inches wide and reclined fifty degrees. Then the recline was increased to sixty degrees.

So much for first class. In the back of the plane, the airlines increased only the seating density.

In the seat wars, airlines constantly add, and occasionally remove, seats. And because of issues of weight, the airlines are always trying to install lighter seats. At one point, United Airlines added twenty-two seats to its short-haul 737s and still reduced the weight of each plane by more than 1,200 pounds.

Many coach seats still recline only a few inches. On some carriers, passengers hope that the seats don't recline at all. The legroom is so tight that knees get scraped, and when the person in the seat ahead pushes the button and sits back, the meal tray of the passenger behind becomes a bulldozer.

Every airline is different, depending on its market and its competition. Don't expect comfortable coach seats on the United Shuttle between Los Angeles and San Francisco, or on America West flights between Los Angeles and Las Vegas.

About fifteen years ago, the ante was upped in the seat wars. Japan Airlines offered "sky beds" on some of its longer 747 flights. For a surcharge of 20 percent above normal first-class fares, the airline provided a curtained six-foot bed and a cotton kimono.

But JAL removed them when too many stewardesses complained of being grabbed and fondled on long flights.

Philippine Airlines then offered beds on all of its 747 flights across the Pacific. The airline's "Cloud Nine" service featured fourteen upper-deck berths.

British Airways went much further. Naval architects were hired to completely redesign the first-class cabin. And, using the same amount of space, these experts developed incredible fully reclining, spacious beds.

Qantas and Singapore airlines jumped in, and Cathay Pacific, United, and American followed.

These single electric/hydraulic seats are engineering marvels; they recline to flat six-foot-six-inch beds.

Indeed, the battle for upscale, first-class passengers is heating up. Virgin Atlantic's Richard Branson announced that, by the end of 2000, his airline would be installing *double* beds, complete with enclosures, on long-haul flights. (Don't hold your breath. It hasn't happened yet, and some observers think it's a fantasy that will be shot down by economic realities of weight, space, and cost.)

In the meantime, British Airways extended the upscale seat battle into business class: flat business-class beds were introduced as well. (In airline economics, 9 percent of travelers—in business class—generate 45 percent of all revenues.)

But what about coach passengers? Remember them? The airlines seem to have forgotten them or are intentionally ignoring them.

In recent years, the space in coach cabins has become even more cramped, if that was even possible. High-density seating configurations by most airlines in coach seemed to conspire to restrict and constrict coach passengers into an uncomfortable—and some would claim unhealthy—ride.

Despite the introduction of newer model planes (stretched versions of the MD-80 and the 737), things didn't get better; they got worse.

The seats didn't get any wider—and, some airline officials would argue, average passengers DID.

Anyone who has flown Southwest airlines knows that it promotes price, not comfort, as a sales perk.

Tell that to the Los Angeles woman who sued Southwest in 2000 for discrimination when the airline insisted she was so fat she had to buy tickets for TWO seats.

The airline claimed in its defense that its policy is that "oversized customers" purchase extra seats "for their comfort and safety." And, the airline said, if a flight was full, the portly passengers could request a refund.

One observer noted: "Fat chance!"

Still, anyone who has flown in the "back of the bus" on a 737, 757, or MD-80 aircraft knows that the old joke of your knees pressing against your chest was never really funny.

To make matters worse, American and Continental, among others, are actually flying stretch versions of the 737, with three-plus-three rows in coach, on long-haul transcontinental flights! Some passengers have been known to refuse to board these aircraft, opting instead to wait for later, widebody flights on the same routes. (But even that is a myth. The cabin of a 737 has EXACTLY the same dimensions as a 757!)

Want to feel confined? The new 737-800 can fly 3,700 miles nonstop and is a very efficient aircraft for the airlines. But its seating configuration crams up to 146 people into a cabin that was designed about thirty years ago for short trips. Not a pretty picture for passengers, not to mention flight attendants who have to work those flights.

Recently, the airlines have been confronted with a problem of excess equipment and excess capacity. In the past four years, airline profits soared, and companies ordered new airplanes. But then the Asian economy plummeted. When OPEC hiked oil prices in 2000 (and air fares started to rise, to adjust for the increased cost of fuel), the airlines found themselves in an awkward predicament.

They had more planes than they needed, and their costs were starting to jump. As a result, the airlines had too many empty planes chasing too few passengers. They had too much capacity.

What did the airlines do with the extra planes? United began using its new Boeing 777s on Chicago-to-Denver flights, something these planes were clearly not designed to do and still remain profitable. On some short-haul routes, the airline even used some of its Boeing 747-400's.

Continental's response: It simply parked its excess aircraft. Enter American Airlines' CEO Don Carty, one of those angered by the excess capacity in the system. Besides the problem of empty seats, the seats that were filled didn't net American enough high-yield revenue.

Translation: Too many discount tickets were being sold. And, last but not least, coach passengers were angry about being crunched in the cabin.

In a surprise move that caught its major competitors off guard, American elected not to park any planes. It decided instead to *park seats.*

In early 2000, American announced that it would begin removing two rows of coach seats from each of its airplanes—

systemwide. The absence of those two rows gains space for coach passengers. The 31-inch seat pitch in the coach section went to as much as 36 inches, a significant and noticeable increase in space and comfort.

On the surface, it seemed to be a win-win for both the airline and its passengers. American claimed that no fares would be increased as a result of the reconfiguration. This was a surprise, considering that the move, which affected more than 700 aircraft and essentially represented 6.5 percent of American Airlines' total seating capacity, cost the airline roughly $70 million.

Why so much money? Removing seats means readjusting air vents, electrical systems, lighting, computer power ports, and carpeting for each plane.

But wait a minute. Why would American suddenly decide to pull seats from its planes and spend $70 million, just to make us more comfortable in coach? Does anyone smell a rat?

Technically, American was correct when it announced that no fares would be increased when the seats were removed.

No fares were increased.

Smell the rat yet? You do if you're familiar with the term "yield management."

Despite the reduction in capacity, American was convinced it could spend the money, reduce the number of seats, and still make a BIGGER profit in the long run.

The method was quite simple. If there were twenty published discount fares on a particular route, American eliminated about eight of them. In immediate effect, passengers got a de facto fare increase!

"The magic of this," one American Airlines executive quietly boasted, "is that it allowed us to reduce the number of seats and then reduce the number of low fares being offered on any one flight, which will get us a higher percentage of full-fare business travelers in coach."

In airline lingo, American was banking on widening the 14 percent revenue premium gap that it has in the industry. In laypersons' terms, the airline was counting on attracting a higher percentage of full-fare business and coach passengers than its competitors.

American's announcement was a major bombshell within the airline industry, but it is not the first time an airline has announced more space in the coach cabin.

TWA removed seats from its coach cabins about five years ago. Indeed, flying coach in TWA soon became a relatively comfortable experience. The marketing folks at TWA loved the idea, but the accountants didn't. Almost as soon as some of us were beginning to settle into the idea of a pleasant coach ride, the airline quietly packed those original seats right back in.

Other airlines—Virgin Atlantic, for example—tried to segment the coach market by dedicating a certain number of slightly larger and more comfortable coach seats on each flight. United also tried to do it on some of its longer-haul flights.

But those attempts, which only offered certain coach seats to higher-fare coach passengers, didn't apply to the entire fleet. The arrangement was confusing and it angered many coach passengers who felt that they deserved the better seats anyway, given the cost of their flight.

Has the American idea worked? Indeed it has. Based on its de facto airfare increase, American recouped its reconfiguration investment in about a year. (The *average* cost of tickets went up.) And, on some of its aircraft (notably, the 777s operating across the Atlantic on European runs), the airline quietly REINSTALLED more than thirty seats in coach. So much for promises.

Seat density remains a problem for other airlines. The United Shuttle operates Boeing 737-300 aircraft with as many as 134 seats—126 of them in coach. In 2001, we have come full circle to the age-old price-versus-comfort threshold. For passengers on short-haul flights, how important is price versus comfort? For those who travel on longer-haul routes, what comes first, comfort or price?

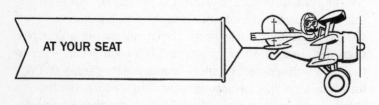

AT YOUR SEAT

You've reached your seat. Expanded legroom or not, you've got to move fast. Put your carry-on into the overhead compartment. Sit down.

Hungry? This moment is key. Look at your airline ticket. Are you on an even- or an odd-numbered flight? It makes a difference on longer flights that offer meals (and choices of meals). This is the time to move quickly.

On most airlines, meal orders on even-numbered flights are taken from the front to the back. On odd-numbered flights, meal orders are taken from the back to the front.

Where are you sitting? If you're on an even-numbered flight and you're in the front, no problem. If you're in the middle or at the back, run up to the galley and get your food order in before the plane pushes back.

That advice presumes you're prepared to EAT airline food, one of the great oxymorons of our time.

Let's be honest. People don't eat airline food because they're hungry. They eat it because they're BORED or because it "comes with the ticket."

You're sitting during the flight. Someone comes to your row and puts a tray down. You stare at it. And, inevitably, you EAT it!

But, like the quality of aircraft air, it's important to know what is on that tray.

"For breakfast this morning, we will be serving an omelette, which can also be used as a flotation device in the event of an over-water landing."

And still, you eat it!

First, some history. In 1955, Northwest Airlines purchased a series of two-page full-color newspaper ads to promote the launch of its New York-to-Chicago service. However, the ads mostly promoted the "Fujiyama Room," Northwest's downstairs lounge on its Stratocruisers. The illustrations showed a white-jacketed steward offering passengers an elaborate tray piled high with shrimp, egg rolls, and other ostensibly Oriental delicacies. The advertising copy was equally fanciful: "Oriental jasmine tea, if you wish. And such meals— juicy steaks, seafood ocean-fresh, salads crisp and cool as salads ought to be." All this bounty was included in the round trip, first-class fare: $85.70!

Veteran frequent flyers have trouble remembering those days; some insist that "those days" never happened.

Well, that was then, and this is now. No one complains about the food anymore. Passengers simply expect it to be bad.

A tally of the amount airlines spend on food might confirm a few more suspicions. Domestic airlines spend from 3 to 5 percent of their total operating budget on food service. The percentages include the cost of china, cutlery, and other utensils.

Because so many ancillary costs are included, it's hard to calculate how much an airline really spends, on average, for the meals it serves. The best guesstimates: Most airlines spend under $5 per passenger, per meal. Southwest spends under 60 cents per passenger per meal.

And whenever the airlines can shave a few cents off a meal, they will. The Olive at American Airlines, a true story, has gained urban-legend status.

Former American CEO Robert Crandall kept noticing that a single black olive was placed on the top of each salad served with the airline meals. But no one ever ate the olive. He ordered it removed. The cost saved by the airline: about $600,000 a year.

The olive, as we have all discovered, was just the beginning. Some airlines are now employing a caste system in coach. The food you get depends on the price you paid for your ticket!

For example, America West quietly developed a five-tier meal system for coach passengers. The routes with the highest concentration of full-fare business travelers in coach got the best-tier meals. They were served to passengers flying at peak times between Boston and Phoenix or from Las Vegas to Newark. Passengers on a late-night discount flight from Los Angeles to Columbus, Ohio, got pot luck.

OK, now that you know how much they spend, can you guess what they are buying?

First, airlines look at detailed time-and-motion studies and compare them with the length of a flight. The goal? Discover which food items can be served on which flights, given the time it takes the flight attendants to prepare and serve a meal, and the time allowed for the passengers to eat it.

During the first twenty years it operated the highly profitable fifty-five-minute New York-to-Boston and New York-to-Washington shuttle flights. Eastern Airlines had no competitors. In the regulated environment of the era, Eastern executives regularly pointed to those dreaded time-and-motion studies that concluded it would be impractical—indeed physically impossible—to offer a meal, a snack, or even a beverage on a shuttle route. So, for two decades, the movers and shakers of American business and government rode the Eastern Shuttle without being offered even an in-flight soft drink.

But during the heady days of deregulation in the early 1980s, an airline called New York Air was launched to compete with Eastern. And its head, the much-despised Frank Lorenzo (he later ran Eastern), did one thing that pleased passengers. He rolled out "the flying Nosh" a small, pre-assembled sack of snacks distributed by flight attendants shortly after takeoff.

Delta and USAir offer snacks on those routes now, and there's hardly a flight that operates more than forty minutes in the air that doesn't at least offer a beverage.

All the market research in the world can't pinpoint passengers' in-flight food preferences. For reasons of cost and simplicity, many airlines have opted to serve cold meals, but they do so at their own peril. For many business travelers, an airline's hot meal may be their ONLY meal on a particular trip.

However, hot meals have many problems, beginning with the atmosphere on the plane. Think the on-board air is tough on you? It's harder on the food. British Airways won't talk about its attempt, many years ago, to serve an in-flight soufflé, except to say that soufflés will never be attempted again. Some bread and rolls will never be served again on Singapore Airlines; the flour used didn't work at the planes' altitude. Successes in test kitchens on the ground often fail miserably in the air.

Sometimes a meal is simply positioned improperly. British Airways was shocked when it put something called "Beef Rangdang" on the menu and no one ordered it. Reason: No one knew what it was. The airline renamed the dish "Malaysian-Style Beef Curry," and people ordered it.

Still, no matter what you call it, food tastes different at 35,000 feet. No one knows exactly why. Charles Lindbergh, after his epic thirty-four-hour solo flight across the Atlantic, commented on what his five sandwiches tasted like.

Today, in-flight catering is a $10-billion-a-year industry. It employs more than 100,000 people. The logistics are equally staggering when the provisioning aspects of a flight are considered.

A jumbo jet preparing to set out on a long-haul flight may be carrying up to 42,000 separate catering items.

British Airways, for example, caters more than 70,000 meals each day out of Heathrow alone. That adds up to 41 tons of chicken, 45 tons of strawberries, 127 tons of tomatoes, and 600,000 pints of milk every year.

So much for the numbers. Next is the moisture problem.

Most passengers don't realize it, but hot in-flight meals have been cooked at least twice before they are served. That may explain why some of the dishes are coated with a thick mystery sauce—a pathetic attempt by the airlines' chef to somehow maintain some moisture in the recooked, reheated food. More often than not, the attempt is a dismal failure.

Sidestepping the quality and the consistency of the food, what are the health concerns?

Many airline meals are downright unhealthy. According to one recent study, a meal of a McDonald's Big Mac, French fries, and a strawberry shake is healthier than a typical airline meal.

Consider these facts. A first-class meal on Delta, consisting of Caesar salad, filet mignon, and ice cream sundae, contained 87 grams of fat, 786 fat calories, 1,505 milligrams of sodium (the real killer), and a total of 1,829 calories. (Most doctors recommend that a person consuming about 2,000 calories a day should consume no more than 65 grams of fat and 2,400 milligrams of sodium daily.)

Add a soft drink to that mix, and the sodium level soars.

Midwest Express meals are delicious, but they are extremely high in fat: 91 grams.

And on Lufthansa, sodium weighs in at 3,477 milligrams for a coach meal.

Yes, you can order ahead and be served a special meal during a flight. Categories include low sodium, Kosher, and lactose-intolerant! And those are just for starters.

My advice: If you MUST eat airline food, order the one special meal the airline can't mess up: the fruit plate.

Next: the drinking issue.

Forget the airborne wine list. It is not your friend. With altitude, pressurization, and dehydration, alcohol is a big no-no. One drink in the air has roughly the same effect as more than two on the ground.

There are also some behavioral considerations.

Alcohol is almost always blamed for incidents of air rage on planes. One survey, at the University of California at Santa Cruz, showed how badly the brain is affected by a combination of low levels of in-flight oxygen, low cabin pressures, and alcohol.

Add to that the general stress of travel, and you have the unmistakable ingredients of trouble aloft.

"The first thing that goes, with drinkers, is their hearing," one flight attendant told me. "So if you are drinking to excess on the plane, you usually begin to speak very loudly, in which case the entire cabin can hear every word you say. It is not very attractive. But it's also the signal for us to cut you off immediately."

Ironically, airlines began serving alcohol in an attempt to relax passengers and create a feeling that the flight might even be cause for celebration.

Just the opposite has occurred.

Most airlines now carry handcuffs as standard operating equipment on each flight, and the handcuffs are used often. Alcohol is involved in almost every incident that results in verbal or physical abuse. Ration or decline the alcohol.

Doctors tell us how important it is to continually hydrate yourself on flights.

OK, we're all agreed on the need for water. But what *kind* of water? When you see the flight attendant walking down the aisle with a tray full of glasses filled with water, don't just reach for a glass.

Instead, ask whether the water is bottled or was drawn from the airline's holding tank. If the answer is the holding tank, don't drink that water.

Airlines have a continuing problem with the bacteria counts in those holding tanks. No one wants to admit this, but those bacteria counts look like the bar scene from *Star Wars*. That's one reason why the airlines dump all those chemicals in the holding tanks and why the water from those tanks tends to have a metallic taste.

If you're at all concerned about where that water is coming from, do what I do. Before flying, go to the store and purchase your own bottled water.

Now, for some safety instructions. Interior aircraft configurations differ on almost every flight. Just be aware of one important fact: how far your seat is from the nearest exit. Count the rows to that exit. Why? In an emergency, it is highly likely that there will be no cabin lights. The cabin will be dark and filled with smoke. You will need to feel (and count) seat backs in order to get to that exit door.

What about the safety instructions themselves? Yes, pay attention, but see whether your seatmate is also paying attention—and understands English.

There's real irony in the "safety demo" done, usually by flight attendants, or via prerecorded announcements. It concerns the exit-row seats:

Here it is, verbatim: "Ladies and gentlemen, we ask that each passenger review the safety instruction card in your seat pocket as soon as you are seated. Please contact a flight attendant for reseating if you are assigned an exit seat and do not meet the selection criteria noted on the card. If you are unwilling, unable, or concerned about injury while performing any of the listed functions, you may also request to be reseated. If you are seated in an exit-row seat, you may be called upon to assist in an emergency. Follow the directions of the crew."

Sounds pretty clear, right? But there's one problem. Who screens the people sitting there to begin with? Under Federal Aviation Administration regulations, no person may occupy an exit-row seat if he or she cannot read, speak, and understand instructions in English—or cannot hear well enough to perform one or more of the applicable instructions. If that person is hard of hearing or can't speak English, what good is the announcement?

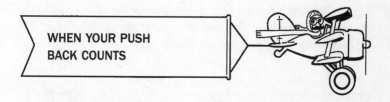

WHEN YOUR PUSH BACK COUNTS

The other day, while waiting to depart from the Orlando airport, I got up from my seat and walked to the first-class lavatory. The door to the cockpit was open and the pilot was involved in a heated argument with the gate agent.

She had come up to tell him the plane was ready to depart and she was closing the door.

"Do not close the aircraft door," he shot back. He pointed to his instruments. "We still have a cargo door open. Why is it still open?"

"We had about thirty strollers, and we had to put them in the hold," she responded.

"Well, don't close the airplane door until the cargo door is shut."

Why was that so important?

Because of the ticking clock. This pilot didn't want to be blamed for a delay.

The moment the aircraft door was shut, an internal fax machine on this American Airlines A300 would have automatically transmitted a message to American's headquarters in Dallas. The "clock" would have been started. A second clock would have started the minute the captain released the parking brakes and allowed the aircraft to push back.

A major disparity between the time the aircraft door was shut and the time the aircraft pushed back would have affected the flight's official on-time performance. "If we're going to be late," the pilot later told me, "I don't want to be blamed when, in fact, they were late loading bags."

Luckily, on at least that flight, they were able to quickly close the cargo door, and we were on time. Well, at least we pushed back from the gate on time!

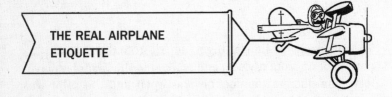

THE REAL AIRPLANE ETIQUETTE

We've all heard about air rage exhibited by passengers. There is also growing air rage among flight attendants. They seem to possess a shorter and shorter fuse in the sometimes not-so-friendly skies.

A flight attendant friend of mine—we'll call her Barbara—has flown for United for more than twenty-five years.

She's seen just about everything, and whether you agree with her or not, here's her advice about airplane etiquette, from the flight attendants' point of view.

It starts as you go through security. Please, be ready to go through security when you get to the X-ray belt. It is not necessary to wait for the guard to say, "OK." Walk through one at a time without touching the sides of the machine. Different security machines are set differently at different airports. Just because you did not set off the buzzer at one airport, does not mean that you won't set it off at another. I have known a tea bag (wrapped in an aluminum package) to set off the alarm, and, of course, we all know about the metal underwires in a woman's bra. After you pick up your carry-ons, move to the side and out of the way of others trying to collect their items. Do not reassemble your luggage right next to the conveyor belt.

Whoever said that your plane would be parked directly next to the security check-in? Some airports are large, and the distance from the check-in counter to your gate could be quite far, and lines could be long.

Once you are at the gate, wait in line until the CSR [customer service representative] is ready for you. Do not be talking on your cell phone and make him or her wait until you are done. Be organized. Have your ticket and ID ready. If you have a particular seat or area of the plane you like to sit in, tell them as soon as you begin to check in. Do not expect to have a seat if you show up after the ten-minute cutoff. This simply means that if you have not checked in ten minutes before the scheduled departure, your seat is subject to cancellation and resale. At the very least, it may be given to another passenger who was waiting for a better seat. Do be pleasant and smile—do not blame the agent if the seat assignment you thought you had is not the one the computer gives you. It is not the agent's fault. Do not make up stories about how you were supposed to be in first class or you were supposed to have the whole row to yourself. Trust me, they have heard it all.

Do not try to impress them with your status. Keep in mind: You get a lot more flies with honey than you do with vinegar. If you truly were wronged by the airline, not your company's travel department or your travel agent or one of the online travel agents, do not take it out on the ticket agent. Ask to see a supervisor or someone higher up. Deal with the people who can make the decisions.

Board when your row number is called, unless you are waiting for a first-class upgrade. Do not carry on your entire household. Especially, do not try to hide your third, fourth, and fifth carry-ons under your coat, or swung way over the back of your shoulder. We can see them. Do not tell us that you got to carry your household on the last flight. Perhaps it had fewer customers and plenty of room, or perhaps it was the type of aircraft that could accommodate more carry-on bags. Please do not drop off your carry-on items at the first open bin. That is the space for the people in those rows. If you see a pillow or blanket in the bin where you are putting your bags, pull them out first. If they get smashed in behind all the bags, etcetera, they will be of no use during the flight because we won't be able to find them. Plus, it will make more room in the bins for more carry-on items. The bin over your head is not your personal storage space. Several other people must share it. When you reach your row, step in so others can pass by you; *then* store your items. The faster the plane is boarded, the more apt you are to leave on time. If you have a briefcase or other small item, put it under the seat in front of you, to free up more overhead bin space. Many airplanes now have the extended overheads so the smaller rollerboards will fit in lengthwise—wheels down and rolled straight in. This also allows for more storage. Please do not come to the flight attendant with a huge item and say, "Where can I put this? It is too fragile to check and it does not fit in the overhead." Most planes do not have that kind of storage space, and the FAA says, 'If it doesn't fit in an approved spot, it cannot be on the aircraft.'" Same goes for large musical instruments, unless you have purchased a seat for them. Also, if you cannot manage your carry-on items yourself, check them. Something too heavy for you to lift is too heavy for the flight attendant. If your bag must be checked planeside, make sure you give the agent your final destination, to help ensure that your luggage arrives when and where you do.

Once your bags are stowed, sit down and plan to stay there for a while. And during the safety demo, if you don't want to listen, at least be quiet. And besides, it is plain rude to talk while someone else is talking. If you are branded rude and/or arrogant by one flight attendant, the word spreads. When we ask you to turn off your computer or cell phone, do it right away—not in four or five minutes but *right then*. When we tell you that we have to pick up the predeparture beverages in first class, we have to pick up the predeparture beverages. The galley must be completely closed up and secure for takeoff, and that takes a few minutes. Also, if you board three minutes before departure, do not expect to get a cocktail at that time.

Respect the seat belt sign. I have many coworkers who have permanent injuries related to turbulence. They have been floating on the ceiling and have come crashing down to the floor on top of people, carts, armrests, and the like. If the seat belt sign has been on for an inordinate amount of time, and the ride seems smooth, and you really need to use the facilities, you might ask the flight attendants how much longer—or some such thing—in a very polite way. Perhaps the captain has just forgotten. But, please, for your own safety and the safety of those you may come crashing down on, stay in your seats, with your seat belt fastened, any time the seat belt sign is on. Personally, I leave my seat belt on all the time I am in my seat, in case of unexpected bumps.

During the service, try to stay in your seat while the carts are in the aisle. We cannot go back and forward, back and forward, constantly to let you by, or we will never finish the service. We realize that you have to sit with your trays for a while—especially on the larger aircraft—and we try to get back to pick them up as quickly as possible, but it takes even longer if you are milling about during the service. Please try not to be upset with the flight attendant if you do not get your first meal choice. We can only serve what we have, and it is impossible to board 100 percent of everything. If you truly have special dietary needs—if you are allergic to seafood or you are diabetic—bring your own food with you in case we cannot accommodate your needs. Many flights do not serve food, so if you think you will be hungry . . . well, you get the idea. If you call the flight attendant over and ask for coffee, please tell him or her at that time if you want cream and/or sugar or another beverage at the same moment. It is really annoying to the flight attendant to make several trips to the same row within two minutes; plus, there are many other people on board besides you. And, a "Please" and a "Thank you" go a long way. You would think that adults would know this, but somehow it is not so. And this applies to first class as well as economy. Remember, you far outnumber us, and we can only be in one place at a time. During the beverage service, please do not hand us a $100 bill and expect to get your drink for free. We are on to this one, and will go to all lengths to get your change; plus, we will do our best to give it to you in singles—just so you won't have to give someone else a large bill. If you do need the flight attendant for something, do not poke her or him—in fact, it is better not to touch the flight attendant at all. If you need her or his attention, raise your hand, say "Excuse me," or ring your flight attendant call button. If you must touch, do so on the arm, very gently.

Do not hand the flight attendants barf bags with dirty diapers in them and do not hand us dirty diapers. We handle food, remember. Dispose of them, in the barf bags, in the garbage. Do not flush them down the toilet. Most flight attendants are happy to hold your child for a few minutes if you need to use the restroom and are traveling alone, but, beyond that, we are not babysitters. We do not change diapers.

Keep in mind the appearance of your area. Can I tell you what the interior of a full aircraft looks like after a flight? We wonder if that is how these people keep their homes. I certainly hope not.

Most flight attendants love their jobs and enjoy being around people. They like to visit with the customers—time permitting. They really do want your flight to be a pleasant experience. Most will bend over backward for you if you are polite, remember to say "Please" and "Thank you," and are generally a nice person. Remember the Golden Rule, and this applies to all persons in the service industry as well: "Do unto others as you would have others do unto you."

OK, kids; got that? Despite the above lecture, if you can avoid the beverage carts, and if the seat belt sign is off, you do need to get up during the flight. I'm not talking about a lavatory run. I'm talking about your general health while in the air.

In addition to the air flow, there's your BLOOD FLOW. Sitting in a cramped airline seat can contribute to some serious circulatory problems, according to many medical researchers.

Get up at least twice on flights of five hours or more, dodge those nasty beverage and meal carts, and take a short stroll around the cabin. Recently numerous reports have surfaced about incidents about what used to be called "economy class syndrome," and is now given a more specific medical term: deep vein thrombosis. Some passengers have reportedly died from it. And it all relates to blood flow and your circulation on board. So you really must take that stroll.

During your stroll, you may want to visit the lavatory. If you thought the holding tanks duplicated the bar scene from *Star Wars,* then this room is central casting!

This airborne petri dish is nothing less than a bacterial wonderland.

On narrow-body aircraft like a 737, there are only three lavatories for about 150 people. The math is easy. On a full flight, 50 people are looking to use one lavatory.

Unless you're traveling with forty-nine members of your immediate family—well, you get the picture.

Before using that lavatory, realize the epidemiological breeding ground you're about to enter. One of the things you can pack in your carry-on bag is a small spray bottle (not aerosol) of disinfectant. Laugh if you will, but it makes total sense.

Spray the toilet seat; then lift it and spray the rim. After wiping off both, you can then sit down.

Then, do what a lot of people forget to do: Spray the faucets on the sink.

Apply a liberal dose of liquid soap (if it's in the bathroom) to your hands; or, barring that, spray your hands with the disinfectant and then wash with soap.

Although there is no hard scientific evidence, anecdotal history indicates that if you don't get sick from the bad air circulating on a plane, a visit to the lavatory usually exposes you to enough bacteria and viruses to last you a couple of months!

Back at your seat, you might be surprised to see that the traditional airsickness bag may still be in the seatback pocket in front of you.

U.S. airlines used more than 20 million of these bags last year. Even though we hardly ever use them for their intended purpose, we've come to expect them anyway.

Why? Because they have so many other practical uses.

We use them to dispose of diapers. With the addition of hot water, a clean bag makes a great on-board baby-bottle warmer. On many Caribbean flights, people take the bags for a later use: to hold their wet swimsuits.

And, strangely, there are people who like to collect them! (Many times, each year, there are conventions for people who love airline "collectibles." Why anyone would treasure a vomit bag from Mohawk or Pan Am is beyond me.)

Some people still do get airsick. But not many.

The biggest problem continues to be: adjustment to the pressurization of the aircraft cabin.

You know the feeling. You suddenly feel pressure in your ears. They almost feel as if they are locking up as the plane's internal cabin pressure changes. (I'm convinced, as are others, that when small children cry on planes, more often than not they're reacting to the changes in pressure.)

On numerous flights, I wasn't able to clear that pressure. I had to wait until I was on the ground. My ears finally did literally "pop" and clear, but a painful headache became part of the process.

There are ways around pressure problems.

First, there's something called the Valsalva maneuver. I learned about it when I was lucky enough to fly F-4s and F-15s in U.S. Air Force war games, at Nellis Air Force Base in Nevada, when I was a correspondent for *Newsweek.* I not only learned about the maneuver; I had to perform it before I was allowed to fly in the high-performance fighter jets.

The minute you feel the pressure start to build, sit straight up. Breathe slowly and deliberately—and deeply. Then pull in your stomach and hold your breath. Close your mouth and swallow as strongly as you can. You should feel your ears start to clear.

What if that doesn't work? One of my flight attendant friends told me her secret, which does work.

Ask a flight attendant for a cup HALF-FILLED with very hot water. Then, hold the cup level on the right side of your head, and tilt your head so that your right ear rests on top of the lip of the cup. After a few moments, move the cup to the left side of your head and tilt your head so that your left ear rests on the lip of the cup. The steam from the hot water should clear your ear passages and relieve pressure. Be sure to insist on the cup's being only half-full, for all the obvious reasons. DO NOT POUR ANYTHING INTO YOUR EAR!).

A WORD ABOUT SEAT BELTS

Every airline will tell you to use a seat belt. You are required to wear them for takeoffs and landings. But here's the real irony: the airlines will hate me for this, but we must always remember that seat belts were installed on airplanes when aircraft rolled down runways at 90 to 100 miles per hour (mph). Today, jets take off at around 160 mph and land at about 150 mph. In the event of a high g-force but a survivable "hard landing," studies have shown that passengers do indeed survive the impact, but then die from the resulting trauma. Most often, the seat belt breaks the passenger's pelvis, there is internal hemorrhaging and the passenger, unable to walk or even to crawl, often dies from the resulting toxic smoke in the aftermath of the "incident."

I'm not going to tell you that you shouldn't wear your seat belts during takeoffs and landings. I'll let you employ your own best judgment. But I WILL insist that you wear a seat belt during the MOST dangerous part of the flight: in the air, when there is a distinct possibility of in-flight turbulence. The most common flying injuries occur at cruising altitude (above 25,000 feet), during moments of unanticipated clear air turbulence (CAT).

Want to become an unguided missile in flight? Then DON'T wear your seat belt.

MORE SERIOUS HEALTH PROBLEMS ALOFT

Ten minutes after taking off from Hong Kong on a nonstop flight to Los Angeles, a woman passenger on a fully loaded Cathay Pacific 747-400 suffered cardiac failure.

A woman passenger on a British Airways 747 flight somewhere over India began to bleed internally and was perilously close to losing consciousness.

One hour into a Lufthansa flight from Miami to Frankfurt, a male passenger suffered chest pains and said he was having difficulty breathing.

The Cathay Pacific flight was too heavy to return to the airport. Luckily, there were two doctors on board. One was an English surgeon returning from vacation; the other was a cardiologist from Duke University, returning home from a medical conference. The captain set a course for Taiwan and released a locked emergency medical kit to the doctors.

As the pilot dumped nearly 100 tons of fuel, the doctors stabilized the passenger. The plane made an emergency landing in Taiwan, and the woman was taken to a hospital. She survived.

There were also doctors traveling on the British Airways flight. Using the extensive emergency medical kit carried on the plane, and crafting a surgical tool out of a wire coat hanger, the doctors performed an operation to reinflate the woman passenger's collapsed lung. Again, a life was saved.

Although the Lufthansa flight was also carrying an extensive emergency medical kit, it was not immediately opened for the passenger with chest pains. When he tried to lie down in a galley, a flight attendant told him to return to his seat. The captain refused to make an emergency landing and continued on to Frankfurt.

The passenger had indeed suffered a heart attack, and a subsequent examination revealed he had suffered permanent heart damage. He sued the airline, and a federal magistrate awarded the passenger $2.75 million.

These and hundreds of other incidents raise questions about the effectiveness of airline medical equipment, as well as individual airlines' procedures in dealing with in-flight medical emergencies.

Emergencies that are considered life-threatening are rare. In a two-year study, the Federal Aviation Administration (FAA) estimated that about three serious medical problems occur per day on U.S. airlines. There are thousands of flights, and more than 1.5 million passengers boarding planes each day.

However, the FAA study was done nearly twenty years ago, and things have changed.

In 1995, for example, Northwest Airlines alone reported 2,000 in-flight medical emergencies, or about five a day. These resulted in eighty diversions or emergency landings.

One thing has not changed: how differently U.S. and foreign airlines approach medical emergencies, train their personnel, and help passengers in a crisis.

All U.S. airlines train their flight attendants in CPR (cardiopulmonary resuscitation), but it is not a requirement among foreign carriers.

That, however, is about the only area in which U.S. airlines have taken the lead in responding to on-board medical emergencies. There is a huge difference in the medical equipment and supplies carried by U.S. carriers and their foreign counterparts.

It would be nice to have a doctor as a fellow passenger, but without proper equipment to help you, the doctor might as well be a circus clown.

Had the Cathay Pacific and British Airways incidents occurred on a U.S. airline, the chances of the patients' survival would have been greatly reduced because proper on-board equipment was lacking.

In the United States, the FAA requires aircraft to have one to four basic first-aid kits, depending on the number of passenger seats. With few exceptions, the contents of this kit haven't changed much since the 1930s: a small assortment of bandages, gauze, tape, scissors, and some new additions— rubber gloves and a bio-cleanup kit.

The emergency medical kit, which is locked in the cockpit, contains no narcotics and can be released by the pilot only to qualified medical personnel. It has a stethoscope, syringes, dextrose injections, and nitroglycerin tablets.

However, until recently, most U.S. airlines had only the minimum equipment required by federal regulators. "Whatever the FAA mandates, that's what we carry," said one corporate medical director for a major U.S. airline. "People need to know that we're not set up to be an airborne ambulance or flying emergency room."

Then, slowly, the airlines started getting the message.

Qantas realized that it made great economic sense to add more emergency equipment on its flights, most of which are long hauls. A flight diversion for a medical emergency will just about wipe out any profit earned on that particular flight. But if a passenger can be stabilized on the plane, the airline and the passenger both win. Qantas began installing emergency heart defibrillators on each of its airplanes, and then trained its flight stewards in how to use them.

Almost immediately, the equipment and training paid off. Within days of the installation, passengers who had suffered heart attacks or seizures were revived and stabilized and eventually recovered.

In the mid-1990s Northwest installed a twenty-four-hour radio patch that let pilots talk with Mayo Clinic specialists. And American Airlines announced it had seven staff physicians on call, to consult with pilots.

But the U.S. carriers still resisted upgrading the emergency medical equipment carried on their planes.

In addition to defibrillators, many doctors felt that U.S. airlines should stock their emergency medical kits with bronchial dilators and with insulin.

The airlines argued that any time a physician uses a kit, it's to stabilize the patient, and that the airline's primary goal at that point is to get the passenger on the ground.

Often, it's as much a legal as a medical consideration. In litigious America, airlines are worried about being sued after the fact. However, every state has a Good Samaritan law: individuals who provide well-intentioned first-aid in emergencies are exempt from liability.

Foreign carriers don't seem to embrace those legal fears. Emergency medical kits on board Air New Zealand, British Airways, and Qantas planes reveal an entirely different approach to handling medical emergencies.

The Air New Zealand kit is a large orange suitcase filled with instruments, diagnostic and ventilation equipment, suction gear, and a veritable pharmacy of injectable, tablet, and spray drugs to treat everything from cardiac arrest to severe allergic reactions, diabetes, and asthma.

And, besides providing the kits, the airline offers a detailed protocol to handle medical emergencies ranging from heart attacks and epilepsy to kidney stones.

The British Airways medical kits contain a "delivery pack" in case a pregnant passenger goes into labor on board.

Qantas and Virgin Airways carry defibrillators. American Airlines finally agreed to install them on its planes, and, in the height of ironies, the man who was so active in pressuring American to equip its fleet with defibrillators was flying as a passenger on the first day the machines were on the planes, and, you guessed it, he suffered a heart attack. An American flight attendant, newly trained on the unit, used it and saved the man's life.

Now that you know all of this, how can become a better prepared passenger?

First, if you take any prescription medicine, exercise common sense. Do not pack it in your checked luggage; put it in your carry-on bag.

Second, if you have a preexisting heart or respiratory problem, remember that aircraft cabins are pressurized to 8,000 feet, and that may contribute to inducing a heart or breathing problem. Always consult your doctor before flying.

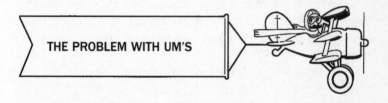

THE PROBLEM WITH UM'S

Last summer, a friend of mine planned to have her six-year-old daughter Sophie visit her grandmother in France. But because of schedule conflicts with her own business, my friend couldn't make the trip. She sent her daughter, alone, on a United Airlines nonstop flight to Paris.

When the plane landed in Paris, a United flight attendant escorted Sophie through passport control and customs, and then delivered her to her grandmother, who showed proper identification and signed a release.

Like hundreds of thousands of other children every year, Sophie flew successfully as a "UM"—airline jargon for "unaccompanied minor."

Exact figures are hard to come by, but United estimates it will carry more than 100,000 unaccompanied minors in 2001. Continental says its figure will be closer to 175,000. Delta's estimate fits somewhere in the middle. Those official numbers appear low. According to the Air Transport Association, the real numbers are increasing almost exponentially. One estimate says that 22,000 UMs take to the skies *every day*.

Why are kids becoming frequent flyers? One big reason is the increase in divorced couples and single-parent families, with each parent living in a different city. "We had one kid check in the other day for a flight to Newark," a Continental agent told me. "And his mother gave us his Gold Elite frequent flyer card. We thought it was a joke until we pulled his records. Sure enough, he was commuting twice a month to see his father."

During the summer months or other holiday periods, there can be as many as thirty unaccompanied children on a plane. In general, they pay full fare and are very well behaved.

Does this make the airlines willing baby-sitters?

Hardly.

The airlines take seriously, but often inflexibly, their responsibility for transporting minors . The airlines' contractual concerns are to fly a child and deliver him or her to a responsible adult who will be meeting the flight at its destination.

No special airline programs or special services are offered for such children, although—as with adult passengers—the efforts of individual crew members and flight attendants can often make the difference between a terrible flight and a great one.

These are the industry's rules:

- No airline will accept an unaccompanied child under age five years.
- Children between ages five and seven years will generally be accepted on nonstop flights.
- Children between ages eight and eleven years will generally be accepted on connecting as well as nonstop flights.
- Most airlines charge between $25 and $30 to escort a child from an arrival gate to a gate for a connecting flight. (More about these costs later.)

Parents can and should do a number of things to help their unaccompanied children get from point A to point B safely and with a minimum of hassles. The preparation is critical. Try to explain to your child what to expect on a flight—what he or she might see and hear (engine noise, landing gear sounds, and so on).

Pack some important extra things. For starters, your child should be carrying cards that clearly show his or her name, home address, phone number, and destination, and the phone number and name of the person meeting him or her. If possible, include a photo of the person who will meet the child. Some parents make a special zippered pocket in their child's jacket to carry a passport, emergency money, and a plastic-coated ID card full of information.

A child's carry-on bags are critical. Fill at least one bag with small toys, crayons, snacks (including small fruit-juice cartons, and granola bars). Depending on the child's age, include an important travel companion: a favorite toy bear or other animal, or a favorite pillow.

Just as important, instruct your child on some of the things adults take for granted, like how to make a collect phone call. Tuck in a phone card (after teaching how to use it), a packet of change, and some small denomination bills.

Nonstop flights are much better (and less expensive) than flights that lead to connections, but that cost keeps going up. In 1998, Northwest and Delta doubled their fees for escorting unaccompanied children to connecting flights. They now charge $30 per child for care and attention on nonstop flights, and $60 for kids who are flying alone and must make a connection with another flight.

The airlines earn a lot of money for simply assigning one of their flight attendants to do a hand-off—walk a child from one gate to another, and transfer responsibility to an attendant there. When American changed its fees for UMs from $30 each way to $60 each way, regardless of connections, the airline realized an annual net revenue increase of more than $767,000!

There is no federal mandate for airborne staffing or for increasing the number of flight attendants based on the number of UMs on each flight.

As a result, on a Saturday flight crammed with kids, harried flight attendants may be unable to serve the adult passengers properly or to supervise the younger ones (or those ACTING like children).

Some other advice: After you put your child on a plane, don't leave the airport. Stay at the terminal and make sure the plane leaves not only the gate but the airport.

People waiting to meet children flying alone should not assume that the airline staff (on a domestic flight) will escort the child through the terminal. Meet the arriving flight *at the gate,* and bring proper identification.

If you're a single parent sending an unaccompanied minor to Canada, Central America, or South America, you must produce a notarized letter of permission from the other parent. (Some countries require such a letter from *both* parents.) Always check, ahead of time, what the rules are.

Apply to your child's journey the same basic common sense you would apply to your own. Especially if a connecting flight is involved, DO NOT book the last outbound flight of the day to that connecting city. Your child then runs the risk of having to stay overnight in a strange city (hopefully, with airline supervision) if the original flight is delayed or the connecting flight is canceled.

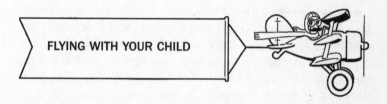

FLYING WITH YOUR CHILD

This situation poses other challenges, not the least of which is safety, especially if you're flying with a child under age two years.

Some readers may remember the tragedy of United Airlines Flight 232, which made an emergency landing in Sioux City, Iowa, in July 1989.

It was a full DC-10 flight. On board were many parents traveling with their young children. A number of the children were under the age of two years.

Think about this: The FAA requires every airline to properly stow all luggage, and to properly lock and restrain beverage carts and other items before takeoff and landing. But, ridiculously, federal law allows parents to fly with their under-twos on their laps and does not require them to purchase a seat and restrain their child.

In the event of a crash or hard landing, beverage carts stand a better chance than those children.

In the Sioux City incident, the plane hit the runway at an excessive speed—a high-G, extremely hard landing. And that's when the inflexible laws of physics took over. It was physically impossible for any of those parents to maintain their grasp on their children.

Many kids became instant missiles. Later, rescue workers found some in overhead compartments, One out of four children aboard died because they were not properly restrained, but many of their parents DID survive.

In the wake of that crash, the U.S. National Transportation Safety Board (NTSB) investigated, and thoroughly researched, the G-forces at work on the doomed DC-10.

The investigation came to a conclusion—and a recommendation the NTSB had made to the FAA after other incidents. The board's "urgent" safety recommendation was: The FAA should require airlines to provide approved high-G safety seats for children under the age of two years.

This wasn't the only time the NTSB looked into the child-restraint issue.

On January 25, 1990, an Avianca 707 crashed off Long Island, after it ran out of fuel. Seventy-three of the 159 people on board survived. The NTSB concluded that, had the one child aboard been in a car seat, it would have survived.

Even when parents want to be responsible, there is confusion and often conflict in the cabin. Since 1982, the FAA has required airlines to let parents bring child seats aboard aircraft, but passengers have complained about conflicts with flight attendants and have reported that some reservation agents dissuaded passengers from bringing car seats on flights.

When I called several airlines to see what they would tell me, I was never dissuaded from bringing a child safety seat aboard because of inconvenience. However, when asked, no representative would say which was safer for a child: lap traveling or traveling in a car seat.

But the NTSB was quite specific. After it evaluated its own tests, it urgently recommended to the FAA:

- For children under twenty pounds, a rear-facing restraint seat should be provided;
- For children twenty to forty pounds, a forward-facing restraint seat was necessary;
- For children above forty pounds, a regular belted airline seat was advised.

Under the current procedures, whenever the NTSB makes a safety recommendation, the FAA has ninety days in which to respond. In this case, on the eve of the ninetieth day, the FAA responded with a technically acceptable statement: It would "study" the issue.

The FAA did, in fact, study the use of restraint systems and seats, and other contraptions for use on commercial aircraft. It's study, remarkably similar in approach and technique to the NTSB investigation, used baby crash-test dummies in simulated 16 G survivable crashes.

Not surprisingly, the FAA reached the same conclusion as the NTSB: Holding a small child in one's lap is an invitation to tragedy, in the event of an emergency. Belting a small child into a regular airline seat would also be useless.

That's the good news.

Here's the bad news. Since it was mandated into existence by an act of Congress in 1935, the FAA has always been troubled by its schizophrenic and impossible dual mission: (1) to enact and enforce airline safety, and (2) to promote the business of aviation. The two goals don't mix, and when they collide, the FAA has historically opted to act in the best interests of cost benefit or economic impact, which are lobbied hard by the airlines. There are countless stories of absolutely obvious and much-needed safety fixes the FAA has chosen not to order, because of their projected cost to the airlines.

The child safety seat issue was no exception.

After doing its own research, the FAA was forced to conclude that the NTSB was right. These seats were needed.

So far so good. But then came one of the lamest reasons ever given for not forcing the airlines to provide these seats for small passengers. The FAA, while announcing that it supported the idea of effective restraint systems, refused to make them mandatory. Why?

(Better fasten your seat belt, so to speak.) The FAA contended that if the federal government required the airlines to provide these seats for young children, the airlines would simply pass those additional costs on to passengers, in the form of higher airfares. The resulting boost in ticket costs would have an undesirable effect: Many people who would otherwise fly would drive instead, and automobile fatalities would be higher.

I'm serious! The FAA actually said this with a straight face. The agency was more concerned with highway safety (clearly not its area of responsibility) than with air safety!

And nothing much has changed, at least on the federal level.

One airline, realizing the importance of the issue, tried to find a middle ground. In 1997, American Airlines announced that although it would not provide these seats, any parent who brought on an FAA-approved seat would be charged a half fare to belt that seat onto the regular airline seat.

How popular is this idea? In one eight-month period, one airline sold 4,400 discounted child-fare seats.

Later, in federal hearings on the issue, FAA Administrator Jane Garvey said the agency was ". . . committed to two things—mandating the use of child restraint systems in aircraft and assuring that children are accorded the same level of safety in aircraft as are adults."

"The FAA goal," she testified, "is getting a child restraint system designed so that it is safe in automobiles and safe in aircraft."

But there ARE seats on the market today that fit the dual requirements. Be aware also that *belt positioning booster seats* don't work and have been banned since 1996.

They are just like booster seats in a restaurant, but the seat belt goes through the bottom and the booster's own padded safety belt goes across the child's lap. These seats are not allowed because airplane seats, unlike automobile seats, are designed to collapse forward. If a crash were to occur, a child in one of these seats would be crushed.

The Sioux City crash was only one of many incidents. In 1994, during a DC-9 accident near Charlotte/Douglas International Airport, thirty-seven people were killed, including a nine-month-old in-lap infant who was held by her mother in the last row of the cabin. The child's mother was unable to hold onto the child during the impact sequence, and the baby died of massive head injuries. The mother survived with fractures to her elbow and arm.

Again, the NTSB issued two safety recommendations to the FAA, urging it (1) to require that all infants and small children be restrained in a manner appropriate to their size, and (2) to develop standards for forward-facing, integrated child safety seats for transport category aircraft.

Again the FAA did nothing, despite additional hard evidence gleaned from the NTSB's investigations of accidents in which child restraint system (CRS) seats were in use and provided protection to children, particularly protection against debris. A family that used a CRS was seated in a row directly behind a row in which two passengers sustained fatal injuries. According to the parents, the CRS protected their daughter from being injured.

Until the FAA acts with stronger resolve, the real responsibility for protecting children on flights is, pun intended, in parents' laps.

Here are the current airline rules:

- A child (under twenty-four months) can sit on a parent's lap for no extra charge. Or, if a parent prefers to bring the child's car seat to the aircraft, the seat next to the parent can be purchased for 50 percent of the regular price.
- After the child has passed twenty-four months, a full fare seat must be purchased.

Continental allows you to bring a car seat down to the plane, even if you have not purchased a seat for it. If the flight is underbooked and there is an empty seat next to you, they will let you use it for free. If there are no empty seats, they will check your car seat for free. They will also allow you to place the car seat in the overhead bin if there is space and if the dimensions of the seat are less than forty-five cubic inches.

TWA has the same policy as Continental but the dimensions of the seat must be: twenty-four inches long, ten inches wide, and sixteen inches high. (This is VERY small!)

Also, the seat must have an FAA approval sticker on it.

United has the same policy as Continental, but the seat is not allowed to be placed in the overhead bins if there is no extra seat.

For a trip that will include a small child, plan in advance. Always ask the airline about its approved seat policy.

Find out the real cost of that seat on the plane, or the airline's empty-seat policy.

Don't arrive at the airport an hour before takeoff and expect that you can (1) bring aboard a child safety seat and (2) have an empty seat for it. Plan ahead!

When you call and indicate that you will be traveling with a small child, ask about all the requirements the airline has for the seat. Ask about the size, measurement, and weight of the car seat, the direction it must face, the allowable weight of the child, and whether it is necessary to buy a seat.

Some people mistakenly believe that if they show up at the airport and there are empty seats, they can have one for free for their child's safety seat. This is not always true. Call the airlines and ask about empty-seat policies ahead of time. Remember, if you don't purchase a ticket ahead of time and the flight is fully booked, you may have to hold your baby on your lap and have your car seat checked at the gate.

FLYING WITH OLDER KIDS

Ask any parent and you're likely to get the same answer: The airlines couldn't care less about kids. From the counter agents to the gate agents to the flight attendants, it's getting a little ugly up there.

Why? The bottom line is: Kids, who don't typically fly first class or business class, aren't big money makers. Child passengers account for as little as 5 to 6 percent of an airline's revenue.

Yet, if you look at the sheer numbers, children should be given proper recognition.

The number of children flying is growing. Children under age eighteen years accompanied adults on more than

26 million air trips in 1998, according to the Travel Industry Association of America. That figure was up 30 percent from just two years earlier. A growing number of children of divorced parents are taking to the skies to see parents and family in far-off locales.

Discount air fares and the growing number of unaccompanied minors have combined to make the flying environment less than friendly.

Ironically, many of these unaccompanied minors are members of frequent flyer programs and have substantially more mileage than some adult passengers.

With the skies getting more crowded, the airlines are cutting down on preboarding or more considerate seating for kids. Once in their seats, children face another problem: inflight entertainment for kids is virtually nonexistent on longer domestic flights.

Some airlines are more kid-friendly than others. For starters, U.S. and foreign airlines treat children differently.

Overseas, Virgin Atlantic and British Airways have excellent special child-safety seats; Swissair is especially kid-friendly. British Airways has a toy chest in its economy sections. Virgin has seatback videos with kid channels. El Al offers both an in-seat TV channel for kids and a special family-seating section.

Singapore Airlines trains its flight attendants in often forgotten arts: changing diapers; preparing formula, milk, and baby meals; sterilizing bottles; and burping a baby. Each aircraft is stocked with diapers, bibs, feeding bottles, milk powder, and baby wipes.

Swissair offers preboarding for families with children. A changing table is in every aircraft, along with children's meals and (on long-haul flights) baby food.

Zurich airport has a LEGO play area, playrooms, and nursery services.

The domestic airlines most friendly to kids are Southwest, Alaska Airlines, Midwest Express, and Air Canada.

For unaccompanied minors, Delta has special supervised play areas called Dusty's Dens at the Atlanta airport, but these are only open seasonally and aren't well publicized. Similarly, Northwest has three Kids' Clubs—in Minneapolis, Detroit, and Memphis. Unaccompanied minors can play games, rest, and have a bite to eat—all under supervision.

The bigger U.S. airlines don't score high marks with parents for their treatment of kids. What can parents do? Is there a way to lessen the hassle?

For starters, plan ahead and choose your flights wisely. Adopt my earlier advice about not booking the last flight of the day, especially if you have to make flight connections en route.

Don't book "direct" flights unless there is no alternative. "Direct" does not mean nonstop; it means the plane will make a stop. When you're on a flight that stops, you increase your chances of a weather- or air traffic-related delay. You want nonstop.

Don't fly on business flights early in the morning. The best times to travel are on a Tuesday or a Wednesday, around noon. The flights aren't as crowded.

Night flights tend to have fewer delays. Some families like to fly at night so their children can sleep, but I don't recommend it. Just because kids *can* sleep doesn't mean they will, and nothing is worse than a red-eye with screaming, wide-awake children aboard.

Choose a good seat. On some planes, a window seat *behind* the exit row has extra room. (I'm not talking about the exit row; children aren't allowed to sit in that row.) Other passengers will thank you if you choose the bulkhead seat. Why? When (not If) your child decides to kick, there's no passenger seated in front of you. Kicking the bulkhead goes unnoticed.

On longer international flights, see whether the bulkheads feature fold-down bassinets that can be used in flight. Sit near the front, close to the lavatory.

Many new or refurbished aircraft have incorporated fold-down changing tables in at least one bathroom on board. A few airlines actually provide extra diapers.

Learn how to stay together. One of the biggest problems these days is that, because of increased passenger loads, a lot of airlines separate families on planes and don't seem to care. If this happens, don't expect gate agents to help you. Your best weapon here might surprise you. I know of one parent who uses a surefire tactic when all else fails and the airline seats her away from her kids. She buys her kids ice cream cones with not one but two scoops. No napkins. As soon as her kids sit down, it's only a matter of seconds before the people sitting next to them volunteer to switch places and allow their mother to sit with them.

Get help to the gate. Can you ask the airline to help you get your child or children from the curb to the gate? Not really. At certain airports, like Chicago's O'Hare and Dallas-Fort Worth, airlines do provide motorized carts for special-assistance cases. That's the good news. The bad news is that these carts are not dependable.

Instead, to get you and your kids and your stuff to the gate in one piece, check in at the curb and tip the skycap more to take you directly to the gate. It's $10 well invested. You cannot depend on any airline personnel to escort you through the airport or to the gate, but skycaps can and will. (Alexander Hamilton talks.)

Get to the gate early, then seek out a supervisor. Remember, there may not be a preboarding announcement anymore, but that doesn't mean the airline won't preboard you if you ask nicely. My last-resort advice (the airlines will love this) is: If, for any reason, you can't preboard with your child, then don't board with the masses either. Instead, wait and board last. Why? You stand a better chance that the airline will realize its mistake and will get you a better seat. Standing in a long boarding line with a small child makes things worse for everyone.

Bring food and games. Never depend on an airline to provide children's meals, even if they're offered. (United offers a McDonald's Happy Meal. But, in the air, the only people I've seen happy to eat one have been the adults!) Instead, bring snacks your child will like—especially snacks that aren't messy. Also bring boxed fruit juices. You can't depend on the flight attendant to make more than two beverage-cart runs during any flight.

Bring games your child likes to play, books, coloring books, activity books, crayons, and that favorite pillow. Extra snacks and activities will be worth their weight in gold in case of unforeseeable delays.

Additional items: Diapers, wipes, formula, and snacks for a full day and then some. Be prepared for extra delays or lost luggage.

Bring one or two changes of clothing for your child and yourself.

Finally, take care of your kids' ears. Children's ears are more sensitive than adults' ears to the changes in air pressure on takeoffs and landings. Older kids can chew gum; younger children can drink a juice box or suck on a bottle.

Taking an antihistamine the day before will clean out the ears. Parents who have a child with ear problems should ask a pediatrician for medication before the flight.

FLYING WITH THE OTHER IMPORTANT MEMBERS OF YOUR FAMILY

Some readers may have already heard this story.

A woman gets off her flight in Los Angeles and goes to the baggage claim area to get her bags, as well as to claim the kennel holding her dog that was loaded into the cargo compartment.

But when airline baggage handlers remove the kennel from the aircraft, they notice that the dog is dead. They panic and go to an animal shelter in hopes of finding a look-alike dog. They present the woman with the living dog, in the original kennel.

She is shocked when she looks inside. "That's not my dog," she exclaims. "My dog is dead. I was bringing it home for burial."

That story is in the urban legend hall of fame.

But among real stories involving airlines' transport of pets, there are many candidates for the hall of shame.

How safe is it to bring your dog or cat on a flight?

According to the Air Transport Association, 99 percent of the 500,000 dogs and cats the airlines handle each year reach their destination in good health and without problems.

That figure sounds impressive, but it means that approximately 5,000 animals *don't* arrive safely.

Transportation of live animals is not regulated by the Federal Aviation Administration. The U.S. Department of Agriculture (USDA) is in charge.

The USDA has levied some heavy fines on airlines that have acted negligently when transporting animals. In 1990,

Delta was fined $140,000 when thirty-two puppies, on a flight from St. Louis to Salt Lake City, died from lack of oxygen. A few years later, the USDA fined TWA for improper handling of live animals.

Some transport problems occur because of aircraft design. Newer planes have pressurized and heated baggage compartments, but older aircraft lack ventilation.

Worse is the lack of proper education among passengers and airline workers. If you're shipping your pet in cargo, call the airline first to learn its specific requirements. Choose an airline-approved shipping kennel that is the right size for your pet, and have your dog's kennel properly tagged.

Ask about health or immunization requirements for your pet. England, for example, requires incoming dogs to be quarantined. So does Hawaii.

How old is your pet? It must be at least 8 weeks old by flight time.

Most likely, you will need to buy an approved carrier/kennel for your dog or cat, but not every airline sells USDA-approved kennels. The design, materials, construction and ventilation requirements are mandated by law. The kennel you buy should have enough room for your animal to stand up, adjust its position, and turn around.

Your pet will probably have to fly in the cargo hold. If its kennel is small enough to fit under the seat in front of you, the airline will allow you to take the animal on board, but two conditions apply:

1. Only one pet is allowed per cabin on any flight. On flights that have first, business, and coach class, three pets may travel in the cabin. Southwest flights, which are all coach, allow only one pet.
2. You are not allowed to take your animal for a walk. Even opening the kennel is a big no-no.

But people cheat all the time.

The biggest offenders of these two rules? People with small dogs or cats. They literally pack their tiny pets inside their carry-on bags. If the pet goes unnoticed, nothing happens. But, more often than not, the owners can't resist taking their animals out, once the plane is airborne.

Some flight attendants, pet lovers themselves, look the other way. Others tend to enforce the rules.

No one was looking the other way on USAir Flight 107, a 757 flight from Philadelphia to Seattle.

In this funny, somewhat bizarre story, the animal that DID make it into the passenger section was much bigger than ANY standard kennel.

For those of you who have always wanted to know whether pigs can fly, the answer is: Apparently they can. Just ask the passengers on that USAir flight.

How—and why—the airline allowed a 300-pound pig to fly first class on this plane is nothing short of astounding.

Apparently, the owners received permission from the airline to bring the porker on board, by producing a doctor's note claiming that the pig was a "service animal"—like a seeing-eye dog.

According to passengers and flight attendants, the crew first tried to stow the pig in the rear of the aircraft, but it blocked an emergency exit. They then chose to wedge the animal between seats 1A and 1C in the first-class section.

The good news: The animal was well behaved during most of the six-hour flight, It slept most of the way. But when the plane landed, the pig not only woke up, it GOT up, and ran wild through the plane as the 757 taxied to the terminal.

It relieved itself as it snorted down the single aisle of the plane. Then it tried to get into the cockpit. Finally, it ran into a galley.

USAir insisted this was a mistake and would not happen again.

Within days of the incident, the FAA made a startling announcement. It ruled that the pig complied with a Department of Transportation policy that allows individuals with a disability to travel with their "service animals."

Excepting that large pig, and turning to a more serious concern, flying is stressful enough for humans, but animals can get really hyper. Some pet owners sedate their dog or cat, but most airlines and veterinarians discourage this practice because the effects of such medications at high altitudes cannot be accurately predicted. Also, a sedated animal may not be able to properly react to the kennel's movements and could get injured.

Law requires that pets be offered food and water within four hours before check-in, but don't overfeed your pet. Make sure you attach a food dish and a water dish to the inside of the kennel. The dishes should be accessible from the outside without having to open the door. To avoid spilling water, just before the animal is loaded, drop ice cubes into the water dish.

Ask if you can watch your pet being loaded. Some airlines allow this.

Next comes some paperwork.

Airlines require you to get a health certificate from a veterinarian within seven to ten days of your flight.

Book your flight well in advance for yourself and your pet. Try, if possible, to book nonstop, or at least direct, flights.

Problems can occur on connecting flights. Animals might be left exposed on the tarmac in extreme weather conditions. (There are rules regarding the temperature at transfer airports—it must be between 10 and 85 degrees

Fahrenheit. USDA guidelines recommend between 45 and 84 degrees.)

What if you discover a problem with your pet after the flight lands?

Call a vet immediately and make sure someone from the airline witnesses the problem.

Remember, the airlines take a tough position regarding an injury or a death of someone's pet. They will only compensate the owner up to a maximum liability of $1,250 (the amount award for damaged or lost luggage). The USDA levies fines, but it doesn't control compensation from an airline to a bereaved passenger.

In a recent court case, American Airlines argued that it was only responsible for that luggage limit. A higher court overruled the decision and said that the passenger—whose dog baked to death at 140 degrees in an American cargo hold—could sue for pain, suffering, and inducement to fraud. The judgment against American was $15,000, opening the door a little wider for passengers to seek higher compensation in cases like this.

As a pet owner, watch out for your furry family member to the best of your ability.

Your last and best hope: that flight attendants, baggage loaders, and airline captains happen to be pet lovers themselves.

Let's hear it for the captain of United Airlines Flight 231, flying from Washington's Dulles Airport to San José, California. Midway in the nearly five-hour trip, an alert United bag loader back in Washington noticed that "Dakota," an African barkless hunting dog, had been improperly loaded into the wrong cargo hold of the Airbus 320. The pilot was alerted by radio, and immediately made the decision to divert to Denver.

The dog survived. The captain was hailed as a hero. Oh yes, the movie shown on the flight was *My Dog Skip*.

But the United story is more than overshadowed by some sadder ones.

A cat stuck in the cargo hold of an American flight suffered a heart attack and stress. Then there was the story of Boris and Delta Airlines. Boris flew from Fort Lauderdale, Florida to New York's LaGuardia, but when its owner went to the baggage depot to get the kennel, all Delta employees could show her was a bloody, empty crate. They told her that Boris had escaped and was running around the runways.

Nearly seven weeks later, Boris was found, suffering from serious injuries to his face, frostbite, dehydration, malnutrition, and infection. But despite the owner's efforts to receive some amount of compensation to cover veterinary bills, the airline reimbursed her only the cost of the dog's airfare and of the crate itself.

This one incident resulted in U.S. Senator Frank Lautenberg's introduction of the Safe Air Travel for Animals Act.

And that proposed legislation, coupled with a dramatic increase in litigation against airlines for mishandling or killing pets, stirred the airlines to impose even stricter rules (to limit their liability) for accepting pets for travel.

For the moment, the airlines are paying strict attention to the thermometer. Depending on the temperatures in both passengers' originating and destination cities, the airline may refuse to carry a pet because of extremes of either heat or cold.

Every airline has different criteria for their live-animal moratorium, so if you plan a trip with a pet, call and pin them down on exact temperature ranges. If the temperature in either city, during summer or winter months, is within five degrees of the limits, be prepared to fly without your pet.

Finally, deal with a little reality yourself. Maybe your dog or cat HATES to fly. Look for a reliable pet sitter or boarding kennel.

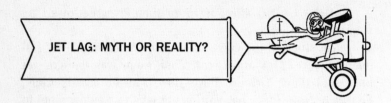

JET LAG: MYTH OR REALITY?

Most of my friends are worried about—some are even obsessed with—the prospect and the effects of jet lag.

How far does that worry extend?

Just ask Saudi Arabian Prince Alwaleed Bin Talal Bin Abulaziz Alsaud. When the prince, with his wife, two children, and a seventeen-person entourage, arrived for an eight-day vacation in South Carolina, he decreed that he didn't want to be affected by jet lag. He had a Hilton hotel install $4,000 worth of lights and a volleyball court so that he and his family could maintain their natural body clocks and remain on local Riyadh time. Not only was there a lot of midnight volleyball and swimming, but lunch was served each morning at 2:00 A.M.

Did it work? He never tried it again.

What about special diets, pills, exercise, or eating regimens?

I have to admit that the ONLY time I ever suffered jet lag was when I actually TRIED one of these "remedies."

Millions of travelers complain about it, and very few claim to have conquered it. Jet lag is not a lot of fun.

A flight from Sydney, Australia, to New York, including stopovers, can easily run twenty-four hours door to door.

But whether you're on a marathon flight to or from Australia, or the shuttle from Boston to Washington, DC, is jet lag your constant travel companion?

Can you prevent it? Can you treat it? Or is it an unavoidable by-product of jet flight?

For some travelers, that may be a rhetorical question.

First, a little history.

Jet lag—some researchers call it "circadian disynchronism"—has certainly had an effect on world history. If you believe such excuses, when diver Greg Louganis hit his head on the ten-meter platform during Olympic trials, he claimed to be suffering from jet lag.

During his presidency, Ronald Reagan's trips to world summits were carefully structured around worries that the effects of jet lag might impinge on the crucial decisions he would have to make.

Some diplomats have even cited jet lag as causing some of their negotiating mistakes. Before he died, former Secretary of State John Foster Dulles actually blamed some of his questionable decisions on jet lag.

Enough about blame or denial. What really constitutes jet lag? Is it, as I sometimes think, merely a state of mind?

Indeed, jet lag is a recognized medical malaise, a disruption of what scientists call the circadian rhythms—the daily individual cycle of sleep and wakefulness. For every continent that you hop, you upset these rhythms.

And for every time zone that you cross, some researchers say it takes one day to adjust your body. Travelers seem to do better flying west. The body has an easier time setting its clock back.

You need to worry about your internal body alarm clock. When you travel three hours or more, your internal alarm clock goes off three hours earlier (or later) than expected. Synchronization among all of the body's rhythms is lost. Instead of hormone levels dropping while body temperature is rising, both may be increasing. And that's when jet lag kicks in.

There's a whole cottage industry of jet lag diets and computer-generated jet lag schedule programs. A number of airlines, including British Airways and Air New Zealand, offer special aromatherapy kits to passengers, or provide treatments once they land.

But a number of researchers and veteran travelers, myself included, believe that what you do before you land makes the real difference.

Doctors have studied the body's internal clock that keeps and controls the body's rhythmic fluctuations, body strength, hormone levels, alertness, sleep, and wakefulness. And they continue to look at how we reset our clock each day with some external cues called *zeitgebers.*

What's a *zeitgeber?* It's a German term for "time giver." Things like light (vs. darkness), social activity, alarm clocks, and caffeine help us reset our body's clock every day.

But rapid time-zone crossings disrupt the usual fit between physiological rhythms and their *zeitgebers.*

Let's start with what you do before you board your flight.

One suggestion that may have merit: Try to hit your body with as many external cues as possible. Stay on the local time of your destination. If it's breakfast time there, have breakfast.

Let's say you're going to England and you're scheduled to arrive the next day at 6:00 A.M. Try to sleep as soon as you get on the plane.

(If I get on a plane and it's midnight at my destination, I pay attention to that. If they serve dinner right after takeoff and I eat, then my body will think it's 8:00 P.M. again. What you do on a plane should mimic what people are doing at your destination.)

Avoid airline food. Most of us eat it not because we're hungry, but because we're bored. The moisture problem, the reheating, and other fun things about airline food contribute to creating a digestion problem for many passengers. I can think of few things more conducive to jet lag than to eat reheated, dry food at high altitude.

When you're on the plane, walk around. (However, if you feel like sleeping, sleep; if you want to watch the movie, watch the movie.)

You already know the drill: bottled water, no alcohol.

Yes, I know the argument: everyone's metabolism is different, and everyone processes alcohol at varying levels of effect. Alcohol is still not a good idea.

OK, so far so good. What should you do at your destination?

This key is the toughest one of all. No matter where you're going, and no matter what time you get there, stay up until at least 11:00 P.M. local time. Needless to say, you will be invariably confronted with an extremely strong urge to take a nap around 3:00 P.M. DON'T DO IT! If you do, you will forget your name, where you are, and why you're even there, for at least two days. My advice: Get up, walk around, get some air, shoot some hoops, do anything except succumb to that powerful temptation to take a nap.

The result? If you can stay up until 11:00 P.M. that night, you'll be well on your way to cycling. You won't sleep your full, normal sleep (about five hours), but you will cycle the next night. Follow this timetable when you arrive at your destination, and again when you return home. It works in both directions.

Even as I advise all this, I acknowledge that everyone is different and is affected, to varying degrees, by the jet flight experience.

Never take any jet lag medication without consulting your doctor. (Some travelers will take, for example, melatonin, and then have wine with their dinner at 35,000 feet. That's nuts!)

Some readers may know that the Sydney-to-Los Angeles flight seems interminable, but it's not the longest. New

York-to-Johannesburg and Los Angeles-to-Melbourne are longer flights. The longest is United Airlines Flight 821, a nonstop service between New York JFK and Hong Kong. At 7,339 nautical miles, United's Flight 821 is the longest nonstop passenger service in the world.

Flight 821 departs JFK daily at 10:30 A.M. and arrives in Hong Kong at 2:10 P.M. (local time) the following day. What time a passenger's body and mind arrive may be a whole different story.

4

On the Ground

SURVIVING THE CHALLENGE OF TAXIS, HOTELS, BELLHOPS, AND THE MINIBUS

I'm going to make a dangerous assumption here: Your flight landed, and you AND your luggage were on the SAME plane.

The next hurdle: the inevitable checked baggage axiom. You checked two bags, simultaneously, for your flight. When you land, the first bag off the plane and onto the carousel will be one of yours. The other one will come LAST.

Why waste your time waiting at the carousel—or waste your money renting a baggage cart? Instead, save time AND money. When you come from the plane, go BEYOND the baggage claim area to the arrivals area at the curb. You'll find there all the discarded rental baggage carts from the previous flight.

In the time it takes you to simply walk out and get a cart, your bags should be waiting for you.

Next, push the cart and your bags to the nearest elevator and head upstairs to the departures area, where it will be less crowded and your friends and/or family can meet you.

Suppose there's no one to meet you and you have to take a cab instead.

At some airports (New York's LaGuardia, Washington's Reagan, Las Vegas) forget the baggage cart (rented or "found") and hire a skycap. Why? The skycaps get a special courtesy at these airports and get to jump the cab line. Tip accordingly; it's worth it.

THE RIDE FROM THE AIRPORT

If you're like me, you want to get from your plane to a taxi in a minimum amount of time.

There are no guarantees that a cab will be waiting, and a huge line of people may be ahead of you.

Here's an idea. Call 1-800-TAXICAB. This clearinghouse will connect you immediately with local cab companies in your destination city.

In effect, you're preordering a cab—booking it like a limo, but at a fraction of the cost.

If you're short on cash, ask which cab companies accept credit cards. Believe me, you'll save time upon your arrival.

What about the rates?

There are only flat-rate cab-ride fares in a few U.S. cities, and, in some cities, they only apply to certain airports. In New York, the flat-rate fare is $30, plus tolls and tip, but that fare only applies FROM JFK, not in the other direction.

It is important—some would say *imperative*—the minute you get into a cab, write down the cab number. Why? You've just come off a long flight and you're not running on all cylinders. You may forget things when you leave the cab—your cell phone, your pocket organizer, or even one of your carry-on bags. Knowing the cab's number may help toward retrieving a lost item.

Also, are you staying in your destination city more than one day?

Tell the driver to make a stop en route. Go to a supermarket or a deli; have the cab wait for you. Even with the meter running, this is a cost-effective decision. Buy some items that you would like to drink and eat while you're in your hotel room.

Why? You are preparing for your inevitable confrontation with the hotel mini bar. (More on that later.)

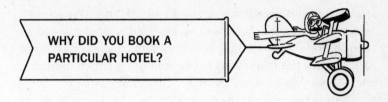

WHY DID YOU BOOK A
PARTICULAR HOTEL?

When you're booking a hotel room, clarity means everything. Why did you choose a particular hotel? An advertisement? Price? Word of mouth? A guide book?

And what do you hope to do at this hotel? Is this a business trip and you only need a room? Is it a vacation? A combination of both reasons to travel?

What price are you willing to pay, and for what
amenities?

Q: What's a four-star hotel? A three-star hotel?

A: No one really knows.

I remember one London hotel's boast that it was the
city's only five-star hotel! How did that happen? The hotel
gave the stars to itself!

In many countries, stars are given to hotels by individual
municipal governments. The stars are based only on the
rates the hotel charges, not on any quality or service criteria.

But the star search continues. Mobil Guides award stars.
AAA gives out diamonds in its rating system of guide books.

Hotels take these awards seriously. I don't.

A top rating in a Mobil Guide supposedly can boost a
hotel's business 20 percent.

Why am I not a fan? Because of the criteria used.

If a guide book gives a hotel five stars because it has a
golf course, what possible use is that to me if I don't play
golf?

I'm more interested in the water pressure in the shower;
how the phones work; Internet access; how fast the valet

parking unit delivers my car; and whether there are enough pillows on the bed. I care less about "fine dining" at hotels. I care more about whether room service can take my order and deliver the food to my room in less than thirty minutes. And there you have my "star" or "diamond" list.

Guide books and ratings have another problem. They are subjective, and I have a healthy cynicism toward any words that end with "st."

I worry when a hotel is voted "greatest," or "best," or "most" or "finest." You get the picture.

Develop your own criteria for what makes a hotel worthy of your business.

For example, what makes a hotel a resort—a swimming pool? Hardly.

What defines a "health club" or a "spa"? One treatment room and an old VHS Jane Fonda workout tape do not make a hotel a spa.

Always ask ahead, especially when you're traveling with your kids.

Virtually every hotel boasts that it has a great children's program. But knocking out the walls between two guest rooms, installing some large card tables, crayons, and LEGOS does not create a great kids' program.

For many years, with the exception of the legendary Eloise at the Plaza Hotel in New York, kids were either ignored or frowned upon at most hotels. They were considered an annoying encumbrance to hotel staff and other guests. Then, a few years ago, a few hotels finally figured out a simple but powerful concept: If you make your property kid-friendly and the kids like it, they're going to bring their parents.

There was another small incentive: the numbers. Children make more than 150 million trips a year, and those trips convert to serious money. So, with great fanfare, many hotels announced they were suddenly opening their doors to kids and offering special children's programs and activities. But, more often than not, the programs were disappointing. Too many hotels converted one or two guest or meeting rooms, set up a few table-and-chairs units, added a few dozen crayons, stacked some cartoon videos on a TV set, and called the offering a children's program."

But some other hotels quietly created comprehensive, properly supervised, and imaginative children's programs that were innovative, responsible, and safe. Wise hotels followed suit. Today, most hotels at least claim to offer a children's program; in fact, the statistics might surprise you. And the demand for such programs has gone beyond just leisure and vacation travelers.

A recent survey commissioned by Sheraton Hotels confirmed that, among business travelers, kids have a lot more to say than one might imagine or admit.

Of the parents polled, 67 percent said they have refused to go on a particular business trip because it conflicted with their children's activities. And 41 percent said they would cut a trip short because of a child's birthday or illness. Thirty-one percent won't travel when a school function is scheduled for their children, and 5 percent would cancel a trip altogether if their children were upset because the parent was leaving.

Translation: As business-traveler parents try to preserve the delicate balance between their work and their family life, the family often hits the road. The kids get to go along.

In many of today's two-income families, executives pack up the kids as well as the briefcase. In the Sheraton study, 60 percent of parents said they have taken a child along on a business trip. (The least significant finding of the Sheraton survey was one of the most amusing. Business travelers who do not take their kids on their trips face a perennial question when they return: "What did you bring me?" Twenty-seven percent reported that they bring home a T-shirt.)

In response to the survey's information, the Sheraton chain offers a family plan. There is no charge for children (seventeen years and younger) who share a room with a parent or guardian, if the children can be accommodated with the existing furnishings. To make business travelers feel more at home, Sheraton is introducing guest rooms that are more like bedrooms at home than hotel rooms. These rooms feature cozy sleigh beds and oversize desks and work areas. The "new look" is being introduced in more than 6,000 hotel rooms as Sheraton renovates its properties in North America. Indeed, Sheraton is just one of a number of major hotel chains rushing to become kid-friendly—and safe for kids. A number of hotels are going out of their way to "childproof" their rooms—not to protect a hotel from children, but to protect children during their stay at the hotel.

At The Breakers, in Palm Beach, Florida, infants and small kids are welcomed to a childproof room that includes a step stool to help kids reach counters and sinks. Families with children under age four years are automatically eligible for childproofing. At check-in, if the names and ages of the children were not given previously, the front desk sends an electronic message to the housekeeping department. Within fifteen minutes, a housekeeping staff member comes to the room and offers to childproof it. Parents may accept or decline this complimentary service.

After the childproofing comes the fun part. The guests can choose either a rollaway bed or a Barney, Lion King, or Aladdin sleeping bag. A majority of the hotel's 569 soundproof rooms are now connected, so families can reserve up to five adjoining guest rooms. This feature gives adults more privacy while keeping the kids in close proximity. If children age seventeen years and younger stay in the same room as their parents, there is no extra charge.

At the Sonesta Beach Resort in Key Biscayne, Florida, when kids check in with their parents, they receive a certificate that invites them to visit the hotel's kids' club room and select a gift from a "treasure chest." The special amenities pack for families—delivered to guests' rooms—often makes the difference: milk and cookies served atop a Frisbee®, or a beach bucket filled with candy, juice, a beach ball, toys, and similar fun stuff.

When the hotel knows a number of children will be staying there at any one time, the staff organizes a pizza party (the kids make their own pizza) and invites all the kids staying at the resort.

Families traveling to the Boca Raton Resort and Club no longer need a van to accommodate their little ones' bring-along items, thanks to the resort's new "Boca Baby" program. The tony world-class golf and beach resort caters to a most discriminating group: babies. From a menu featuring freshly made baby food, to strollers, high chairs, and other paraphernalia available upon request, the Boca Baby program is designed exclusively for those age three years and under. Nearly 10 percent of its guests have babies, so the resort wanted to make traveling with little ones less stressful and more enjoyable for both the babies and the parents. The program was inspired by the resort's executive chef, James Reaux. He made healthy and delicious baby food for his own children and now does so for resort guests. Meals at the resort come complete with a Boca Baby bib and bottle.

But the program goes beyond recipes to more important aspects, such as child safety: As part of the program, guests can request the following items upon arrival: quality cribs with extra-firm mattresses; high chairs; baby bath amenities; child-friendly sunscreen and baby sunglasses; a hooded towel and a washcloth; a baby bathtub; age-appropriate toys; a diaper pail; instructions for reserving baby-sitters through the resort; a baby monitor (for guests staying in suites); a car seat; a stroller; a humidifier; baby spoons; pacifier/teething toys; diapers (including swim diapers) and wipes; and children's videos.

In Canada, the folks in British Columbia are actively involved in servicing the growing family travel market with an aggressive kid-friendly campaign. The program, run by Kid Friendly Services, a Vancouver company, goes beyond distribution of cute children's amenities.

"It's more important than just marketing 'Kids stay free' deals," says founder Cheryl MacKinnon. "We are encouraging airlines, hotels, car rental companies, and other attractions to consider elements like safety and accessibility. These range from colorful footstools at counters to kid-friendly play areas in info centers, family parking spots near the front door, interactive/educational games, and giveaways that invite and inspire kids to explore the destination more fully." MacKinnon also has lobbied hotels to: start emptying the mini bars and using them for storage of formula and other food for babies and young children; ensure that cribs, playpens, skycots, and high chairs meet current safety standards; and provide emergency diapers, blankets, and bottles. "It may sound silly," she says, "but as a parent who traveled with a baby, sometimes—for whatever reason—you need these things to tide you over till the next morning, when the stores open."

THE STAY

In the United States, some hotels agree that it's not silly. Radisson has developed Family Approved Hotels. Families traveling with children are offered special features, services, and amenities to enhance their stay. There are more than seventy participating hotels in the United States, Canada, the

Caribbean, Central America, and Asia. Participating hotels offer, in at least one restaurant and through room service, a children's menu featuring kids' favorite foods. Child-care services are either on-site or are made available via a list of qualified baby sitters.

Cots, cribs, and playpens are available upon request. Popular award-winning books and games for children ages three through twelve years can be checked out from a special library. A professional children's librarian from Baker & Taylor Books, the leading supplier of book and related services to more than 100,000 bookstores, schools, and libraries worldwide, recommended a balanced selection of books specifically for Radisson Hotels.

. A swimming pool is the most popular hotel feature for children, according to family travel research. Child-proofing/safety kits are available at the front desk. Families traveling with small children may use them during their stay. Family movies are available on the in-room movie system.

The Hyatt hotels also are trying to be more kid-friendly. At the Grand Hyatt San Francisco, kids can receive a Tonka toy dump truck filled with candy, fruit, and small toys, and they get to keep the truck. At The Resort at Squaw Creek, at Lake Tahoe, guests can request child seats on the Squaw Valley Shuttle, which transports guests from Reno/Lake Tahoe International Airport to the resort. Childproof safety plugs for a room's electric sockets are available for guests who request them.

The Loews hotel chain does an excellent job in catering to families with children. It starts with childproofing. Every Loews property has kits available for guests with small children. The kits include: a night light; electrical outlet covers; padding for furnishings' hard edges; a sliding-glass-door lock; and a soft water-spout cover. All kids ages ten years and under receive a complimentary "Loews Loves Kids" gift bag upon arrival. There's a discount on a children's room adjoining their parents' room. (Children ages eighteen years and under stay free when they share a room with their parents.) Guests have complimentary use of cribs, roll-away beds, and children's sheets. Restaurant menus, room service, and mini bars offer children's menus and child-friendly snacks. A "Kids' Kloset" offers games, books, car seats, strollers, night lights, potty seats, baby bathtubs, baby blankets, and electrical outlet covers for guests to use during their stay.

Can your child say "Upgrade?" If so, check into the new Loews Portofino Bay Hotel at Universal Studios Escape, in Orlando, Florida. It features a new room concept for the hotel's eighteen kids' suites: an adjoining room for children, which can be accessed only through the main room. Each of the suites is designed with childhood themes and features two single beds, a small table-and-chair set, a beanbag chair, and a separate closet with children's bathrobes and hangers.(Here's a somewhat dangerous thought: Parents also can give their children a separate room card that allows access to the room and lets them make purchases, throughout Universal Studios Escape, up to a preloaded spending limit set by the parents.)

Although U.S. hotels have clearly begun to embrace children, most foreign hotels still believe that children should be neither seen nor heard. But there are, of course, exceptions. In London, The Athenaeum Hotel and Apartments launched a children's program the summer of 2000 for children ages six to twelve years. Each child is to receive Arthurnaeum (a lovable brown bear that is the hotel's furry hospitality ambassador), a kiddies' pack containing a coloring book and crayons, a rubber duck for the bath, and a range of children's toiletries (soap, shampoo, bubble bath, talc, mini toothbrush, and toothpaste). A special children's menu has been developed in the Windsor Lounge, and room service and turndown service will include milk and cookies. The children will also receive a gift voucher to Hamley's, considered London's best-known toy store. Also, children stay free when staying with parents in one of the hotel's thirty-four one- and two-bedroom apartments.

IS THE HOTEL PET-FRIENDLY?

More and more of us travel with our pets. And more and more hotels are developing flexible policies toward allowing pets in guests' rooms.

Even if you are told a hotel is pet-friendly, always ask, ahead of your stay, whether the hotel will require a damage deposit for your animal. Also, are there special pet services? At some hotels, they range from dog walking (by hotel doormen) to wilder offerings. A hotel in Mexico has installed special exercise treadmills for dogs!

The factors that count here are not only supply and demand but also location and season. A special rate at a hotel in Hawaii during the Christmas season? Forget it. However, getting a rate in March may be easy because there are empty rooms.

You need to know how to cut a deal, either before you get there or when you arrive at the hotel. Some desk clerks will throw out a room rate just to see if it will fly; treat it like the first price quoted at the covered bazaar in Istanbul. You know the drill. After hearing the first price, you immediately shake your head and walk out of the stall. If the hotel is 50 percent full at eleven o'clock at night, and the clerk says that rooms are $159, you simply respond: "I'll give you $79 or forget the deal." For most hotels, something is always better than nothing.

What about calling ahead? If it's a convention hotel, it's the beginning of the week, and you're in New Orleans or Chicago and the town is packed, of course you're going to call the hotel before you go there. The question is: Whom do you ask to speak with? The reservations agent? No. Ask for the director of sales. You want to let him or her know you're a corporate person, not some yokel off the street. You might say: "Listen, I was going to talk to the reservations people, but I'd rather talk to you, because I'm going to be coming to Chicago quite a few times over the next several months, and I'd like to work out a rate with you."

Note: Before you contact the director of sales, *do call* the reservations desk and find out the hotel's prices, just to get a basis of comparison. Then see whether you can cut a deal with the director of sales. If so, (1) you've got a deal with someone who's highly placed in the hotel, (2) you've got a contact at the hotel, and (3) you've got a rate that's substantially below what you'd pay if you walked in off the street or telephoned for a reservation. A hotel has the same goal as an airline frequent flyer program. It wants your loyalty and your repeat business. If you can give it that loyalty, or at least a perception of it, you will get some deals.

Now that you've been clear with the hotel—and, with luck, have received clarity in return—it's equally important to know the right way to make your reservation.

The hotel business engages in the dark science of yield, aka *revenue management.* At some hotels, there may be as many as forty different rates for any one room.

How can you get the best deal? The key factors are: what number or extension you call, what day of the week and what time of day you call, how many days you are staying, and to whom you speak.

Let's start with the number that you call.

Many of us have been tempted to call a toll-free 800 number for reservations, especially when a booking is desired at any number of large-chain hotels.

It's convenient, the call is free, and you can quickly make a reservation at any of the chain's hotels, anywhere in the world.

Technically those facts are correct. Still, you should avoid toll-free 800 numbers for reservations.

A case in point. I had been invited to a wedding of a close friend in Albuquerque, New Mexico. I needed to fly in on a Friday, attend the wedding late on Saturday afternoon and the reception that evening, and fly out early on Sunday morning.

Opting for expediency, I called the toll-free number for Hilton. I asked whether I could make a reservation for a room for two nights, "at the lowest rate," for the Albuquerque Hilton.

No problem. The lowest rate they could offer me was $89 per night. Would I like to guarantee that, and hold the room via a credit card? Sure. I gave the agent my American Express card number, got my confirmation number, and, in less than four minutes, I had made the reservation.

Nine days later, I hopped on the short flight from Los Angeles to New Mexico, grabbed a cab at the Albuquerque airport, and arrived at the hotel.

Armed with my confirmation number and prepaid room reservation, I walked into the lobby and headed for the front desk.

There were two people ahead of me in line. The man directly in front of me, also there for the wedding, seemed nervous. He told me, while we waited, that he had decided at the very last minute to come to the nuptials, and didn't have a reservation. He was taking a chance, hoping there might be a room available.

I tried to act concerned, but that wasn't easy since I already had my confirmed reservation.

When it was his turn, he walled up to the front desk clerk and asked if the hotel had any rooms for that night, and, if so, what was the lowest rate?

Yes, she replied, they had rooms.

And the rate?

"Thirty-nine dollars."

What? The lowest rate was $50 *less* than I was paying?

There was only one thing to do.

When I approached the desk, I conveniently forgot to mention my earlier reservation and asked the same questions the "walk-in" had asked. Sure enough, rooms were $39.

"Fine," I said, "I'll take one, for two nights."

I whipped out my American Express card and completed the transaction for the much cheaper room.

In the end, both the hotel and American Express still charged me $89 for the room. I disputed the bill, and my claim was simple: The hotel had failed to disclose that there was, indeed, a lower rate available at the time I had made my booking. Therefore, the charge was invalid. In addition, I did not receive the service for which I had contracted—the lowest rate at the hotel. And under the terms of my credit card agreement, I was not liable to pay the charge. Finally, the proof here was easy: I DID PAY the $39 charge—for the same room—with my American Express card. American Express removed the larger charge from my bill.

The lesson here: *Never ever* call a toll-free 800 number advertised by hotel chains like Hilton, Hyatt, and Sheraton. The 800 numbers are nothing more than clearinghouses for blocks of rooms, which are put on the market at the highest rate the hotels think they can get away with.

It's almost always cheaper to spend a dollar or two on a long-distance call to an individual hotel, and negotiate your own rate. There may be thirty-five separate rates that can be used for any room—corporate rate, weekend rate, senior rate, student rate, auto club rate, and so forth. The "rack rate" is the highest possible tariff published for that room. It's what the hotels charge people who don't know any better.

If you pay the rack rate, you should be quietly taken away and put to sleep.

Another word about 800 numbers. The large hotel chains now argue that they have revamped their 800-number reservations systems to provide "rate integrity." The 800 service will offer the exact same rate that would be quoted by the individual hotel if you were to call it directly.

Is that really true? The answer is yes, if you just call the hotel directly and ask to speak to a reservations agent. But, once again, it gets down to WHOM you call and, more often than not, WHEN you call. Remember, EVERY RATE IS NE-GOTIABLE. Usually, when a hotel is booked to about 92 percent of capacity, it is much less inclined to lower its rates. But when bookings are under 92 percent, the rate game is definitely on.

THE BEST TIME TO CALL

What's the best time to call to get the lowest rate? If you're simply walking into a hotel without a reservation, it's a no-brainer: 10:00 P.M. on a Wednesday night in February will usually get you an incredibly low room rate. You may even be upgraded to a suite.

For the rest of us, who tend to phone ahead, try 4:00 P.M. on a Sunday. Why? Because the folks who run "revenue management," the people who set the sliding rates for any hotel room, are off on Sundays, and you stand a much better chance of getting a front-desk clerk who just needs to sell a room. The result: a lower rate.

Because hotels tend to be overbuilt in today's travel economy, there are plenty of opportunities for bargaining. In fact, more than three-quarters of all business travelers negotiate with hotels and never pay published prices. Keep in mind that, in recent years, the average daily room rates for hotels in major cities grew by 4.4 percent per year. Still, an unsold room is the last thing a hotelier wants; it represents revenue the hotel can never recoup. (It's like an airplane flying with an empty seat; the fare is lost forever.) The hotelier will figure that earning something is better than nothing. As an example, in some big-city hotels, the weekend rate may go as low as one-third of the regular nightly rate. Suggest cutting a deal in which that rate is extended throughout the week if you stay in that hotel.

OTHER QUESTIONS TO ASK

When you ask for a price quote on a hotel room, most hotels neglect to mention that the official rate—the rate offered to you, even if it is the lowest available rate—doesn't include occupancy tax or sales tax. Because they're trying to be competitive, the hotels quote only the price for the room. The taxes are add-ons and, in many cities, they are excessive.

In the United States, hotel taxes average 12 percent. The most abusive hidden fee in at least seventeen U.S. cities, including Atlanta, Chicago, and Miami, is a surcharge to finance a local stadium or a convention center.

Not only do these charges add a significant amount to travelers' bills, but no one warns that they are coming. Cities get away with burdening travelers with a disproportionate amount of the costs of building arenas because we don't vote there.

How high are these taxes? Here is a tally of occupancy tax in some cities:

Chicago	14.9 percent
Dallas	13
Los Angeles	14
Houston	15
Anaheim (California)	15
Seattle	15.2
Columbus (Ohio)	15.75

If you call a hotel and the room rate quoted is $150, you know you will be paying more, maybe MUCH more.

Overseas, the tab can be worse. The dreaded value added tax (VAT) is slapped onto just about anything, especially hotel rooms.

Be sure you arrive at a mutually agreeable definition of terms. Was the $150 rate quoted to you the cost for double occupancy or for the room? If it was for double occupancy, the real rate is $300 per night. You'd be surprised how many people don't ask about the room rate and don't define the terms ahead of time, only to find out, too late, that their rate is actually double.

Are there other extras? Is there an additional charge for your kids? Many hotels now have a deal where up to two kids under age sixteen can stay free. But you need to know these details up front, even if the rate quoted is for the room.

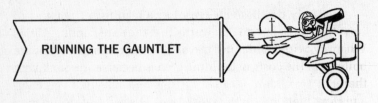

RUNNING THE GAUNTLET

Your cab has brought you to your hotel. In big cities like New York, Chicago, and Miami, where unions rule, be prepared to run the gauntlet of the limited-distance, limited-responsibility army: doormen, bellhops, and others who will help you get from point A to point B but, you learn, each pair of points measures about ten feet.

The doorman opens the door to your cab, helps with lifting your luggage out of the trunk, and then moves your bags about five feet.

Hand extended: Tip opportunity 1.

Then a bellman appears, places your luggage on a cart, and wheels it roughly twenty-five feet from the curb: through the doors and into the lobby.

Hand extended: Tip opportunity 2.

Your luggage sits there until you check in. Another bellman then brings your luggage up and places it in your room.

Hand extended: Tip opportunity 3.

America is a wonderful country. Three separate people to do the job of one person.

Is it any wonder that most savvy business travelers insist on carrying their own bags? The money isn't the issue here. Being forced to support ridiculous excess violates many travelers' principles.

I do not tip the doorman or the first bellman. I tip the second bellman according to the amount of luggage I'm carrying. The amount of the tip is sufficient for him to split the tip with the other two, and I announce that fact when I give him the money.

BACK AT THE FRONT DESK

What happens after you walk into the hotel lobby is almost boilerplate in design and function. You present yourself at the front desk, announce your name, and state that you have a reservation.

The desk clerk checks the hotel's records, and, with luck, has you in the system.

"Yes, Mr. Jones, we have your room right here."

The clerk will then, more than likely, verify your name and address, and the length of your stay.

This is inevitably followed by a routine question: "Could I see a credit card so I can make an imprint?" The request sounds normal, painless, and innocent.

It's anything but.

More often than not, the clerk is NOT making an imprint of your credit card. Instead, without informing you, the clerk swipes the card through the credit card authorization terminal, and does something called "blocking."

This is bad news. When the clerk swipes your card, he/she then punches in an arbitrary dollar amount, ranging from your room rate to a wild multiple of that rate. At that moment, anywhere from $100 to $3,000—or more—is "blocked" on your credit card account.

The hotel does this to protect itself in case you go beserk at the mini bar or steal all the towels.

But here are the problems. First, the hotel doesn't tell you it's doing this. And second, if you use a credit card that has a preset credit line—like Mastercard, Visa, or Discover, you may be in for an embarrassing moment later, when you go to use your card. Unbeknownst to you, your credit line has been maxxed out simply by checking into the hotel! But whatever you do, NEVER use an ATM or debit card to check into a hotel. Those blocking charges never get reversed. Your checking account is debited, just like cash. And getting that money back can not only take a long time, then there's the issue of all those NSF charges on your resulting returned checks.

My advice: If you have another credit card with no pre-set spending limit (for example, American Express or Diners Club), even if you have no intention of paying your hotel bill with it, use it when you check in. In that way, when the hotel blocks charges, it hasn't ruined your day.

When you check out, ask the hotel cashier to rip up your Amex or Diners Club invoice. When you see that has been done, pay your REAL charges, and nothing more, with your Visa, Mastercard, or Discover card.

FIVE ESSENTIAL QUESTIONS

After you present a credit card at check-in, but before you go up to your room, five key questions MUST be answered at the front desk. They will affect not only the kind of room you get, but your overall safety and comfort while staying at the hotel.

1. *How close is my room to the construction?* Sound strange? Not in the least. Virtually every hotel is run on cycles of renovation. At any given time, at least one floor, or sometimes an entire wing, is closed down for refurbishment or renovation.

   The last thing you need is to be booked next to an early-morning jackhammer.

2. *How close is my room to the ballroom? (Or, How far ABOVE the ballroom is my room?* There's usually no problem with noise from the ballroom when there's a party. AFTER the party, about 1:00 A.M., there's often a problem. That's when hotel workers are cleaning up—

throwing out the used wine and champagne bottles. Ah yes, the blissful sounds of breaking glass.

3. *How close is my room to the elevators?* Some travelers think it's a good idea to be close to the elevators, for both convenience and security reasons. But if you're too close to the elevators, you hear them all night long.

An aside about room height. There is absolutely no benefit to getting a room above the eighth floor at any hotel.

- Reason A: The higher you go, the longer it takes to get there—and to get down from there. At peak morning and afternoon times, a room on a hotel's fortieth floor means an extra ten minutes waiting *for* the elevator, and more time waiting in the elevator as it stops on almost all the floors.

- Reason B: Safety. There's not a fire department in the world that can get above the eighth floor. If you're in one of the high "great view" rooms in the event of a fire, your great view will be of the fire department's being unable to reach you!

4. *Is the heating a two-pipe or a four-pipe system?* If it's a two-pipe system, you will either freeze or burn. The newer four-pipe system allows better control of room temperature. Not all hotels have converted to the four-pipe system, which means that not all rooms at many hotels have it. You've got to ask.

5. *Could you do me a favor: Call engineering and ask what floors have booster pumps?* This is usually my first question, because good water pressure is so important to me. (When you ask, the desk clerk may give

you a deer-in-the-headlights look.) " Most high-rise hotels have been unable to maintain great water pressure
in the rooms. So, on different (not necessarily alternat-
ing) floors, the hotels install booster pumps. Get a
room on one of those floors. When you turn on your
shower, the pressure will match a fire hose!

Back to the front desk. You asked the right questions,
you got the right rate, and you got the best room for your
money.

What next? You go to the room with the bellman, even if
you have no luggage. Why? For two reasons.

1. Ask the bellman to remove your hotel bedspread. Hotels do NOT clean bedspreads after each guest. In fact,
   they may not clean them for weeks. You don't need it,
   you won't use it, and you don't need me to tell you
   why. Also, call housekeeping and ask to have three pillows brought to your room. (There's nothing I like less
   than a hotel bed with just two skimpy pillows.)
2. Remember that supermarket or deli stop you made en
   route to the hotel?

The minute you enter the room with the bellman, ask
him to immediately empty the minibar and inform the front
desk.

I *HATE* minibars. They are seductive but mean-spirited
(I've had too many dates like that!). Seriously, you must acknowledge the inevitability of a snack attack in your room,
but your wallet shouldn't be raped in the process.

Minibars are among the best profit makers in a hotel.
Paying $6 for a mini bottle of soda should be a felony for
both parties: the hotel, for charging the outrageous fee, and
you, for being stupid enough to pay that amount.

Instead, load up your minibar with the items you bought at the store. During an average two-day stay, you'll save more than $50. Believe me, those overpriced candy bars add up.

The minibar wars have gotten so bad that some hotels have installed Darth Vader minibars. If you even open the door and slightly MOVE an item, you are automatically charged for that item, whether you use it or not! You are now forewarned.

The minibars are indicative of the boom in nickel-and-diming at many hotels. These establishments slip insidious, extra, undisclosed charges onto guests' bills, and if you're not careful, you might not even see them or know what they are.

Or, you might only discover the charges after the fact, when you're checking out.

Here's my hall-of-fame nomination for nickel and diming.

I was checking into the Hyatt Regency Hotel in Houston for a one-night stay. I went through the usual ritual, and before handing me my room key, the clerk said, "Oh, you received a Federal Express package. Would you like us to deliver it to you?"

(I love stupid questions like this one. I was tempted to respond, "No, please share it with the other guests.")

The bellman walked over, got the FedEx pack, put it with the rest of my luggage, and up we went to my room.

The next morning, when I was checking out, I reviewed my bill. Without explanation, there was an additional $5 charge.

When I asked what it was, the reply was a shock. I had been charged to RECEIVE a FedEx package!

I complained. The charge was taken off the bill.

Two days later, at the Hilton in Las Vegas, I was called and told I had received a fax. Would I like it delivered? (Again, I was tempted to respond, "No, please post it in the lobby.")

The fax was delivered, and I tipped the bellman.

When I checked out, my bill showed a charge for receiving a fax. Again, I complained, and again, the charge was removed from the bill.

A week later, at the Anatole Hotel in Dallas, I got hit with a double whammy. I had received a fax. The hotel would NOT deliver it. I had to walk about a half-mile to get it, AND I was charged a fee for receiving the fax!

There's also a nickel-and-diming ripoff involving the in-room safe. Many hotels and resorts now offer these security devices. But many of them don't tell guests that they charge upward of $4 a day for use of the safes. Think about what an in-room safe is saying to you:

1. The hotel doesn't trust its own security system.

2. The hotel doesn't trust its staff.

3. We're going to charge you up to $4 a day to use a safe, when, under every state's innkeeper laws, the hotel is not held liable for the loss of any valuables from that safe. (Hotels are only liable—in a limited way—for theft or loss from their safe deposit boxes, which are available to guests, free of charge, at the front desk.)

Then there's the ripoff of room service, or, more precisely, of what comes WITH room service: the double-dipping receipt.

Let's start with a definition of room service. It is a premium service, usually at a premium price, for the luxury and convenience of eating inside your own hotel room. OK; so far so good.

Understanding that you will likely pay a little more for this service, you pick up your phone and place your order.

And soon—hopefully—there's a knock at your door, and a room service waiter is delivering your meal on a cart. After doing the setup, he presents you with the bill.

On the surface, most room service receipts look like a standard white-and-yellow copy of a credit card bill.

As an example, you've ordered a cheeseburger, a salad, a glass of wine, and perhaps a fruit plate for dessert.

Now, look carefully at that room service bill.

It lists the food items ordered, and their prices.

Next, there's a "service charge" (usually under $5) and a state sales tax.

And then, the hotel arbitrarily imposes a 15 to 18 percent gratuity.

Ready for the surprise?

Below that space on the slip, is the word SUBTOTAL. SUBTOTAL?

Yes. Right under the subtotal listing is another word, and the space to its right is left blank: "TIP."

Another tip? What was the 18 percent gratuity?

If you simply look at the subtotal and add a tip, you've just been ripped off. The hotel has double-dipped, courtesy of you.

Now for the biggest ripoff of them all: hotel telephone charges.

In the past few years, hotels have been forced to fully disclose—or I should say, MORE fully disclose—their phone charges to their guests.

As a result, many hotels now place "disclosure cards" in guests' rooms. They delineate what you will pay to make local and long-distance calls.

I remember one hotel that—quite seriously—put in each room a phone disclosure card that essentially said the following: "Please be advised that the ONLY free call you'll ever have at this hotel is if you call another guest room."

The card itself was ludicrous. Many of the guests, myself included, ended up grabbing the card, calling other guest rooms, and asking, "Do you believe this crap?"

Indeed, in any roundup of guests' grievances, nothing else even comes close to the outrageous phone charges—and surcharges—levied by many hotels.

If you're like me, you first learned about these charges the hard way: when you got your hotel bill, the phone charges exceeded your room rate!

Hotels often sell their phone services to the highest bidder, often known as AOS (alternate operator service), and they don't disclose this arrangement to guests.

Or, they block calls to 800 numbers or toll-free numbers overseas, and often charge as much as $4 per call (not per access) to get these numbers.

In a number of foreign hotels, even when I was able to get through to my MCI or AT&T number to make a call, the call was diverted from the hotel to another operator who asked what number I wanted. When I insisted that the operator identify herself, she revealed that she was a third-party operator for an independent telephone company. Translation: Her company would be placing the call, and when I received my MCI bill, there would be an even higher charge for that call.

Why do hotels do this? By not telling you about the third-party company, they essentially delay your anger by a few weeks. You are not billed a surcharge by the hotel. You get your bill and pay your other charges at the hotel.

Only when you get home and get your phone bill does the phone arrangement hit you. And the damage has been done.

Now, let's do the math. Say a hotel charges a minimum of $1 per call, even for toll-free numbers.

If you average just ten calls a day from your room (that total is not considered excessively high), you've added $10 a day to your charges.

Is there a solution? Actually, there are a few. Hotels and many governments don't like these ideas, but their greed created these solutions, and I heartily endorse them.

1. Use your cell phone at hotels. On the highly competitive cell phone market, prices for air time are at an all-time low. Make your cell phone your only contact phone, and you'll save a bundle.

2. Investigate any number of long-distance phone services that let you program their systems to CALL YOU. This is an ingenious response to hotel and governmental greed.

Here's how one system, KALLBACK, works. You become a member of the service, and you register your credit card to pay your phone bills.

Next, KALLBACK (800-338-0225) gives you a special number to call in the Seattle area (where they're based) and your identifying code number.

When you're ready to travel to Topeka or Tokyo, you simply call that number and punch in your code. A computerized voice then asks what number you want it to call. Punch in the number of your hotel. Then it will ask whether you want it to call now, or later. Punch in "later." Then hang up.

When you get to your location and are settled in your hotel room, go to the phone. Pick it up and proceed to do what others might consider financial suicide: Make a direct-dial call to KALLBACK's number in Seattle. Let it ring once, then hang up.

This signals the computer to call you back at the number you originally gave it.

Within 30 seconds, the phone rings at the hotel. When the connection is established and the operator answers, the computer voice asks to speak to you (by name). Your phone rings in your room. You hear the same computer voice asking to speak to you. Simply punch in your code, and the same computer voice then asks which number you want. Punch in the area code and the number, and you're connected. Make as many calls as you want, and pay competitive MCA/Sprint/AT&T rates, without excessive surcharges and taxes.

As far as the hotel and the local and/or foreign government are concerned, the call is recorded as a free, incoming call.

One final word about hotel ripoffs. Here, I'm talking about fire safety and security.

During the past two decades, there have been some disastrous hotel fires: the 1980 blaze at the MGM Grand in Las Vegas (85 dead); the 1986 New Year's Eve conflagration at the Dupont Plaza Hotel in San Juan, Puerto Rico (at least 97 fatalities); and the 1988 fire at the Heliopolis Sheraton Hotel & Towers in Cairo, Egypt (17 dead). In the 1990s, the sad trend continued, with a number of serious and catastrophic hotel fires in Asia.

The National Fire Protection Association reports that about 8,000 hotel and motel fires occur each year. The fires have focused attention on a serious travel question: How safe is your hotel room from fire, and how well-protected are you?

Some of the answers may not be comforting. Worse, other answers may not be readily available. This much, however, is known. Cigarette smokers account for 21 percent of hotel and motel fires, and fires of suspicious origin (arson) account for 19 percent.

Many hotels are not equipped to report or retard fires effectively, and most hotel guests have no idea how to give themselves a fighting chance before a fire breaks out, or how to escape a burning hotel safely.

Think back to the last time you checked into a hotel. Did the bellman point out the fire escapes or exits? Was there a smoke detector or sprinkler head in your room? And if the fire escapes weren't pointed out, was there a map or sign in the room to tell you their location?

A lot of the problem can be blamed on outdated municipal and state fire codes. Inadequate codes, combined with a historic unwillingness on the part of many individual hotels (and chains) to upgrade their fire-safety systems, have led to well-documented tragedies. The MGM Grand fire was the catalyst for finally getting officials to strengthen fire-safety codes throughout Nevada. Now, sprinkler systems are required in all hotels—old and new—statewide.

In 1987, a bill was introduced in Congress that would have forced most hotels to install sprinklers in rooms. Many hotels, along with the American Hotel and Motel Association, successfully lobbied against the legislation.

Even when laws are passed, they are full of loopholes that allow grandfather clauses to exclude hotels already built or to give older hotels many years to make the needed changes.

These days, nearly all hotels have smoke detectors, but many don't have sprinklers.

Some of the larger hotel chains have developed serious guidelines for their properties:

1. Fire prevention through controlling the quality of construction and interior-finish materials.
2. Design features to retard the spread of fire and smoke.
3. Detection alarm systems to alert staff and guests.
4. Escape routes and an emergency power supply.
5. Fire-extinguishing systems—specifically, sprinklers.

If a fire breaks out in a hotel where you are, many firefighters suggest that you do everything you can to get out of your room, if possible.

But first, don't just open your room door. Instead, feel the door. If it is very hot, don't open it. Instead, stay in your room. Shut off the air conditioner, stuff a wet towel under the door and remove all the curtains or draperies from the window. Next, head for the bathroom. Fill the tub with water—and wait.

If the room door doesn't feel hot, however, drop to your knees before opening it. Then crawl out the door and head for the nearest *stairway,* not the elevator.

The next time you check into a hotel, ask about its fire-safety system, smoke and heat detectors, and sprinklers. Also, inquire about the location of exits. If the staff can't answer these questions satisfactorily, you owe it to yourself to stay somewhere else.

And speaking of leaving your room, a note on security.

Put the Do Not Disturb sign on the outside of your door. Turn the television on. Why? An intruder or burglar has to think twice before entering a room with both the Do Not Disturb sign AND the TV on.

As an added protection, call hotel security and ask to have someone come to your room to engage the deadlock bolt to the room from the OUTSIDE when you are leaving the room. (Yes, they can do this easily.) This means that no one can enter the room—including you—without the assistance of a hotel security officer. But few guests know about this tactic, and it really makes your room secure.

SOME UNUSUAL
DOLLAR-SAVING LODGINGS

You're traveling to Houston or Hong Kong, Peoria or Paris, Los Angeles or London. You have secured an attractive air fare. But where will you stay? You start checking around, only to learn that your four- or five-night stay at a hotel will cost twice as much as the air fare—or more. Even the discount hotels' rates are prohibitive at your destination. What are the alternatives? University dormitories, youth hostels, private apartments, U.S. Forest Service watchtowers, and even coastal yurts are available, at tremendous savings.

Youth hostels have gone considerably upscale, and they're no longer limited to the prepubescent and postadolescent crowd. Today, many hostels offer private rooms ranging from $25 to $60 a night. For more information and a listing of hostels' locations and rates, call 800-444-6111.

Among the world's YMCAs and YWCAs are some surprises, including the Hong Kong YMCA, located next door to the legendary Peninsula Hotel. It offers good rooms, great views, and even a health club, at about $108 a night (a fraction of the Peninsula's price). In New York, a room at "the Y" can go for as low as $54; in London, where an average hotel room will cost you more than $200 a night, a room at the Y is $66. For more information, call 212-308-2899.

Another great hotel alternative is college dormitories. Dorms eagerly welcome paying guests during summer and vacation periods when students aren't there. More than 70 percent of U.S. colleges offer dorm rooms for rent. In California, UCLA has two on-campus hotels. To get a complete listing of dorm rooms available across the United States, order a copy of the Budget Lodging Guide. Call 800-525-6633. It costs $14.95 plus $2 for shipping.

If you're a business traveler, one of the most attractive hotel alternatives (especially for extended business trips) is an apartment rental. More and more folks are reserving flats in London and apartments in Paris instead of booking a hotel. Short-term apartment rentals in Europe and Asia are becoming more popular, for a number of good reasons. The first reason is price. A weekly London apartment rental averages about $875. Amenities include a kitchen, a living room, a dining area—and no minibar. Go to the market, buy what you want at local prices, and stock your own refrigerator. A number of U.S. firms specialize in finding and renting apartments overseas. Among them are: Barclay International Group, 800-845-6636; B&V Associates, 800-546-4777; Chez Vous, 415-331-2535 (specializes in France), and In the English Manner (British manor house agency), 800-422-0799.

Want a really strange hotel alternative? Contact a British company called Distinctly Different (011-441-225-866842). These folks offer former schools, windmills, jails, even a former brothel, all scattered throughout Great Britain, France, Germany, Belgium, and the Caribbean.

Perhaps the strangest hotel alternative can be found at a place called the Ice Princess in Jukkasjarvi, Sweden, known as the world's largest igloo. The temperature in the rooms ranges from minus 3 degrees Celsius to minus 8 degrees Celsius (27 degrees Fahrenheit to 18 degrees Fahrenheit). That's *cold.* But, amazingly, guests sleep well on beds of (you guessed it) ice covered with reindeer skins and sleeping bags. There are only eleven rooms at the ice hotel, and, yes, there is a sauna. Call 800-528-1234.

There are a number of great lighthouses and light stations around the United States where you can spend the night. Among them are the Lighthouse Inn in West Dennis, Massachusetts, 508-398-2244; the Saugerties Lighthouse in New York state, 914-246-4380 (rooms go for $73 a night); and the upscale East Brother Lightstation in Point Richmond, California, one of the great lighthouses built around San Francisco Bay. Rates here start at $235 a night; call 510-233-2385.

My favorite hotel alternative is unique lodgings, such as lookouts and yurts. Scattered throughout U.S. forests are lookout towers and structures built to house rangers looking for fires. With the advent of specialized radar systems and other technology, lookout officers have become obsolete, but the towers still stand. Lookout towers provide the barest of essentials, but they offer one of the more extraordinary ways to experience the wilderness. A room with a view is as low as $25 a night. Check out Oregon, but also Montana.

Yurts are circular domed tents. In Oregon, they are located at nine of the most popular state parks along the Pacific coast. They have plywood floors, lockable doors, electricity, indoor lighting, bunk beds, and space heaters. Rents are as low as $25 a night. For information on the fire-station lookout towers and the yurts in Oregon and Washington, call 800-452-5687. For a Montana lookout tower, call 406-821-3201.

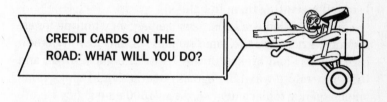

CREDIT CARDS ON THE ROAD: WHAT WILL YOU DO?

It's a famous American Express commercial: a tourist loses traveler's checks in the Gobi Desert.

If you believe the ads, one phone call gets an American Express courier to slosh through a forest, climb a peak, or tool through desert sands in a HumVee to bring you your replacement checks, cards, and emergency cash.

Visa and MasterCard make similar claims. Those commercials, as well as many printed cardholder agreements offered by MasterCard, Visa, and American Express, promise quick global assistance within twenty-four hours in an emergency.

I decided to test those companies' claims. Did I pick the Gobi Desert? Albania? The Falkland Islands? No. I stayed right here in the good old USA. And I chose Rhyolite, Nevada, a ghost town at the gateway to Death Valley. Population: zero.

Boasting one working phone booth, Rhyolite is nine miles from Beatty, Nevada, which has hotels and banks.

I used four of my own credit cards:

1. A regular MasterCard from my University of Wisconsin Credit Union.

2. A Gold MasterCard from General Motors.

3. A First Card Visa Gold card affiliated with United Airlines.

4. A Gold American Express card.

I started by cutting them in half.

When I called each company's emergency hotline for assistance, I narrated the same scenario: I had lost my credit card, my car had broken down, I was in a ghost town, and the temperature was 120 degrees outside. Could they get me an emergency replacement card and $300 emergency cash?

The University of Wisconsin MasterCard accepted my third collect call. After I was on hold for twenty-five minutes, a supervisor told me to call back in an hour. I did so and got another supervisor, who told me she was "at a loss" and I should call back. I called her an hour later and she suggested I call 911!

Gold MasterCard offers emergency services, including a replacement card within twenty-four hours, and emergency cash—or so the ads proclaim. "Sorry," the representative said, "you're six dollars over your limit, so there's nothing we can do for you."

Perhaps Visa Gold would come to the rescue. After an hour of waiting, I was put through to a supervisor, in Elgin, Illinois, who told me they could—and would—get $300 in emergency cash to me in the desert.

Could I call back in an hour? I could. But sixty minutes later, a supervisor said all they could do was wire the $300 to the nearest Western Union office.

How was I supposed to get there? I asked the woman on the phone. "Don't you folks at Visa say you're everywhere I want to be? So where are you?"

She said, "I don't know."

"So you're saying I've got to take a hike in the desert?"

"Yes," she answered.

My last hope: American Express. But they too would only wire the money to Western Union.

I suggested that they call Western Union in Beatty and ask whether someone could come to me. After all, there's that indelible advertising image of the Amex representative navigating the sands.

The American Express representative called the Stage-coach Hotel and Casino, where the Western Union office was situated, and called me back. "Sorry," she said. No one would do it. So, realizing that, in every case, I would have been stranded in the desert (misleading advertising claim number one), I got into the car and drove into Beatty in search of the Western Union office. Assuming—in my scenario—that a Good Samaritan had rescued me from the heat, the sand, and the sagebrush, I wanted to see whether any money was indeed waiting for me.

When I arrived at the hotel in Beatty to collect my $300 emergency money from First Card Visa Gold and Gold American Express, I got a final shock.

The $300 had indeed been wired to Western Union by First Card, but there was no record of money from American Express. Both the hotel receptionist and the manager said they'd never received a phone call from Amex asking whether they would come out to the desert and get me.

"We get calls from stranded folks all the time," I was told. "We would have been glad to run the money out to you."

So, were these credit card companies lying about their emergency services?

Advertising claims notwithstanding, you need to read the fine print of your cardholder agreement, something few of us ever do. There is nothing in the regular MasterCard cardholder agreement that mentions emergency replacement cards or emergency cash. Under the Gold MasterCard agreement, because I had violated the terms by being over my limit—even by six dollars—they were under no obligation to help me.

The Visa Gold agreement reads: "We will work with you to arrange direct delivery or a convenient location for you to pick up your replacement card or emergency cash." Convenient to whom?

The American Express agreement says: "Just request an Emergency Replacement Card, and Customer Service will offer you one of these options:

—Regular or Overnight Mail,
—Pickup at an American Express Travel Service location,
—Hand delivery by courier (in an extreme emergency)."

Being stranded in the desert isn't an "extreme emergency"? What about common sense? Not one credit-card customer-service representative suggested charging my account and hiring a taxi, tow truck, or rental car to get me out of my predicament. There is an implication in credit-card commercials that these companies will help you immediately, no matter where you are. But unless you're actually shooting one of their commercials, I wouldn't count on their help.

OTHER MONEY ISSUES

Do you carry travelers' checks? Do you really need them?

First, let's put them in perspective. With the proliferation of ATM machines worldwide, the need for travelers' checks should diminish. Still, thousands of travelers buy them each year, for their own peace of mind. I understand this. But I don't necessarily accept the concept of travelers' checks in the new global village in which we live and through which we travel.

Indeed, since 1995, annual sales of American Express travelers' checks have declined or remained flat. Visa's travelers' check sales have plummeted to only half of what they were in 1994. What exactly does a travelers' check mean? When you buy the checks, you are giving the check issuer an interest-free loan. Ever wonder why you get that handy little plastic wallet when you carry them away? The issuer is hoping you NEVER use the checks. Or, if you use some of them, they're counting on your placing the rest of the checks in a bureau drawer for later use.

If you're still worried about money security issues while traveling, purchase a minimum number of travelers' checks for emergency purposes only.

FOREIGN CURRENCY EXCHANGE

Use your ATM card worldwide. There are a number of good reasons for this advice. First, you get the current-day exchange rate offered by the local bank to all of its customers; you are not paying an excessively high exchange commission. And the rate you do pay will be 2 to 7 percent better than the rates when exchanging cash or travelers' checks.

(However, if you're using credit cards, be careful of the recent trend, among some companies, to add "transaction fees" for purchases made in foreign countries.)

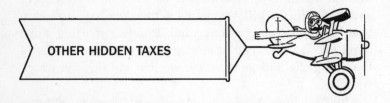

OTHER HIDDEN TAXES

Earlier, I mentioned the dreaded value added tax (VAT). When you shop overseas, you are almost always paying extra, without knowing it. At last count, about seventy-six countries apply some form of a value added tax, and this can boost the prices for many goods and services between 3 percent and 25 percent.

That's the bad news. The better news is that a growing number of countries, many of them in Europe, have several ways for travelers to reclaim the taxes they've paid on items they take with them when they leave, and, in some cases, the taxes they've paid on their hotel rooms.

When you're making a purchase, always ask about VAT refunds. The stores, and some hotels, will be only too willing to provide you with the proper forms. Some establishments charge a service fee to process those forms, but this is still found money, and it DOES add up.

In case you're wondering, France's VAT can be as high as 30 percent. Ditto in Thailand. In Argentina, VAT is 21 percent.

In most countries, you need to present these completed, postage-paid forms at the departure airport when you leave. Many countries require that you have the goods with you to show customs officers. This isn't always possible, but bring all of your receipts with you.

Just drop the properly stamped forms in a post box, and, within about four weeks, you will get either a check for the VAT refund or a credit to your credit card. At some airports, the VAT refund is instantly disbursed in cash. (The easiest option: the credit-card credit. After all, why would you want to change even MORE foreign currency at that point?)

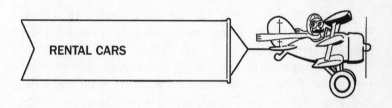

RENTAL CARS

Each year, millions of us rent cars—55 million of us, to be exact. Rental fleets now exceed 1.6 million vehicles.

There's a very good reason that rental cars are an $18 billion industry. More often than not, we overpay for the car and for gas, we buy insurance and other protection services we don't need, and we don't understand other rental requirements and disclaimers.

First, let's look at the rental car and the rate you pay.

Think airline fares are confusing? Not long ago, rental car rates at companies like Hertz, Avis, and National filled books the size of municipal telephone directories.

Rates have since been consolidated and simplified, but it's still a confusing world out there.

First, how do *you* make a rental car reservation? That dreaded 800 number again?

If you use the 800 number, you may get a low rate, but not the lowest rate or the best car. You are calling a national reservations system that displays a rental company's inventory and prices but cannot give you a better deal.

What's the best day to rent a car? Saturday, especially in summer months. Do you think airlines consistently overbook? The rental car companies are just as guilty. If a rental car agency tells you it has no cars available on a Friday, chances are excellent it suddenly will have cars early on Saturday morning, when some of the "committed" weekend reservations don't materialize. Also, weekly renters tend to return cars late on Friday nights.

And, just as suddenly, the car also comes with a deal. Again, an empty car sitting unused on a lot is not what the company had in mind.

Deals can only be done at the local level. Why? Rental cars move like a flock of birds; there are seasonal and holiday movements. Also, local agency operations are better judges of their own inventory and pricing.

Airport locations have different pricing than in-city rental lots, and, depending on fleet size, they may be more expensive.

So, do everything you can to rent locally, but get ready for some sticker shock. The National Association of Attorneys General estimates that the actual cost of renting a car may exceed the advertised rate by as much as 75 percent. Car rental companies can tack on all kinds of additional fees, from airport taxes to car wash facility surcharges. The best way to avoid surprises on your bill? Ask a lot of questions about hidden charges before you sign on the dotted line.

HAVE YOU RENTED A CAR LATELY?

At one time, there were fifty different rates for any one rental car. The good news now is that most rental car companies have simplified their basic rates.

Consumers can also save money by seeking out standard corporate discounts or membership discounts available from alumni associations, automobile clubs, and frequent-flyer alliances.

Official rates now seem simpler, but ask a lot of questions *before* you rent your next car, or you will be unpleasantly surprised when you get your bill.

What a number of car rental companies don't fully disclose when quoting you *any* rate, discount or not, are the extra fees and surcharges—and they can really add up.

Don't believe me? The National Association of Attorneys General (NAAG) has started its own task force in response to consumers' complaints across the country.

This is not the first time the NAAG has looked into possible abuses in the rental car industry. In 1989, the NAAG adopted its first guidelines on the industry's practices. It addressed the issue of "unbundling" (making the advertised price of a rental car appear artificially low).

Now, more than ten years after the original guidelines were issued, consumers have been hit with additional (and increased) surcharges, fees, taxes, and other surprises sprinkled among the rates. The NAAG now estimates that the actual cost of renting a car may exceed the advertised rate by as much as 75 percent.

Consider this recent scenario. I called Budget Rent-a-Car and asked about reserving a compact car in Aspen, Colorado, for a midweek rental of two days. Before I could speak to a reservations agents, a recorded voice cautioned me that if I was under twenty-five years of age, restrictions could be imposed, as well as additional surcharges. And, if over twenty-five? "The rate does not include concession fees or surcharges, and your driving record may be checked."

I was then connected to a live agent who quoted me a two-day rate of $109.90 for a Ford Escort, complete with unlimited mileage. That worked out to a daily rate of about

$55 per day. A little expensive, but I did get unlimited mileage. "Would you like me to make the reservation?" the agent offered.

"Not yet," I responded. "Are there any other charges?" I asked.

"Well, yes," she answered. "There's an eight-and-a-half percent sales tax, as well as a twelve percent surcharge for airport tax."

That's it? I asked again.

"Yes," came the response.

Well, not necessarily.

Let's do the preliminary math here. The Ford Escort rental fee in Aspen is *not* really $109.90 for two days. Not counting my possible subsidizing of a car-wash facility, and counting the 8.5 percent tax plus the 12 percent surcharge (a 20.5 percent hit at the end of the bill), the real basic cost of that rental car is more like $131.88.

Ah, but we're not finished yet. When I showed up to rent the car, I was offered (renters at a number of companies have claimed they were pressured into buying) the collision damage waiver (CDW).

Many of us who already own a car and are insured are probably already covered by our own automobile policy. And at Budget in Aspen, CDW will cost you an extra $16.99 per day.

If I hadn't checked with my insurance company before I flew to Aspen, I might very well have thought that I needed that CDW, and the cost of my two-day rental would have jumped to another $33.98.

With more than 20 percent tax added, plus $33.98 in CDW, the tab would rise to $165.86.

But we weren't through yet.

Recently, some Budget renters in Aspen were hit with a $3 per day "car washing facility" charge. That's right, they were helping to build a car wash and only discovered it when they received their bill.

As part of my shopping and disclosure test, I called Hertz, Avis, National, Thrifty, and Budget—not just once, but a number of times—to determine whether there was any pattern to disclosures or to rates.

The answers: No. Four calls to Budget, but only twice did they disclose the extra charges. Three calls to Thrifty; only one disclosure of the charges. And when I called Thrifty to rent a compact car in Boston, I received no such warnings or disclaimers. The agent simply quoted me the basic rate of $33.90 per day with unlimited mileage. Only when I asked did the agent then acknowledge, after a pause, that yes, there seemed to be additional charges: a 10 percent airport "access fee," a 4 percent excise tax, and a 5 percent sales tax. Once again, the basic rate, without insurance or other goodies, was pushed to nearly 20 percent above the quoted rate. (Then, add CDW, at Thrifty's rate of $16.95 per day.)

In the four calls to Budget, the rate quoted changed four times. Each subsequent call netted a lower rate!

Also not quoted: a $10-per-rental charge from the City of Boston to fund its new convention center.

Some rental car companies will offer to sell you something called PEI—personal effects insurance. In theory, it sounds great. If, while renting a car, something is stolen from that car, you're covered.

Not only is it not a great deal, it's insulting. PEI is about the most worthless insurance policy you can buy. Why? Read the fine print. For rental PEI policies to pay off, you car has to be locked, there has to be a forced break-in to the car, and, announced in finer print; most of your valuable items are excluded from coverage anyway. There's a low dollar cap on the amount of coverage, you have to file a police report, and, last but never least, many drivers are already covered under homeowner's or renter's insurance policies.

A review of the PEI offered by Hertz reveals that the maximum coverage for all claims is $600 per person, and the total for all individuals in the car is capped at $1,800.

Ready to laugh? Here are the exclusions:

Animals, contact lenses, currency, tickets, documents and perishables. Two other items also excluded from coverage: artificial teeth and limbs. With Hertz cars, the message is clear: If you have a dog that has false teeth and legs and is carrying an airline ticket and wearing contact lenses, DON'T LEAVE IT IN THE RENTAL CAR!

Moral to this story: Before you sign a rental car agreement/contract—or, better, before you make that reservation—demand to know any and all "pass through" charges. In Seattle, for example, there's a 2 percent car rental tax—in addition to the local sales tax. In Atlanta, the car rental tax is 3 percent.

SOME OTHER AVOIDABLE "SURPRISES"

Always ask if there is a drop-off charge. Sometimes (and I'm not kidding) the fee can be as high as $1,000! A few companies, like Alamo and Hertz, do not charge for a drop-off in Florida or California if the car was rented within that state.

Then there's the ticking clock. You have to watch out for the twenty-four-hour rate. If you rent your car, for example, on a Wednesday and return it on Thursday, you would expect to be charged for a one-day rental. But what's the grace period? Return it *after* twenty-four hours, even one hour after, and most companies hit you with a second-day rental fee.

Everything I just told you becomes one big foreign-language problem overseas. There, rental car companies, even those bearing familiar U.S. brands, operate as feudal fief-doms and, more often than not, ignore the rates quoted on U.S.-based reservations.

If you are renting a car overseas, you absolutely MUST keep a paper trail of evidence. Get a confirmation faxed to you. Always reserve and pay with your credit card.

It's your only defense against the highway robbery many foreign rental car "local" locations employ to recognize your reservation, and perhaps even to confirm it, but not the terms of the deal. Remember the dreaded VAT? This is a big whammy on foreign car rentals; it often adds as much as 25 percent of the rental cost. And, should you be charged the VAT, ask in advance whether it is at least partially refundable.

A final word about insurance. Many major credit card companies say that if you rent a car and use their card, your insurance is covered.

Not necessarily. Again, it's time to take a walk through the fine-print forest. And on this journey, with few excep-tions, you have to be particularly astute. Most credit card companies do, in fact, offer some kind of insurance when you rent a car and use their card. But be careful. Most of this insurance is considered "secondary" insurance; it kicks in only after you've exhausted all your other insurance. If you don't have insurance to begin with, it doesn't kick in at all.

Before you rent, investigate your own automobile insur-ance policy to determine whether it covers rental cars. If so, you're in.

If not, check directly with your credit card and deter-mine whether it is offering primary or secondary insurance. Hint: If you're renting with a gold or platinum card, there's a better chance you have primary insurance coverage.

Again, overseas it's a different story. Even if your card of-fers primary coverage in this country, overseas it might not. At last count, American Express no longer offers collision coverage in Australia, New Zealand, Jamaica, Ireland, Israel, or Italy. (There are also highway charges for cars driven in Austria or Switzerland. You'll need to purchase a sticker to avoid paying a fine.)

Watch out for some other rental car whammies.

At some resort locations, rental car companies issue cash deposit waivers for some pretty weird things.

Not long ago, I was going to Hawaii. Like many island-bound travelers, I fancied myself wearing a tropical shirt, sunglasses, and driving a convertible. The rental car agency offered a "Jeep" at an attractive rate.

Excited, I jumped at the deal.

Stupid me. First, it wasn't a real "Jeep" but a small Geo version of a Jeep, with no storage space or luggage security. Second, everyone renting a car—Jeep or otherwise—should know that there is no approved off-road driving anywhere in the fiftieth state if you're in a rental car. Off-road driving voids your insurance and rental contract.

Third, I was given a surprise "waiver." I had to put down an additional $50 deposit and sign a waiver. And what was that all about? The convertible top! Under the terms of the waiver, if I didn't return the "Jeep" with the top fastened in the up and closed position, I forfeited the $50.

That seemed absurd. I took the rental agent along an obvious verbal route. "Either the top is really easy to put up, which should mean there would be no waiver, or it's impossible to put up, and that's why there's a waiver."

"No, man," he replied. "It's real easy."

"Then show me," I responded.

He shrugged, and then walked out to the parking lot with me. He hit two buttons, two levers, yanked back a handle, and the top was down. "See?" he laughed. "Easy."

But that maneuver put the top DOWN. What about putting the top back UP?

"Here," he said, handing me a two-page instruction book and retreating back to the office.

Well, the top WAS down, I WAS in Hawaii, and so I drove off.

I went to a hotel that prided itself on individual service. They even provided me a butler, something of an absurdity in Hawaii.

Every morning, he would ask if there was anything he could do for me, and I would thank him and decline.

Until the last morning, when it was time to drive to the airport and return the infamous "Jeep."

"Yes, there's just one thing I need." I asked him nonchalantly, "Could you just put the top back up on my 'Jeep?'"

"No problem," he said, eager to please, and went outside my room.

Twenty minutes later, when I looked out from my bedroom window, the butler, two men from engineering, and a room service waiter were surrounding the "Jeep," trying desperately to return the convertible top to the UP position.

A half-hour later, they succeeded. I tipped accordingly, and proudly drove the car back to the airport.

I had beaten the rental car agency. I walked confidently into the office, returned the car keys, and asked for my deposit back. A curious rental car agent looked out the window and seemed surprised: I really had returned the car with the top UP. He returned my deposit.

Hooray for me. No waiver fees.

But I had not reviewed any of my "refueling options." Most rental car companies now offer the choice of bringing the car back with either a full tank of gas or with the same level of fuel as when the car was first rented. Other companies will allow you to prepurchase a tank of gas at the time of rental for a flat fee, but there's a catch to this. Unless you're bringing the car back on the fumes from an empty tank, it's not an economical choice.

And some companies seem to make all of their money on the gas, not on the rental itself—as I was about to find out with my "Jeep."

I had escaped the convertible top "waiver," but was about to be shocked by the gas policy.

After giving me back my deposit for the absurd waiver, the rental car agent recorded my mileage and the half-full tank of gas still in the car.

He punched a few buttons, out came the receipt, and when I scrutinized the rental car bill, the company had charged me a $52 refueling charge for 13 gallons of gas!

I had brought the car in with a half a tank, and they were charging me for a full tank at $4 a gallon!

Something had to be wrong. I told the agent I wanted to see the supervisor.

He smiled. "I AM the supervisor."

How could they charge me this much?

"It's our policy to charge for a full tank of gas."

"Even if I bring the car back with half a tank?"

"Yep."

And he wouldn't budge.

Later, I called General Motors and talked to their fleet sales division. First, I asked if they had sold a fleet of rental cars to that company in Hawaii. They had. I asked if the model of the GEO "Jeep" they sold was different from any model I could otherwise buy at a GEO showroom. Yes, there were some differences: the seatcovers, the carpeting, and the quality of the radio. That was it.

Everything else was standard? Yes.

Including the gas tank? Yes.

And what is the capacity of that gas tank? 11.1 gallons!

Does the rental company's gas refueling policy constitute a ripoff? Considering I brought the GEO back with half a tank AND they were charging me to fill it up AND they were charging $4 a gallon, the answer would be *Yes*. Now, compound this with the crime—yes, the crime. They were charging me to literally OVERFILL a tank by nearly two gallons. This was more than a simple ripoff. It was a corporate policy of robbery.

I kept the receipt and wrote about the incident. The company, under penalty of a consent decree hammered out with that state's attorney general, then stopped the practice.

Bottom line: You have rights as long as you keep receipts, get names, and develop an evidentiary paper trail.

Here's another little rental car surprise: In at least twenty U.S. cities where rental car companies are charged for being on airport property, a $2.00 to $2.45 charge is passed on to the renter.

There's also something called a "turnback" charge for folks who don't buy the loss-damage waiver that rental car companies often force upon consumers, many of whom are covered by their own auto insurance policies.

Let's say you rented a car, didn't buy the company's loss-damage waiver, and had an accident. When you returned the car, the company could hit you with a huge charge for "loss of turnback."

If you don't buy the collision damage or loss damage waiver, a rental car company does have the right to charge you for the cost of repairs, plus a "loss of use" fee to cover the income it would have derived from renting the car during the time it was being fixed. But most car insurance policies held by consumers cover repair and loss-of-use fees.

Loss of turnback, however, is different. It's the money a rental car company expects to lose when it sells a damaged (but repaired) car back to the manufacturer. In some cases, the loss of turnback has run to thousands of dollars.

Budget Rent-a-Car had been doing this, and the Federal Trade Commission found out because Budget failed to disclose the "turnback" charge to renters. No rental car companies are doing this now.

Rental car companies try to impose other insidious charges. Some that they CAN and do impose are within their legal rights. Others are more questionable.

YOUR DRIVING RECORD

Car rental companies can and do ask individual U.S. states to check on your driving record. If you have an abnormal number of accidents, these companies can and will either charge higher deposits or deny you the rental completely.

There's also an extra-drivers fee. If you're renting a car and you have even the slightest notion that another person might drive the car at any time during your rental period, you MUST register that person and provide his or her license at the time you rent the car. It is a legal and insurance nightmare if an accident then occurs and you're not behind the wheel. Some rental car companies simply want you to register the second driver. Others insist upon registration and payment of an additional fee. The companies can legally charge these fees, and as excessive (at least in principle) as they might seem, you must pay them if someone else is going to drive the rental car. You're asking for a heap of trouble if you don't.

Another problem is age discrimination.

Many rental car companies make it extremely difficult to rent a car if you're under age twenty-five years. Under twenty-five and asking to rent from Avis or Hertz? Forget it. (Unless you live in New York State. Hertz lost a New York court case on age discrimination. As a result, renters between ages eighteen to twenty-four years can indeed rent a car. But Hertz slaps them with a $56-PER-DAY fee for the under-age privilege. It calls it the "under-age insurance differential.")

Other companies' policies vary. If you're between ages twenty-one and twenty-five years, you can rent from Alamo, but at a higher rate. The same deal applies with Budget and Dollar.

SPECIAL DEALS

In some instances, if you look at fleets of rental cars like flocks of migratory birds, you can get some great seasonal deals.

Magically, rental cars tend to drive away from Florida or Arizona every spring, only to return there in late November. Magic? No; oversupply. Companies that own their own fleets are desperate to move those cars in spring and late fall. And who better to do that than YOU?

Hertz, National, Budget, and Avis often offer one-way "drive-away" deals, sometimes for as low as $9 a day, to have renters do them a favor.

If you're interested in a one-way rental, check (or have your travel agent check) with Avis (800-230-4898; www.avis .com), Hertz (800-654-3131; www.hertz.com), or National (800-227-7368; www.nationalcar.com) to see which has the best deal for your preferred itinerary.

WHERE AIRPORT DEALS ARE BETTER

Most of the time, renting a car at an airport boosts the rate because of additional taxes. But there are some strange deals in unlikely places. For example, for reasons that no one understands, a three-day rental from Hertz at the Dallas-Fort Worth airport runs $89, but, in downtown Dallas, the same car will cost you $147.

There are never any discounts on car rentals in New York City, especially at an airport, right? Not necessarily. At LaGuardia, a one-day rental of a midsize car from National Rental Car will set you back $76.98, but the same car at Newark costs $42.99. Go figure.

5

At Sea

PLEASE! IGNORE THE BROCHURES

CRUISE SHIPS

In case you haven't noticed lately, the seas are on sale. Virtually every cruise line is substantially discounting, and, in the world of supply and demand, supply is definitely on the consumers' side. Result: A strong buyers' market—worldwide—for any possible cruise vacation.

One of the reasons: an unprecedented boom in shipbuilding.

And why is that happening?

The cruise industry has been insisting that nearly 69 million Americans are interested in taking a cruise, and another 43.5 million are "definitely" or "probably" going to take a cruise vacation within the next five years.

Seven years ago, the same industry officials claimed that 44 million people intended to take a cruise within the next five years.

Guess what happened? They exaggerated. At least 15 million of those 44 million projected cruise ship passengers never arrived at the docks.

Despite the no-shows, the cruise ship industry didn't stop building new ships.

In the past, cruise lines built new ships to replace "old tonnage." But now, in anticipation of (1) a boom in the public's apparent desire to cruise, and (2) a lowering of the median age of cruisers, cruise lines are expanding their fleets almost exponentially.

In the cruise line business, the number of available berths increased by a whopping 12 percent in 2000.

And, as anyone in the cruise business can tell you, an unsold cruise ship cabin is revenue the cruise line will never recoup once the ship sails. Result: Cabins are being offered at 1980 prices. The cruise lines will do just about anything to get people aboard.

It all gets down to basic financing. When a new ship is built, the only way a cruise line can amortize its investment is to make the ship a series of profit centers. If the ship sails with about 80 percent on-board capacity, the line has a pretty good handle on how much it needs you to spend in the casino, on shore excursions, at the spa, and in the gift shop (I should say *shops*) in order to begin to turn a profit.

That's all well and good if demand can support an average occupancy rate of 80 percent.

But today, with so many new ships coming on line, that figure has quickly eroded, despite the fact that about half of the more than 6.6 million North Americans projected to book a cruise in 2001 will be first-timers.

And therein lies the problem. Only 12 percent of the American public (according to the cruise industry's figures) has ever taken a cruise. Somehow, more than a few cruise lines have converted that figure into an assumption that 88 percent of Americans suddenly want to try a cruise. Wishful thinking perhaps, but the industry claims that its own studies show that nine out of ten people who take a cruise plan to do it again; a record 43.5 million cruise "prospects" plan to cruise in the next five years; and 68.8 million people have expressed "a healthy interest in the concept."

Healthy, indeed. In 2001, Carnival cruises will entertain two million passengers, and 250,000 of them will be children. And 50 percent of those booked will be first-timers.

Still, the increase in supply is quickly outpacing demand. And that's good news for anyone who seriously wants to take a cruise and save significant money in the process.

In the past three years, dozens of new ships have begun sailing. They have ranged from the 388-passenger *Silver Whisper* (Silversea Cruises) to the mammoth 3,100-passenger *Adventure of the Seas* (Royal Caribbean). That's a lot of berths to fill—in addition to the berths the lines need to fill now.

Get ready to make some deals. The ships are waiting for you. And the deals are so wild that some lines are literally "dumping" cabins at rates that now average about $75 a day!

One cruise line dumped prices even further. Forget what it says in brochures. No one pays those prices, especially when you consider that, at one point, Carnival unloaded some cabins for a week-long cruise on its ship *Sensation* for $260! In October 2000, Princess was selling seven-day Caribbean cruises for as little as $499.

The other good news is that, as the new ships come out of the shipyards, cruise lines are repositioning some of their older ships to different, more exotic ports, and discounting those cruises as well.

Here are some great examples of cruise discounts on the market today—and reasons to ignore the brochures. For example, the brochure rate for one *Explorer* seven-day sailing was $2,424. But the real selling rate was $1,574. Savings: 35 percent.

Take a look at one *Grand Princess* cruise. The brochure rate: $2,583. The real rate: $1,199. Savings: 54 percent. The brochure rate for one Carnival *Triumph* departure was $1,925. But the going rate was $900. Savings: 53 percent.

An important message: If you pay the brochure rate, you just PAID FOR all those brochures!

Travel agents and cruise consolidators offer great last-minute deals. For example, Liberty Travel recently offered the following deals:

- A three-day Bahamas cruise for $249 on Carnival.
- A seven-day Caribbean cruise (also on Carnival) for $549.
- On Holland America, a five-day Caribbean cruise for $399 (unheard-of pricing).

- A twelve-day South America cruise for just $1,099. That's less than $100 a day!

The consolidators, like World Wide Cruises (800-882-9000), offer wilder deals.

- A seven-night Barcelona/Athens cruise for $1,199.
- A fourteen-night Athens/Dubai cruise for $1,599
- A fourteen-night Sydney/Auckland cruise for $1,799.

BOOKING A CRUISE

You have to know what you really want in a cruise. Are you booking the ship to take you to a destination, or is the ship a destination in and of itself?

How physically active do you want to be (or are you allowed to be) on the ship and on shore?

Do you like kids? Will you cruise with your kids?

Or do you want a quiet romantic cruise?

What kind of cabin do you want? Ignore the wide-angle photography in the cruise line's brochures. If you didn't know any better, you'd think you could entertain the entire State of Rhode Island in your cabin.

Try to remember that you are only in your cabin to shower, sleep, and change clothes. Most people fantasize about spending time in their cabin. The reality is that they are hardly ever there.

After you've determined that you don't need the most expensive cabin on the ship, ask yourself about the view from your cabin. Romantic notions about portholes and gentle sea breezes are nothing but nice memories of historic ship crossings. Today, there are few portholes, and cabin windows do not open. You're in a hermetically sealed, air-conditioned cabin; period. So, how important is the view, especially if you're never there?

The view notwithstanding, there are also center-of-gravity considerations.

Think about this: The cabins with the best views tend to be on the higher decks of the ship. A better view, but a rougher ride. Why? Center of gravity. In rough seas, which part of the ship will move the most? Higher decks will roll and pitch endlessly. Lower decks won't.

Embrace a realistic view of your cabin, and book a lower-deck inside cabin. It will be cheaper, you'll like it more if you're prone to motion sickness, and, with very few exceptions, you're entitled to the same restaurants and on-board activities/experiences as every other passenger. Some important requirements when you book your cabin: you do not want a room under the disco or the gym, and if you insist on a cabin with a view, make sure it is not blocked by lifeboats or tenders.

There are other important questions you need to ask; they all concern what the extras will cost. Once again, the brochures can be misleading. Many cruise ships have brochures that feature beautiful photographs of the officers and the crew. There, in dress whites, alongside the other officers, is the ship's doctor. But the doctor is not an officer of the ship. More often than not, he or she is an independent contractor and a separate profit center on the ship.

This means that any medical care you may need on the ship—even the dispensing of an aspirin tablet—will be a separate and often expensive charge. (Not to scare you unnecessarily, but remember that you need to practice some preventive medicine before you board any cruise ship. The potential for the rapid spread of communicable diseases on ships is great, for all the obvious reasons: close quarters, a single air-conditioning system, and so on. Before you sail, get immunized against influenza, typhoid, and Hepatitis A.)

It is imperative that you get your own health insurance, and make sure it covers you while at sea. It should also include—as with a land trip—medical evacuation and repatriation insurance. (In an emergency, the insurer will evacuate you from the ship and return you to the best available medical care in the United States.)

Ask about the medical facilities on board the ship. Princess Lines, for example, has a state-of-the-art satellite medical link with the emergency room of Cedars Sinai Medical Center in Los Angeles. Ship doctors can consult via satellite, review tests, x-rays, et al., and make a more effective diagnosis.

Do you have a physical disability? To their credit, cruise lines were quick to recognize the absolute need to be accessible to physically challenged persons.

I have yet to see a cruise ship sailing from a U.S. port that isn't ADA (Americans with Disabilities Act) compliant. Corridors and passageways have ramps. Rooms are accessible to the handicapped.

That news is refreshing. However, what the cruise lines, for the most part, have neglected to do is use their vast influence to make their port cities accessible to the handicapped. Many passengers confined to wheelchairs must stay confined to the ship at each port. Ask whether the ports you'll visit are as accessible as your cabin.

Shore excursions are major profit centers for cruise lines and are not included in your cruise fare. Do your homework here. Where are you visiting?

Look for "repositioning" cruises; they're the hottest deals around. These are deeply discounted oddball itineraries that are offered when cruise lines need to—literally—reposition their ships from one location to another. More often than not, these cruises are crossings. This the way cruising was meant to be: long stretches at sea instead of one Caribbean port after another. And the rates are well below others because, after all, the line needs to get the ship somewhere, and you just go along for the ride.

CANCELLATION POLICIES

In addition to medical insurance, you might want to investigate trip cancellation insurance. If you—or the cruise line—do not or cannot leave as planned, most cruise lines have very tough cancellation and refund policies. The premium charged for these separately purchased cancellation policies is nominal, and worth your investment.

Consider the fine print on one Norwegian Caribbean cruise ticket. In the event the cruise is overbooked or accommodations are oversold, the passenger agrees that: "Although space has been booked and confirmed, the accommodations may be withdrawn or boarding denied."

Here's something else. Unless you're an experienced cruise passenger—in fact, unless you're an experienced cruise passenger on a particular ship—beware of booking a cruise online. I'm not saying that you won't get the price you want, but booking a cruise only begins with the fare you pay. Remember, you need to choose a ship, an itinerary, a cabin category, shore excursions, and other options.

Finally, one additional tip that really works. With so many new ships coming on line, book an inaugural cruise. Yes, it will be more expensive, but here's a little discussed fact. The shipyards building these ships are batting almost 1.000 for never delivering them on time. The result: The ships are delayed going into service. The inaugural cruise is delayed, and the cruise lines give you a full refund and a discount on their next cruise. What a deal!

If you're booking a cruise that includes airfare, be particularly aware of what rights you're giving away to the airline and your route to get you to and from the ship.

Some cruise lines insist that booking your air transportation is totally within their discretion. For example, a family of four living on Long Island, New York booked a cruise out of Puerto Rico ten months in advance on Princess. Then, shortly before departing on their cruise, the Princess sent them their itinerary. Princess had booked them, in the middle of winter, on an itinerary almost guaranteed to cause trouble. Instead of putting them on a number of available nonstop flights from either Kennedy or Newark airports, Princess put the quartet on a flight from the most delayed airport in the U.S.— LaGuardia. To make matters worse, the family was booked on a LaGuardia to Chicago flight, and then from Chicago to Puerto Rico. (Any look at a map easily shows how ludicrous this route is, even in good weather flying into and out of airports without delay and cancellation problems).

Would Princess or their travel agent help them? No chance. Apparently the family didn't pay something called the "airline deviation fee," an extra charge that means the cruise line would have guaranteed to put them on a nonstop flight.

Now that you know the questions to ask, here are some questions to avoid.

At about 11:00 P.M. one night, a passenger called the bridge of the cruise ship and asked to speak to the officer on duty. "I'm having trouble sleeping," he said. "Could you please ask the captain to drive between the waves."

On a Caribbean cruise, a passenger asked whether the outdoor swimming pool was filled with fresh water or sea water. When told it was sea water, she nodded knowingly.

"Ah, yes," she said, "that explains why the water is sloshing around."

How about the woman who approached the cruise director on the first night of the cruise and asked, "What time is the midnight buffet?"

Then there was the couple who were into their second week at sea, as part of an 89-day around-the-world cruise. They walked into the dining room and asked their maître d': "Do the waiters live on board?" When told by the slightly dumbfounded maître d' that yes, all the waiters did indeed live on the ship, the couple asked, "Does that mean you make all this food here?"

Here's one of my favorites. A cruise passenger walked up to the shore-excursion officer as the ship was sailing from Dubrovnik on its way to Venice, Italy. "Why," he demanded, "didn't they speak English here?"

"Because this is Yugoslavia, sir," the officer calmly replied.

"Well," the passenger shot back, "what about Venice? I suppose we'll have the same problem there?"

Then there was the passenger who pointed to the stairs leading to the upper and lower decks and asked, "Do these stairs go up or down?"

On a cruise into Glacier Bay, Alaska, one passenger asked the ship's officers if they could stop so she could mail a letter.

On another Alaska cruise, after being told the correct temperature, one of the passengers walked up to the captain and inquired, "If it's that cold, what's our altitude?"

Not surprisingly, many silly cruise-ship questions are asked during shore excursions. On a tour of Dalian, a port city in mainland China, one passenger asked her guide, "How much are the condos here?"

Another passenger asked if it was illegal to wear jewelry in Peking.

Upon docking in Piraeus, Greece, a passenger asked, "How many draculas are there to the dollar?"

On one cruise, a male passenger boarded with five tuxedos, convinced that it was the only outfit he was allowed to wear at sea. On the second day of the cruise, he was gently directed to one of the ship's boutiques, where he could purchase some more casual garments.

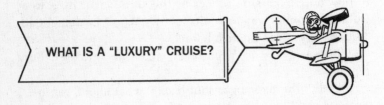

WHAT IS A "LUXURY" CRUISE?

In 1985, when the Italian liner *Achille Lauro* was hijacked by terrorists in the eastern Mediterranean, most of the press described the vessel as a "luxury cruise ship." But the ship was fifty years old when the hijacking occurred, and it had a history of severe problems—a number of fires and at-sea collisions. In 1982, its parent company had declared bankruptcy. The ship itself was seized after Italian government authorities determined that there had been "irregularities" in its casino operations.

So, the *Achille Lauro,* seized, abandoned and bankrupt, lay idle in an Italian port. The Italian government was no longer in the shipping business, and the days of its great liners—flagships like the *Michelangelo*—were long over.

The government didn't want this old ship, so it was leased—for $1—to Chandris Lines, which then marketed the old ship as a down-market, discount cruise ship in the eastern Mediterranean.

So much for "luxury."

For a while after the hijacking, the *Achille Lauro* was one popular ship. People booked it not only because of its notoriety, but because they were betting that the odds the same ship would be hijacked twice were extremely slim!

But soon, its hijacking history wasn't enough to keep the curious passengers coming. It was chartered to bring Irish and Egyptian soccer fans to Italy for the World Cup games.

A few years later, the ship sank under mysterious circumstances.

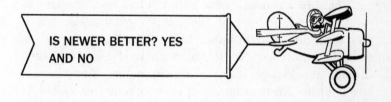

IS NEWER BETTER? YES AND NO

The only new ship is a newly BUILT ship, not a newly NAMED ship.

Making that distinction doesn't necessarily mean that an older ship is less seaworthy, less comfortable, or less safe.

In fact, in a rough sea, I'd much rather be on the old *Rotterdam* than on some of the newer, boxy ships that look like a condominium fell over and somehow learned how to float.

In this era of full disclosure, you have a right to know the genealogy of your cruise ship. It might help you make a better informed decision.

"You'll sail on a classic," reads one cruise ship brochure.

"A ship rich in history," boasts another piece of promotional literature.

It all sounds good, but two questions remain unanswered:

1. How old is your ship?
2. Should its age worry you?

Often, the answers are not easy to find. An "old" cruise ship is not necessarily a floating fire trap or a rust bucket on the verge of submerging. But it's nice to know where your ship has been and how old it is. Such information can help you decide what cruise to take.

Some cruise line brochures and advertisements have been guilty of using misleading words to sell their cruises. For example, a few years back, one Greek cruise line advertised sailings on the South American Riviera aboard its "new" ship, the *Pegasus*.

The ship was hardly new. In fact, it had already sunk—as the *Sundancer,* on June 29, 1984, near Vancouver, Canada. It was then resold to Epirotiki Lines (based in Athens), refloated, towed past North America's west coast and then through the Panama Canal and across the stormy winter swells of the North Atlantic—a slow journey that ended 52 days later in Piraeus, Greece. The ship was fixed and then heavily advertised as the "new" *Pegasus*.

It later sank again and was never refloated.

When the *Sundancer* sank the first time, it was declared a total loss and the insurance company paid off. The parent cruise company then bought a Scandinavian ferry, converted it to a cruise ship, renamed it the *Stardancer* and brought it to Los Angeles, where it replaced the *Azure Seas*.

The *Azure Seas?!*

I first saw the *Azure Seas* about twenty years ago. It was introduced in Los Angeles as a "new ship" sailing from California to Mexico on three-day cruises.

But a quick check revealed it wasn't a new ship. In fact, it was built in Scotland in 1954 and named the *Southern Cross.* It was built to take British holidaymakers to Australia.

The jet age destroyed that market, and it was pulled out of service in 1971. Two years later, a Greek family bought the ship, registered it in Panama, and it became the *Calypso.* In late April 1975, she started cruising in the Mediterranean as a low-class tourist ship. Some cruise ship aficionados re-member that the "captain's dinner" offered passengers a choice between fried chicken and "frankfurter sausages in mustard sauce!"

The *Calypso* was then chartered by a French company—Paquet Cruises. In 1980, it showed up in Los Angeles as the *Azure Seas,* promoted as a new ship doing Mexico cruises. For ten years, she went between Ensenada and Los Angeles.

Then *Stardancer* came in and the *Azure Seas* dis-appeared.

Where is the *Azure Seas* today? Now, nearly fifty years old, the ship has been renamed again—this time as the *Ocean Breeze,* running budget cruises in the Caribbean.

And what happened to the *Stardancer?* Its parent com-pany was absorbed by Royal Caribbean Cruises, which re-named the ship *Viking Serenade.* It still sails from Los Angeles but may soon be repositioned to Asia.

To understand a cruise ship's history, look at how often it has changed hands, and who has owned it.

With few exceptions, most cruise ships older than ten years have probably been owned at least twice. They are, in-deed, rich in history—and poor in continuity.

In functional areas, older ships are potentially more troublesome. Plumbing is a major headache on older ships. Electrical problems are a close second. Maintenance costs, not surprisingly, are higher, which might mean that certain maintenance items are deferred because of the expense.

An important question to ask: Was the ship you're booked on built by the line that operates it?

If so, chances are the crew has been thoroughly trained on its equipment, and the engineering staff probably wrote the manuals.

If it wasn't, how many years has the ship sailed with this line? If the answer is less than three years, you're dealing with a crew that is still getting to know an older ship.

Interestingly, Carnival Cruise Lines (now the largest in the world) began with an older ship. In 1972, the company bought its first vessel, *Empress of Canada.* On its maiden voyage, the ship ran aground. After an extensive refit (and subsequent renovations in recent years), the ship sailed again. It was called the *Mardi Gras.*

In 1975, Carnival bought the *Empress of Britain* (now called the *Carnivale*). And in 1977, the company purchased a ship called the *S.A. Vaal,* a liner that had been sailing between England and South Africa, and renamed it the *Festivale.* Since then, Carnival has built all its new ships.

Royal Caribbean Cruise Lines has built all its ships to specifications particular to its markets and cruise areas.

Holland America has built many of its ships, the most famous of which is the *Rotterdam.* The first *Rotterdam* sailed in 1873. Since then, there have been four other *Rotterdams,* including the current *Rotterdam V,* which was brought into service in 1959 and retired in 1997 (but not scrapped; it became the *Rembrandt*), and now the *Rotterdam VI.* Companies like Holland America maintain the names of their ships, although the ships themselves are different.

The original *Westerdam* (which sailed between 1946 and 1964) was built during World War II as a passenger and cargo carrier, but didn't sail until 1946 because the ship was sunk twice in harbor. The first time, the ship was sunk by the Dutch because they didn't want the Germans to be able to use it. The Germans refloated it and then sank it a second time, near the close of the war, because they didn't want the Dutch to get it.

The next *Westerdam* was once the *Homeric,* purchased by Holland America in 1988.

Problems can sometimes occur with successive ownership changes. Perhaps needed renovations—especially safety standard improvements—are not performed because the new owner lacks capital or is not required to upgrade the ship under current laws.

"We've pushed hard to force cruise lines to report incidents, accidents, and ownership changes," says one U.S. National Transportation Safety Board (NTSB) inspector. But the NTSB lacks jurisdiction, in most cases, to demand accurate and current reporting. NTSB records are not accurate because ship companies don't have to report to the NTSB incidents that occur in international waters. The companies can pull a vessel, fix it up, paint it, and sell it. The new owners can give it a new name and no one will know its former history.

One of the more interesting histories belongs to a ship called the *Regent Sea.* It was built in 1957 for the Swedish American line as the *Gripsholm,* and it sailed for seventeen years as a transatlantic liner. In 1974, it was sold to a Greek firm, Karageorgis Cruises. Renamed the *Navarino,* it cruised Mediterranean, South American, and South African waters until 1981, when a fire broke out. After the ship was repaired, it was put up for sale. The prospective buyer—Commodore Cruise Lines—insisted on a dry docking and thorough inspection before the deal was finalized. As the *Navarino* was being lifted out of the water, the supports gave way and the vessel leaned against one side of the floating dock. The wall collapsed, and the ship flooded through open side ports and foundered with a thirty-five-degree list. Many of the accommodations and all the machinery spaces were underwater. The ship was declared a total loss.

At one point, the ship was going to be towed to Brazil to be used as a stationary floating hotel in San Paolo. But the deal never happened. Instead, it stayed in a shipyard near Athens for a few years.

Then, on November 12, 1985, after undergoing extensive repairs, the ship was sold to Regency Cruises and entered service as the *Regent Sea.* (The ship was later seized when the parent company couldn't pay its bills.)

Anyone remember the *S. S. Monterey?* The ship, which formerly sailed for Pacific Far East Lines out of San Francisco, was sold to a U.S. company that planned to begin cruising around the islands of Hawaii. But the line went bankrupt. The ship was sold again to a Panamanian company and then chartered to Star Lauro of Italy for twelve- and fourteen-day cruises of the Mediterranean.

Some older ships will never sail again, but they're still floating.

Remember the Italian liners, *Michelangelo* and *Raffaello?* In 1977, the ships were taken from Genoa to Iran to be used as floating barracks.

The *Victoria,* operated by Chandris, was built in 1936 as the *Dunnotar Castle.* The *S.S. Britannis* was built in 1932. The 58-year-old ship was once the *Monterey,* then the *Matsonia,* and finally the *Lurline.*

There are some benefits to sailing on an older ship. For one thing, it actually looks like a ship. Older ships seem to have usable passenger space, plus promenade decks where passengers can truly promenade. On older ships, the passenger cabins can be considerably larger.

In general, older ships usually carry fewer passengers, display a more thoughtful interior design (often using wood), and offer a feeling of making a passage rather than simply taking a cruise.

6

Final Thoughts on
Resources, Tools, Web Sites

AND WHAT TO DO WHEN IT
ALL GOES WRONG

There are those of you who are convinced, perhaps correctly, that the process of travel will only get worse before it gets better.

There are those who also remember, less than fondly,that cold January day in 1999 in Detroit. That was the day when thousands of passengers were kept trapped inside their planes at the airport—some for as long as nine hours.

It was a catalytic moment of passenger rage and justifiable anger. Within weeks of the incident, no fewer than 13 separate pieces of legislation were introduced in Congress aimed at formalizing the concept of airline passenger rights.

And the airlines moved just as quickly to beg Congress not to do that. Instead, the airlines asked to be given a chance to make some promises of better customer service and improved passenger rights.

And what about all the lawsuits filed in the Northwest Detroit incident? On the eve of a large trial, and more than two years after the snowstorm, Northwest suddenly agreed to pay $7.1 million to thousands of passengers to settle the case (payments ranged from $1,000 to $2,500 per passenger, depending upon how long each was stranded). And while the airline lobby is still winning in its fight to keep Congress from legislating passenger rights and airline responsibilities.

The airlines have issued nicely packaged "customer care" manifestos, which officially claimed they would then tell the truth about offering the lowest fares, improve the flow—as well as the quality—of information to passengers when there were delays.

Callers to Delta Air Lines' reservation centers soon began to hear a prerecorded voice saying that the airline will always offer them the lowest available fare on their desired routes.

American Airlines' customer service plan promised the same thing, saying that the airline would endeavor to provide the lowest fare.

And then there was the reality. . . . The language used by the airlines was a textbook course in disclaimers: "Try," "all best efforts," "do everything possible."

Really? I decided to test the promise. I called American Airlines to book the ideal discount coach flight: more than three weeks in advance and staying over a Saturday night. The reservations agent asked me what kind of ticket I wanted. I responded "discount coach." The fare quote, for the "lowest" fare, for a flight leaving Los Angeles at 10:00 A.M. and returning six days later from New York at 3:00 P.M., booked three weeks in advance and staying over that dreaded Saturday night: A staggering $785!

That's the lowest fare?

Well, not exactly. What the airline didn't volunteer (so much for "endeavoring") was that if I took their 8:00 A.M. departure on the same day and returned at 8:00 A.M. from New York (again on the same exact dates as the original desired flights) the fare suddenly dropped to $499! Almost a $300 savings. Just to make sure they hadn't simply forgotten to mention this deal, I called two times again over the next three days with the same desired flights. Not once were the "flight specific" deals mentioned. (And what are those deals? On transcontinental flights, if you depart LAX before 8:15 in the morning, or between 11:45 A.M. and 1:15 P.M.—or if you return from JFK to LAX between 6:45 A.M. and 8:15 A.M. or between 5:45 P.M. and 7:15 P.M., the fares drop dramatically.)

But you are not told this. You have to somehow divine it.

Another airline promise made to Congress is better communication when there are flight delays. Another case in point involves American Airlines. I was booked on a flight leaving Los Angeles for Las Vegas. Scheduled departure time: 5:05 P.M.

But when I arrived at LAX, I was told the flight was delayed until 6:00 P.M. The reason: Weather.

Now, here's the real question (or questions):

1. When did the airline know there was a delay? And why didn't they call me? (Yes, they had my number. In fact, every time you make a reservation, the airline asks for your number.)

2. Was it really weather related?

3. Was the new departure time fictitious as well? Where was the plane assigned to my flight at that particular moment?

The answers, as I soon discovered, were less than truthful.

First, the airline knew my plane would be delayed at 3:00 P.M., more than two hours before my flight was scheduled to depart. They just didn't call. And yes, they did have my number.

Second, it wasn't weather related. The aircraft was coming in from Las Vegas, where there were in fact no weather problems.

Third, and perhaps most disturbing, was the new departure time information. A further check with American revealed that the plane was then due in to LAX at 5:53 P.M.

Assuming the incoming plane was carrying no passengers, needed no fuel, no replacement crew, and no catering, a seven-minute turnaround time was equally absurd.

Then, the news got worse. I asked a few more questions and learned that the new arrival time was also a lie. The aircraft hadn't even left Las Vegas when they posted the amended arrival time in Los Angeles.

So . . . what were my options? An American Eagle flight "scheduled" to leave Los Angeles at 5:30 P.M. I raced over to the Eagle terminal, only to discover a plane sitting on the ground with no activity. At 5:20, I asked, "Is the plane leaving at 5:30?"

The counter agent nodded.

"Then when are you boarding?" I asked. "They're just servicing the aircraft," she assured me. I looked out and saw baggage handlers removing luggage from the plane. "Why are they doing that?" I asked. "Oh," she reported, "they are weighing each bag individually."

That was, I'm sorry to report, another lie. In fact, the baggage handlers were taking the bags off the plane because they were taking the plane out of service. And, as they towed the plane away from the gate, the departure board was adjusted—unrealistically to read a new departure time (for a gate that now had no plane) of 5:45 P.M.

At this time, my original—delayed—flight was beginning to look pretty good. The departure board now said it would be leaving at 6:10.

A hopeful sign?

Not exactly. I called American and discovered that the flight had only gotten airborne out of Las Vegas at 5:33 and wouldn't be landing until 6:30.

Then, American adjusted the departure board to read that the plane would be leaving at 6:30, another impossibility since the plane didn't actually touch down until 6:22.

At this point, I decided to lodge a complaint, and I called the airline. My complaint: I forgive the airlines for weather delays. I certainly forgive the airlines for mechanical delays. I do NOT forgive them for not calling me to communicate their problems, and worse, I do not forgive them for misinformation or false statements.

In every one of these cases, the behavior of the airline limited my options and those of my fellow passengers. So . . . what happened when I complained? The airline representative said someone would get back to me. And, a few months later, someone did. I received a form letter of apology from American along with additional credited mileage to my frequent flyer account. Wow . . .

Here's the question: Could I have done better?

Answer: Yes.

And that's what this section is all about: tools, resources, and ammunition. What to do when it all goes wrong.

On the surface, it might seem harder to seek redress. For the moment, the airlines have been able to effectively deflect any federal legislation mandating them to keep their promises. Most cruise ships are officially registered in Liberia, or Panama, or the Bahamas, making enforcement of safety or service issues that much tougher.

As a result, frustrated passengers are left to write angry letters—to the airlines, to hotels, to cruise ships, to me, and to a growing number of Web sites devoted entirely to travel complaints.

America's $541 billion travel industry needs to be more responsible. And in many cases, so do you. Toward that end, here are some resources, tools, phone numbers, Web sites you should keep handy—and use!

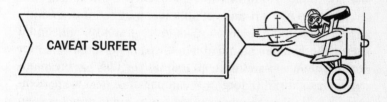

CAVEAT SURFER

Not a day goes by without at least five new Web sites appearing that are devoted to travel for a specific interest or group, whether it is bicycling tours, art galleries in Cyprus, or one-armed fugitives. There are now more than 11,000 travel Web sites out there. If you believe current estimates, there are more than 332 million people connected to the Internet worldwide—and it seems that almost every one of them wants to—or is—traveling.

But therein lies the promise—and the problem—of the wild new e-frontier. Sites that at first glance seem to be informational may actually be thinly disguised attempts to get us to buy travel services. Sometimes what they're selling is good. But when we're seduced by apparent access to quick and easy information, we may not be getting what we really want or need.

Which isn't to say travel sites aren't working overtime to deliver your heart's desire—or at least to figure out what that is. They'll have to in order to survive. The Net has had a seismic effect on the underlying architecture of the travel business, now the largest industry in the world. We're in a brand new territory, and to determine where the borders are, we're going to need a map.

Let's start with some staggering numbers. In 1998, Americans spent $1.9 billion on Internet travel purchases. What's expected by the end of 2001? A whopping $6.5 billion. It doesn't take a brilliant analyst to calculate how powerful the marriage of the Internet and travel has become. And the honeymoon is just beginning. According to PhoCusWright, an industry research firm, only 3 percent of all travel transactions currently take place online (a figure expected to grow to 8 percent by 2001). But there are plenty of window shoppers: the 52.2 million of us now researching trips online. The Web has become a sophisticated profiling tool that can point out remote spots we never knew existed and can enhance our entire travel experience. We use the Net as exactly that—a net to gather information and to see the places we're planning to visit. Then we ask it to get us there with the least amount of effort and cash.

Not surprisingly, the Web's most aggressive transformation has occurred in the airline industry: Of all of last year's online travel transactions, 73 percent were for plane tickets. And since the cost of processing an e-ticket is just 30 cents, compared with $9.49 for a ticket purchased from a traditional travel agent, the sector will continue to explode. One key to playing the Internet travel game is to look closely at the new airline marketing partnerships, which will no doubt affect your ability to get the best price online.

Consider AOL AADVANTAGE, the recent marriage between AOL and American Airlines, which lets you earn miles by shopping online at AOL partner sites. Besides offering frequent flyer perks, the program lets you convert your miles into e-dollars and then use them to buy select products or swap them for AOL service. AOL Aadvantage seems to want you to think about the Internet as a means of accruing travel credits without actually having to buy a trip! This shows how far e-travel has already evolved beyond mere ticket transactions.

Which isn't to say ticket sales don't count. The merger between travelocity.com and previewtravel.com will result in $1.2 billion in total annual revenue, easily placing the new entity in the top five of all e-businesses. Challenging that behemoth will be a beefed up expedia.com, which acquired travelscape.com and other key properties. Then there's the impending consortium of airlines, which, if approved, will combine America's largest carriers and leading foreign airlines into one supersite that offers deeply discounted fares, along with a full menu of other travel services. Meanwhile, priceline.com is acting as both ticket broker and airline—or airlines, rather—by partnering with United, Delta, and American on its name-your-price site.

Sound confusing? It is, even to travel professionals. And until the dust settles, it's all too easy to be dazzled by the technology. It's essential to remember that a visit to the Net doesn't guarantee the best price—or the best of anything. Nor does it take the place of common sense.

The greatest advantage of the Internet is that, with few exceptions, it lets you browse before you buy. So don't assume that just because United teamed up with Buy.com to form buytravel.com, you'll get the best United prices there. You may find better deals at cheaptickets.com or itravel.com, or even in the newspaper. There are always other places to look, online and off, when you don't find what you want at one of the big Net agents.

Here's an inside tip: When traveling internationally, don't assume that a direct route is necessarily the cheapest one. Let's say you want to fly from New York to Nairobi. No discount fares are available, so your round-trip coach ticket could run upward of $2,000. Airfares from New York to London are dirt cheap, though, with some as low as $298 roundtrip. Next stop: lastminute.com, a British Web site offering some great travel deals that originate inside the United Kingdom but are available to anyone who logs on. Lastminute.com can't deliver? No problem. Spend five bucks on a London paper, such as *The Daily Telegraph* or *The Evening Standard,* and check the travel section. You're likely to find at least a dozen ads offering London-Nairobi round-trip fares for under $400. And yes, you can call them; they take credit cards and will deliver your tickets.

To get the best deals, it's always good to consult the locals. This is true in the United States as well. Want a cheap ticket to Phoenix from New York? Don't look for fares from New York on the usual Net suspects. Instead, log on to 12news.com, the site of the NBC affiliate in Phoenix, and check Internet Travel Deals. The Web sites of many local TV stations offer similar services and are worth checking out if the bottom line is your top priority.

Once you get to where you're going, you'll need a place to stay. Hotels came to the Web a bit later than the airlines and are still playing catch-up; only 1.5 percent of all rooms booked last year were booked online. So far, small enterprises that have banded together to make themselves marketable, such as the properties featured at travelpresskits.com, have had the biggest impact on Net bookings. But it's not only bookings that can benefit hotels. A well-designed hotel site serves a purpose far different from that of an agent's or airline's site: It attracts you, the consumer, by showing you exactly what you'll be getting for your money. And it's much more entertaining than a brochure.

Go to any Four Seasons site and you'll see an example of what I'm suggesting. Many of their locations offer virtual tours that let you look at room interiors or the spa. The best news is that there is little of the pressure to buy that you inevitably feel with most airline sites. And when you do want to book, you're not doing it in the dark.

If price is your main motivator in booking a hotel, the Hotel Reservations Network does a reasonably good job of discounting excess inventory. Want to bid for the room instead? There's Priceline, of course, but now Expedia has Hotel Price Matcher, a feature that works the same way: Enter how much you're willing to pay for a room that meets your specs; if the site finds a match, it charges your credit card for a nonrefundable reservation. If you do decide to bid, just remember that there's often a hidden price to pay. With airfare auctions, your flight may not be nonstop and you may not get frequent flyer miles. With hotels, you may not get the miles or frequent-stay points. But if the deal is good enough, the trade-off may be worth it.

What about booking cruises on the Web? The cruise business was one of the last travel sectors to go online, in part because more than 96 percent of all cruise sales are made by travel agents, who can help novices decipher what is often an expensive and complicated purchase. The industry has made a real effort in the past year to come onboard the Web, though. Previewtravel.com just announced that its cruise bookings for the first two months of 2000 exceeded all of last year's sales. Cruises still constitute only a fraction of online transactions, but such a dramatic surge signals something significant.

Perhaps because they were last to launch, many cruise sites are among the best in terms of visual entertainment. One of my favorites is Princess cruises & tours. Check out its onboard Web cams, which give you instant live access to any of its ships around the world. Talk about aspirational travel! Another great site, Renaissance cruises, offers video-enhanced virtual tours. For cruise bargains, try onsale auctions and deals, which recently offered a Celebrity cruise for two to Alaska for $1,199—about $200 less than the same cruise on Celebrity's own site. Because of unsold ship berth means lost revenue that the cruise line will never recoup, companies have begun to dump inventory directly onto the Net. If you want to actually speak to a travel specialist when booking a cruise (and if you're a first-timer, I absolutely recommend it), uniglobe.com has agents available to answer your questions via a toll-free number. More often than not these days, however, traditional agents are being bypassed. The industry has been thoroughly shaken by Darwinian economic forces: The Net will eliminate all vendors that cannot match excess supply to potential buyers with the Net's speed and efficiency.

Does this mean that travel agents will become extinct? No, but they are starting to see themselves as an endangered species. The American Society of Travel Agents recently petitioned the Justice Department to investigate possible antitrust violations by major airlines that are partnering in Orbitz, the new low-fare site. Agents are particularly concerned about cruise sites, because commissions on ship bookings are the biggest they receive.

Technological advances will also continue to transform how the Internet delivers and promotes travel. According to

Forrester Research, some 27 million people will have broad-band access within the next year. As this trend accelerates, transaction sites will begin to make more and more use of video-streaming technology to better inform visitors and to provide greater entertainment value, in the hope that you'll stick around long enough to buy. Smart travel agents will use the same technology to deliver a video e-mail message about where the bargains are.

It won't stop there. Vodaphone (UK), the world's largest wireless manufacturer, has already forged partnerships with Travelocity and Expedia. The handheld wireless booking engine will arrive in the near future. Travel agents will then be able to stream themselves to your PalmPilot. This person will be speaking directly to you, wherever you are. When that happens, the Net will truly have changed the travel industry, by putting you in contact with a real human being. Wow, what a concept!

Worried about the security of the last message you had to send from some college kid's laptop in Jakarta? Log on to Cybercop, which offers many different ways to encrypt your files and online correspondence. If you don't want anyone to intercept your naughty e-mail from your sweetheart or the access codes from that novel you're trying to broker to Hollywood, these guys can handle your needs. Go to the freeware section and download their product [www.pgp.com].

Road warriors John Tedesco and Jeff Grass loved logging on while traveling, but hated coming home to a stack of unpaid bills. So they created a site that lets you pay your bills online from anywhere. This was not a breakthrough innovation (many banks allow you to do the same thing). But these folks built a better mousetrap. They don't just deduct automatic payments from your account—you're notified by e-mail when a bill is due, and you decide what you want to do and when [paymybills.com].

Thanks to the Internet, we can take a sneak peek at what awaits us before we decide to head off for Tahiti. But what about, say, Columbus, Ohio? Sites like citynet do a good job of covering America's major cities, but information on smaller towns can be more difficult to come by. Poke around a little, though, and the Web yields some surprises.

BEST READ GUIDE INTERNATIONAL

It's globe-trotting moniker notwithstanding, this site concentrates on small U.S. cities, from Amarillo, Texas ("an outdoorsman's paradise!"), to Traverse City, Michigan (where "life's a breeze aboard the Tall Ships"). The towns provide lively features and good photos, along with guides to nearby attractions. Angler's alert: Free fishing seminars are being held throughout the summer in Brainerd, Minnesota, where walleye and pike are jumpin' in area lakes [bestreadguides.com].

BOULEVARDS; WILLAMETTE WEEK

A good way to suss out information about larger cities is to consult their free alternative weeklies. *Boulevards* acts as an intersection for dozens of such papers around the country. One of the best of these is *Willamette Week* (published in Portland, Oregon), which gives you an inside line on artsy gatherings and live club dates. Residents use the print version to make their plans. With a quirky town like Portland, it's a good idea to tap into the underground [boulevards.com]; [www.wweek.com].

Austin, Texas, is another city with a vibrant alternative scene. A small dose of local knowledge helps unlock its best features, and Austin360 delivers. In one quick visit, we learned the show times for the Alvin Ailey American Dance Theater, where the best bands were playing, what the garage sales were selling—and, most important, where to find the cheapest gas. Now, that's good juice for the traveler [austin360.com].

Columbus, Ohio, may not have the hip cachet of Austin. But dig into Cowtown and you'll find a surprisingly happening scene. Webmaster Mark Gunderson turns you on to everything from Bernie's Distillery, where hot local bands rock out, to the best thrift stores. He even includes a section on "illegal tours" through abandoned buildings of architectural note, such as the Street Maintenance Facility at the "dead end of Dublin Avenue" [myohio.voyager.net/markg/Columbus.html].

Note: Remember, a growing number of dot.coms can quickly become NOT.coms. With so many new sites being added (and disappearing) every day, I can't guarantee that all of these will be there for you. But it's a start.

So with that as my ONLY real disclaimer in this book, here are some other choices I particularly like, with the proviso that the Internet is *a* tool, not the *ONLY* tool!

PLANNING A TRIP

Two sites to watch: www.hotwire.com, a site backed by a consortium of American, American West, Continental, Northwest, United, and USAir.

The other site which I really like is www.sidestep.com. These guys search ALL the airlines Web sites for low fares, and then link you to those Web sites.

LAST MINUTE TRAVEL

One very creative site is www.site59.com. These folks offer last minute discounted package deals (it doesn't matter if you get a cheap airfare if the hotel will be $500 a night). They aren't just great last minute deals financially, but experientially.

FLIGHT DELAYS

The U.S. Department of Transportation can help—a little. It now requires all major domestic airlines to make their on-time record for *every* flight available to the public. Just check online at www.dot.gov/airconsumer.

Want to know where your flight is right now? www.fly.faa .gov has real-time information on flight status and airport operations.

Other useful sites include www.google.com, then punch "flight tracker" as keywords, or try www.thetrip.com /flightstatus.

Traveling on a charter? There's even a Web site that lets you check on which charter carrier has the worst on-time performance: www.auc.org.uk/news/delay99.html.

THE REAL RULES OF AIR TRAVEL

Punch up www.onetravel.com and look for "rules of the air." You'll find simple, easy to understand explanations for dozens of airline rules, tariffs, and that document of Talmudic complexity—the airline "contract of carriage." Or try www.onetravel.com/rules/rules/cfm.

THE REAL TERMS OF AIR TRAVEL

Here's an esoteric site I like. Call me crazy, but I actually know seating configurations and airplane histories, thanks in part to www.planespotter.com. This site will sell you (about $8) a great, laminated fold-out that gives you a basic explanation and great visual cues to identifying different kinds of planes, configurations, and sizes of aircraft.

WEATHER AND TRAFFIC

Here are some very useful "before you go" sites:

www.weather.com/travelwise

www.nws.noaa.gov/

www.onlineweather.com

And even if the weather is cooperating, there's always the problem of traffic. So log onto www.trafficstation.com for real-time traffic updates from twenty-eight North American cities.

TIME

Just in case you know where you are, but have no idea what time it is where you're headed: www.timeanddate.com will give you the local time in 130 cities around the world.

DIRECTIONS

Try a site called www.mapsonus.com. The site prints driving directions for the way you want to get there—either the fastest route, the geographically shortest, or, if you have the time, the most scenic routes. Another good site—www.mapquest.com—is very user friendly.

Lost at the airport? Then click on www.trip.com, look for "tools for travel" and pick your airport.

MONEY

Want to know how many drachmas it takes to make $20? Do Zlotys confuse you? Then log onto www.oanda.com and you'll get fast conversion rates for more than 160 different foreign currencies. You can even print out one of their conversion charts to take with you. Another good universal currency converter: www.xe.net/ucc.

If you're like me, you use your ATM card when you travel. So log onto www.mastercard.com/atm/ or www.visa.com/pd/atm/main.html to get ATM locations worldwide.

Want foreign currency *before* you leave town? Visit www.currency-to-go.com. This service promises to get you any one of 75 foreign currencies to your doorstep overnight for a $10 fee if you order by 3:00 P.M. Eastern time. Order $500 or more and the service even waives the fee!

INSURANCE

Check out these sites for important information on virtually every kind of travel insurance:

www.travel.state.gov/medical.html will give you information on medical evacuation services.

www.worldwideassistance.com is a good resource for family travel insurance.

Here are some others:

www.worldaccess.com
www.berkely.com
www.intsos.com

Most of these sites will try to sell you insurance, but when it comes to travel, you probably aren't covered and need it. Perhaps most important, investigate a company called Medjet, which provides medical evacuation and repatriation insurance (I strongly advise you to consider this). Call (800) 963-3538.

Also check with www.travelguard.com—these folks even sell trip cancellation insurance and offer storm and hurricane hotline information.

PREVENTIVE MEDICINE

Before leaving home, try out www.medicineplanet.com. It's a great resource of country-specific medical information, where to find medical clinics abroad, and it is country/gender/disease specific in its listings.

Also, look at www.tripprep.com which can get you up-to-date information on travel-related diseases and maladies ranging from nausea to yellow fever.

OTHER DETAILS

Want more details about your destination, but you don't want the typical brochure promotions? Try www.geocities.com /thetropics/2442/database.html.

This will get you on the inside track with locals who are willing to answer e-mails about their cities.

The Zagat guides are great (www.zagat.com) when it comes to restaurants, but now, you can get staff views of those same establishments at http://flyinthesoup.com.

PETS

www.dogfriendly.com gives you a great fifty-state break-down on which hotels, restaurants, and local cities welcome dogs, not to mention tips about flying with Fido.

PASSPORT INFO

There are 275 million Americans. But only 32 million of us have valid passports! Do you have one? If you do, is it valid? If you need a new one, or don't have one to begin with, here's what you need to know:

Get one. Period. As hockey legend Wayne Gretzky once said, "You miss 100 percent of the shots you never take."

Need a passport fast? Try www.travisa.com. This site cuts through the red tape, whether you're applying for a new passport or replacing one that you lost. Travisa's stated guarantee is to process your complete application within five hours of receiving it; in some cases, it can have a new passport to you in 24 hours. Extensive background resources include visa requirements for U.S. travelers to literally every country, links to government travel advisory sites, and an excellent health section that details which illnesses are prevalent in various parts of the world and how to avoid them [travisa.com].

VISAS AND FEES

It's not just getting the passport, it's knowing which countries require an additional visa before they'll let you in. For that, log onto www.embassy.org/embassies to get a list of every embassy in Washington, DC. Then link to those Web sites for the information you need.

LANGUAGE

You've got to start somewhere, so try www.travlang.com—sixteen translating dictionaries that convert basic words and phrases. At least you'll know how to find the right words to find the bathroom! Need translations of trickier phrases? Try www.freetranslation.com.

MEDICAL INFORMATION

Check out www.onhealth.com. Also www.cdc.gov/travel /index.htm (The National Center for Infectious Diseases Travelers Health information).

SAFETY

Get all the U.S. State Department consular information sheets, announcements, warnings, bans at: www.travel.state .gov.

Is "danger" your middle name? For practical info ranging from what to pack to what to do if a rhino attacks, there's a site that is a stellar resource for anyone heading off the beaten track. Detailed overviews of global hot spots use a "jump to" box that lets you move from country to country; in Algeria, for example, you'll be warned about bomb attacks in the markets of Algiers. Even those travelers choosing to stick to comfort zones can benefit from handy data like long-distance access codes from dozens of countries.

www.fieldingtravel.com will land you at a place called "DangerFinder." Before heading to Somalia, or other less than desirable places, you'll find out what you may really be up against.

CRUISE SHIPS

A basic guide to some important information is www .cruiseopinion.com. This site contains more than 4,000 cruise ship reviews, and it doesn't pull punches.

This is the vessel sanitation program run by the centers for disease control for any cruise ship sailing in U.S. waters that visits U.S. ports. A score of 86 or higher is good. Below that, well . . .

Another link: www.cdc.gov/travel/cruiships.htm (cruise ships is intentionally mispelled on this site).

Overall safety: http://psix.uscg.mil/vesselsearch.asp.

CUSTOMS

Worried about what is/isn't duty free? What you really can bring into the country? Visit www.customs.ustreas.gov /travel/trtext.htm.

Also, what food can you bring back? www.aphis.usda .gov.

And remember, those Value-Added Taxes (VAT) can kill you. But most of us can recoup that VAT by getting a customs stamp when we shop. Which countries, stores, and purchases qualify? Call Global Refund at (800) 566-9828 to know before you go.

GOING UNDERGROUND

www.subwaynavigator.com will get you all the routes of all the subway systems around the world.

PROTECTING YOUR LUGGAGE

www.securewrap.com will help you find which airports
have services that will shrinkwrap your luggage before you
check it in.

IF YOU'RE DRIVING . . .

www.speedtrap.com/speedtrap—You have to love this site.
It actually tells you where "smokey" is—where the cops
and/or highway patrols around the United States have set up
radar traps to catch speeders.

AIR SAFETY FOR THE TRULY NEUROTIC

If you're truly afraid to fly, if you're obsessed by bad airplane
movies, then there's one Web site—at least for entertainment
purposes—you need to hit: www.amigoingdown.com. You
tell it what city you're flying from, and to, which airline,
which aircraft type, and in seconds, it calculates your odds
of crashing.

And, finally, as long as you're surfing the Net, this list
wouldn't be complete without the best surfing sites on the
Web!

www.surfline.com (the current surf conditions, even surf
cams!)

And, when all else fails, there's always the simple notion of picking up the phone and actually calling someone.

Some useful numbers:

Access Air (877) 462-2237

Aer Lingus (800) 223-6537

Aero California (800) 237-6225

Aeroflot (800) 736-4192

Aerolineas Argentinas
  (800) 333-0276

Aeromexico (800) 237-6639

Air Afrique (800) 456-9192

Air ALM (800) 327-7230

Air Aruba (800) 882-7822

Air Caledonia (800) 677-4277

Air Canada (800) 630-3299

Air China (800) 982-8802

Air Europa (888) 238-7672

Air Fiji (877) air-fiji

Air France (800) 237-2747

Air India (800) 442-4455

Air Jamaica (800) 523-5585

Air Madagascar (800) 821-3388

Air Mauritius (800) 537-1182

Air New Zealand (800) 262-1234

Air Pacific (800) 227-4446

Air Sunshine (800) 327-8900

AirTran Airways (800) AIR-TRAN

Air Vegas (800) 255-7474

Air Zimbabwe (800) 742-3006

Alaska Airlines (800) 426-0333

Alitalia (800) 223-5730

All Nippon Airways (800) 235-9262

Aloha Air (800) 367-5250

America West Airlines
  (800) 235-9292

American Airlines (800) 433-7300

American Trans Air (800) 225-2995

Ansett Australia Airlines
  (888) 4-ANSETT

Asiana Airlines (800) 227-4262

Atlantic Airlines (800) 879-0000

Austrian Airlines (800) 843-0002

Avianca (800) 284-2622

Avioimpex—Interimpex
  (800) 713-2622

Bahamas Air (800) 222-4262

Balkan Bulgarian Airlines
  (800) 852-0944

Big Sky Airlines (800) 237-7788

British Airways (800) 247-9297

British Midland (800) 788-0555

BWIA International (800) 538-2942

Canada 3000 (888) 226-3000

Canadian Air Intl (800) 426-7000

CanJet Airlines (800) 809-7777

Cape Air (800) 352-0714

Cathay Pacific Airways
  (800) 233-2742

Cayman Airways (800) 441-3003

Chalk's Ocean Airways
  (800) 4-CHALKS

China Airlines (800) 227-5118

China Eastern Airlines
  (800) 200-5118

China Southern (888) 338-8988

Colgan Air (800) 428-4322

Comair (800) 354-9822

Condor (800) 524-6975

Continental Airlines (800) 525-0280

Copa Airlines (800) 359-2672

Corporate Airlines (800) 555-6565

Corporate EXPRESS—Canada
(403) 216-4050

Corsair (800) 677-0720

Croatia Airlines (888) 426-7628

Czech Airlines (800) 223-2365

Delta Air Lines (800) 221-1212

East Coast Flight Services
(800) 554-0550

Ecuatoriana (800) 732-8277

Egyptair (800) 334-6787

El Al Israel Airlines (800) 223-6700

Emirates Air (800) 777-3999

EVA Airways (800) 695-1188

Finnair (800) 950-5000

Frontier Airlines (800) 432-1359

Garuda Indonesia (800) 342-7832

Gulf Air (800) 433-7300

Gulfstream Intl Airlines
(800) 992-8532

Hawaiian Airlines (800) 367-5320

Horizon Air (800) 547-9308

Iberia (800) 772-4642

Icelandair (800) 223-5500

Island Air (800) 323-3345

Japan Airlines (800) 525-3663

JetBlue Airways (800) 538-2583

Jet Express (800) 806-8833

Kenya Airways (800) 343-2506

KLM (800) 374-7747

Korean Air (800) 438-5000

Kuwait Airways (800) 458-9248

Lacsa Costa Rica (800) 225-2272

LanChile Airlines (800) 735-5526

Lauda Airlines (800) 588-8399

Leading Air Logistics (800) 552-5323

LTU International (800) (888) 0200

Lufthansa (800) 645-3880

Lynx Air International
(888) LYNX-AIR

Malaysia (800) 552-9264

Malev Hungarian (800) 223-6884

Martinair Holland (800) 627-8462

Mesa Airlines (800) 637-2247

Mesaba Airlines (800) 225-2525

Mexicana (800) 531-7921

Midway Airlines (800) 446-4392

Midwest Express Airlines
(800) 452-2022

Nantucket Airlines (800) 635-8787

National Airlines (888) 757-5387

New England Airlines
(800) 243-2460

Nica Airlines (800) 831-6422

North Vancouver Air (800) 228-6608

Northwest Airlines (800) 225-2525

Olympic Airways (800) 223-1226

Pakistan Intl Airline (800) 221-2552

Pan Am (800) 359-7262

Philippine Airlines (800) 435-9725

Polish Air-Lot (800) 223-0593

Polynesian Airlines (800) 644-7659

Proair (800) 939-9551

Qantas Airways (800) 227-4500

Royal Airlines (888) 828-9797

Royal Air Maroc (800) 344-6726

Royal Jordanian Airlines
     (800) 223-0470

Royal Nepal (800) 266-3725

Royal Tonga (800) 486-6426

Ryan International Airways
     (800) 727-0457

Sabena (800) 955-2000

SAS Scandinavian Airlines
     (800) 221-2350

Saudia Arabian Airlines (
     800) 472-8342

Shuttle America (888) 999-3273

Singapore Airlines (800) 742-3333

Solomon Airlines (800) 677-4277

South African (800) 722-9675

Southeast Airlines (800) 222-1201

Southwest Airlines (800) 435-9792

Spanair (888) 545-5757

Spirit Airlines (800) 772-7117

SriLankan (877) 915-2652

Sun Country Airlines (800) 752-1218

Sunflower Airlines, Fiji
     (800) 707-3454

Suriname Airways (800) 327-6864

Swissair (800) 221-4750

TACA Airlines (800) 535-8780

TAM—Transportes Aereos
     Regionais (888) 235-9826

TAP Air Portugal (800) 221-7370

Thai Air (800) 426-5204

Transbrasil (800) 872-3153

Travelair (800) 948-3770

Tropic Air (800) 422-3435

Turkish Airlines (800) 874-8875

TWA (800) 221-2000

Ukraine Intl Airlines (800) 876-0114

United Airlines (800) 241-6522

US Airways (800) 428-4322

USAir Shuttle (800) 428-4322

Vanguard Airlines (800) 826-4827

Varig (800) 468-2744

Vasp Brazilian Airlines
     (800) 732-8277

Virgin Atlantic (800) 862-8621

WestJet Airlines (800) 538-5696

Remember, since these are toll-free numbers, if you don't like what you hear on your first go-around, hang up, and try again. Since airlines update their fares more than 300,000 times a day, what may not be available at 10:00 A.M. may suddenly become available four minutes later. As long as you are outside the ticketing and payment restrictions window, you lose nothing by calling back.

Car Rental Agencies, National Numbers:

Avis	(800) 331-1212
Budget	(800) 527-0700
Dollar	(800) 421-6868
Hertz	(800) 654-3131
National	(800) 328-4567

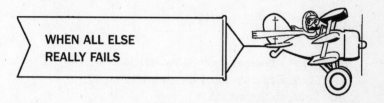

**WHEN ALL ELSE
REALLY FAILS**

THE POWER AND THE FINESSE
OF THE COMPLAINT

When something goes wrong, you want to complain, and, more important, you want something done about it.

I'm a great letter writer, but sending a letter to an airline, cruise line, or hotel may just not be enough.

You need to develop and maintain a paper trail.

When something goes wrong, you need to be a good reporter. Get names, dates, addresses, phone numbers, witnesses. Then write a letter to the airline, but then send a copy to the appropriate federal agency.

If it's safety related:

Assistant Administrator for System Safety ASY-100
Federal Aviation Administration
800 Independence Avenue, SW
Washington, DC 20591
(800) FAA-SURE, (800) 322-7873, or
the Aviation Safety Hotline at (800) 255-1111.

If it's service-related:

> Office of Consumer Affairs
> U.S. Department of Transportation
> 400 Seventh Street, NW
> Room 10405
> Washington, DC 20590
> (202) 366-2220.

And then copy:

> Aviation Consumer Protection Division
> C-75 U.S. Department of Transportation
> 400 Seventh Street, SW
> Washington, DC 20590
> E-mail the Aviation Consumer Protection Division at
> airconsumer@ost.dot.gov.

IF YOU REALLY NEED TO VENT . . .

Looking to bond with other angry travelers. There's help. A growing number of Web sites designed to let you rant and rave, scream, use capital letters, the works to vent your anger and frustration.

There's the mild www.passengerrights.com complaint site. Also www.travelproblems.com.

A little angrier? Anytime you think you've been treated badly, just log on to www.airlinessuck.com and you'll soon discover your flight wasn't that bad after all!

INDEX

A

Achille Lauro, 344–345

advance-purchase
  requirement, waiver of,
  124–125

advisories, from State
  Department, 13–17, 371

Aer Lingus, 85

Aerolineas Argentians, 121

AeroMexico, 152

Afghanistan, travel to,
  13–14

Air Canada, 265

aircraft, 24, 131–132, 134,
  224. *See also* airplanes
  Boeing 707, 226
  Douglas DC-2, 225
  Douglas DC-8, 226
  MD-80, 219, 228
  707, 226
  727, 219
  737, 219, 223, 226, 228,
    246
  737–300, 232
  737–800, 229
  747, 223, 226–227
  747–400, 249
  757, 228
  777, 224–225, 229, 231

airfare, 47–49, 52, 115–122
  air passes, 66
  back-to-back ticketing,
    111–115, 117
  bereavement, 123–127
  competitive shopping,
    69–72
  coupons, 66–67
  e-tickets, 81–84, 189
  information resources,
    108–109
  legislation, 117–118
  mileage programs, 54–55
  open return, 55–56
  positioning flights, 68,
    118
  Saturday-night stayover
    requirements, 29,
    111–113, 115
  split tickets, 86–89
  standby, 56–57, 110

Air France, 85, 87, 152

ABOUT THE AUTHOR

Peter Greenberg is considered the nation's preeminent expert on travel and travel-related issues. Currently the travel editor for NBC's *Today* show, the Emmy Award–winning writer and producer is also the chief correspondent for Discovery Network's Travel Channel as well as editor at large for the *National Geographic Traveler* magazine.

A former *Newsweek* correspondent, Greenberg also writes a weekly column for MSNBC.com and hosts a weekly radio show on KABC-AM in Los Angeles.